Handel und Internationales Marketing / Retailing and International Marketing

Edited by

Bernhard Swoboda
Thomas Foscht

The book series focuses on the fields of Retailing and International Marketing. These two areas represent the research fields of the editors — each of them as a single research area, but also in combination.

Both of these research areas are widely understood. Consequently, the series provides a platform for the publication of doctoral theses and habilitations, conference proceedings and edited books, as well as related methodological issues that encompass the focus of the series. The series is broad in the sense that it covers academic works in the area of consumer-oriented marketing as well as the area of market-oriented management.

In addition to academic works recommended by the editors, the book series also welcomes other academic contributions. These may be submitted to the editors and will be published in the book series after a positive assessment.

Edited by
Professor Dr. Prof. h.c. Bernhard Swoboda
Professor Dr. Thomas Foscht

Stefan Elsner

Retail Internationalization

Analysis of Market Entry Modes, Format Transfer and Coordination of Retail Activities

Springer Gabler

Stefan Elsner
Universität Trier, Germany

Dissertation Universität Trier, 2012

ISBN 978-3-658-01095-9 ISBN 978-3-658-01096-6 (eBook)
DOI 10.1007/978-3-658-01096-6

The Deutsche Nationalbibliothek lists this publication in the Deutsche Nationalbibliografie; detailed bibliographic data are available in the Internet at http://dnb.d-nb.de.

Library of Congress Control Number: 2013943460

Springer Gabler

Printed on acid-free paper

Springer Gabler is a brand of Springer DE.
Springer DE is part of Springer Science+Business Media.
www.springer-gabler.de

Foreword

With the process of retail internationalization gaining momentum since the 1990s, retailing is more and more becoming an international industry. Indeed, many of the world's prominent retailers already derive a significant proportion of their sales from international operations. This occurs for leading grocery retailers (e.g., Walmart, Carrefour and Tesco) in the largest retail sector according sales volumes, for leading fashion retailers (e.g., Inditex, Hennes & Mauritz and The GAP) in the second largest retail sector, and also for service retailers (e.g., McDonald's, KFC and Starbucks). Those retailers face specific challenges when going abroad, which are not relevant if a retailer works in its home country only. For example, they have to choose a general international strategy, country markets for foreign expansion, they have to decide on the market entry mode, the market servicing or on the coordination of foreign units or foreign activities (across countries) in general. These decisions could be done in different manners what significantly determine the performance of firms in international markets. However, research on retail firms' internationalization is still limited, especially compared to the research on internationalization of manufacturing firms.

The study by Dr. Stefan Elsner analyzes empirically three important decisions in the retail internationalization process:

- The choice of the market entry strategy,
- the successful transfer of the retail format from home to host countries and
- the standardization of marketing-mix/ marketing strategy and the centralization as well as formalization of international decision making.

All three topics are under-researched in the literature on retail internationalization in general or in particular concerning their specific research questions, analyzing, for example, institutionalized entry strategies as basis for the choice of current entry modes or analyzing the relationship between the transfer of visible marketing mix instruments and internal processes (supply chain and marketing) with retailers' performance in a host country. Scholars and managers could learn about the relevance of institutionalized entry modes for the subsequent entry mode choice and how processes and marketing elements interact.

Managers could learn how competitors and successful retailers operate abroad and what the central parameters are in order to archive success in foreign countries.

With his work Dr. Stefan Elsner makes a significant contribution to international retailing and international business research. He advances knowledge on international retailers' core decisions and significantly disentangles the interrelation of important decisions and retail firms' performance in foreign countries. On the one hand, his work impresses with the extent of attention paid to the conceptualization and sample design in a difficult field of research. On the other hand, he derives valuable insights for future research as well as for retailing expansion managers. Finally, he presents a dissertation in one of the core research fields of my chair in Trier.

I am particularly pleased with Dr. Stefan Elsner work, as he presents the ninth dissertation at my chair for Marketing & Retailing at the University of Tier. I am especially thankful for over three years of working as a research assistant at my chair for Marketing & Retailing. In those years Dr. Stefan Elsner worked very hard, overcame many challenges and used all the freedom as well as financial and personal resources I was able to offer him. At the end of this time, he is able to present this outstanding piece of work. I thank him very much for his time and I wish Dr. Stefan Elsner all the best for his future professional endeavors as well as his private life.

Trier, November 2012 Prof. Dr. Prof. h. c. Bernhard Swoboda

Acknowledgements

Writing a doctoral thesis is a considerable challenge – beginning with the conceptualization phase, followed by data collection and ending with the analysis and interpretation of the results. I am proud that I have mastered all these challenges and that all three parts of this dissertation have been considered for presentation at renowned conferences, such as the Academy of International Business (AIB), the European International Business Academy (EIBA), the Australia and New Zealand International Business Academy (ANZIBA) and the Summer and Winter Marketing Educators' Conferences of the American Marketing Association (AMA), where I received important feedback to improve my work. I have enjoyed this exciting and instructive time, and I am very thankful to the different groups of people who supported me considerably in this process.

First of all, I wish to thank my supervisor, Prof. Dr. Prof. h. c. Bernhard Swoboda (University of Trier), from whom I received a significant amount of support. From the very beginning, I was pushed to submit my research to several conferences in order to improve my work and network with other researchers all over the world. I am also very grateful for his support during the data collection phase, in which he helped me to establish contact with the managers of retailers with international operations wherever possible. This support was certainly an important foundation on which to build the satisfying result of this doctoral thesis. Finally, I thank him for his intellectual input and challenging discussions, which also played an important role in making this thesis a success.

Furthermore, I would like to thank Prof. Dr. Dirk Morschett (University of Fribourg) for his valuable feedback during the preparation of my doctoral thesis and also for evaluating my work as a second advisor in a very short period of time. A thank you also goes to Prof. Dr. Jörn Block (University of Trier) for taking over the chairmanship of the thesis defense committee.

I also received a considerable amount of professional and personal support from my colleagues at the Chair of Marketing and Retailing of the University of Trier. For this I am very grateful as it facilitated my work by providing important research and teaching know-how, and, not least, a lot of fun. Therefore, I would like to thank my former colleagues, Dr. Sandra Sommer, Dr. Markus Meierer, and Dr. Martin Jager for introducing me to work at the university and also for paving my future academic development. A big thank you also goes to my current colleagues, Bettina Berg, Karin Pennemann, Edith Olejnik, Eileen Blanke, Margot Löwenberg, and last, but not least, Ursula Fassbender, who all contributed to this exciting time. Thank you very much for the long and fruitful discussions, your helpfulness, both professionally and personally, and finally for a lot of funny and unforgettable experiences. I appreciated my time at the Chair of Marketing and Retailing a lot and you are the people responsible for me enjoying the work. I would also like to thank my new colleagues, Julia Weindel, Cathrin Puchert and our student assistant Christoph Seibel, for supporting me in the final phase of my dissertation. Moreover, I am very grateful to my students who supported me in several seminars with stimulating discussions and challenging questions, as well as to the students that I have co-supervised during their diploma theses. Here, special thanks go to Eva Schneider, Kateryna Grabovska, Christiane König and Friederike Döbel, with whom it would have been possible to develop interesting conference contributions.

Finally, my biggest thank you goes to my family, who supported me during critical phases of my dissertation process. This kept me motivated and built the foundation for the success of my doctoral dissertation. In particular, I would like to thank my parents, Edith and Reinhard Elsner, who supported me at all times during my education, from the early beginnings right up to the present day, as well as Sandra Hinzen, Dennis Hinzen, Julian Hinzen, Hilde Elsner, Gerda Joeken, Dr. Thay Tong Thi, Dr. Quy Duong Dinh, Tuan Anh Duong Dinh and Ngoc Huong Luu Thi for their understanding when I was absent due to work obligations and also for taking over personal tasks and obligations, which took a lot of pressure off me. Special thanks go to my wife, Dr. Hai Van Duong Dinh, who supported me not only personally with her patience and encouragement, but also professionally, which influenced my work significantly. Last, but not least, thanks go to my recently born daughter Mila Sa Châu, who showed me what I am working for. I am very grateful for the support by all of my family and wish to dedicate this book to them.

Trier, November 2012 Stefan Elsner

Table of Contents

List of Figures

List of Tables

List of Abbreviations

%...................................percent
& ....and
χ^2...................................Chi-square
€...................................Euro
AIC................................Akaike Information Criterion
ANWR...........................Ariston-Nord-West-Ring
AVE...............................Average variance extracted
B ....Beta
BE ....Belgium
Bn ....Billion
C&A ....Clemens & August
CEE ....Central and Eastern Europe
CEO ....Chief executive officer
CH.................................Switzerland
CMP..............................Core marketing processes
CRM..............................Customer Relationship Management
CSCP............................Core supply chain processes
DE.................................Germany
DIY................................Do-it-yourself
e.g.................................Exempli gratia/ for example
EFA...............................Exploratory factor analysis
ERP ....Enterprise Resource Planning
ES ....Spain
et al. ....Et alia/ and others
etc. ....Et cetera
EU ....European Union
Exp................................Exponent
F^2 ....Effect size
FDI ....Foreign direct investments

FFR .... Flexible Format Replication
FR .... France
GB .... United Kingdom
GDP .... Gross domestic product
GEE .... Generalized Estimating Equations
GMS .... Global Marketing Strategy
H .... Hypothesis
H&M .... Hennes & Mauritz
i.e. .... Id est/ that is
IEM .... Institutionalized Entry Mode
IGD .... Institute of Grocery Distribution
IKEA .... Ingvar Kamprad Elmtaryd Agunnaryd
Incl. .... Including
I-R .... Integration-Responsiveness
IRP .... Intelligent Resource Planning
ItTC .... Item-to-total correlation
JP .... Japan
KFC .... Kentucky Fried Chicken
KMO .... Kaiser-Meyer-Olkin
Log .... Logarithm
m .... Million
M&A .... Merger and Acquisition
MANOVA .... Multiple analysis of variance
M-Markt .... MediaMarkt
MNC .... Multinational companies
MNE .... Multinational enterprises
MV .... Mean value
N .... Number of sample size
n.a. .... Not applicable
n.s. .... Not significant

NL ....Netherland
OLI ....Ownership-Location-Internalization
p.....................................Significance level
p.....................................Page
PCC ....Proportional chance criterion
PLS ....Partial Least Squares
PMP ....Peripheral marketing processes
PMT ....Profit maximization theory
POLCONV ....Political Constraint Index V
POS ....Point-of-sale
PSCP ....Peripheral supply chain processes
Q^2 ....Prediction relevance
QIC ....Quasi-likelihood information criterion
QICC..............................Quasi-likelihood information criterion corrected
R^2 ....R-square
RBV ....Resource based view
SE ....Sweden
SME ....Small and medium enterprise
std ....Standard deviation
TCA ....Transaction cost analysis
UK..................................United Kingdom
US..................................United States
USA ....United States of America
VIF ....Variance inflation factor
vs. ....versus
WOS ....Wholly owned subsidiary
β.....................................Beta

A. Introduction

1. Relevance and Focus

Retailers are internationalizing increasingly, although retail internationalization is not generally a new phenomenon. In a historical context, internationalization by Dutch and English trading houses was reported as far back as the Middle Ages (Zentes, Swoboda and Foscht 2012) as well as during the age of industrialization, when the first foreign direct investments (FDI) in the British retail market were documented (Godley and Fletcher 2000). However, internationalization of modern retailing only began after the Second World War, as Figure A-1 illustrates for the accumulated market entries of the 18 largest grocery retailers today worldwide.

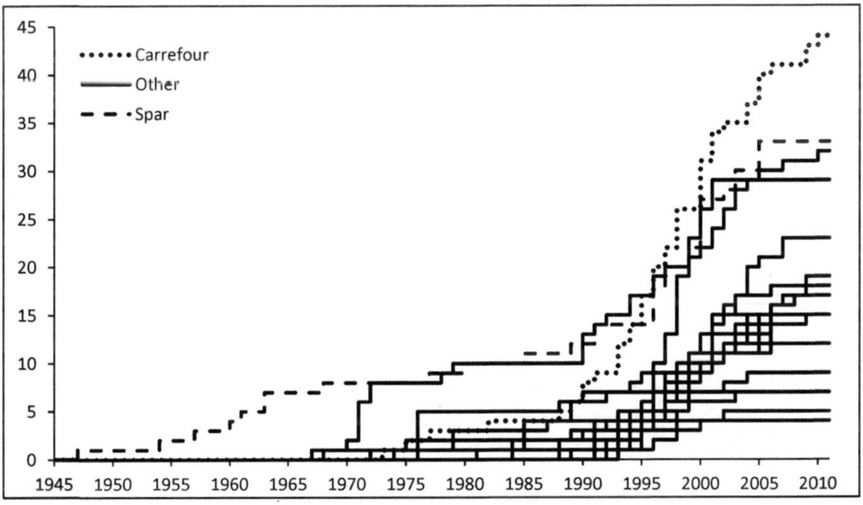

Figure A-1: Accumulated Market Entries of the 18 Largest Grocery Retailers Worldwide
Source: Planet Retail (2011a).

Spar started to internationalize in 1947 and was one of the first large grocery retailers worldwide to expand into foreign markets. Aldi and Metro followed much later in the sixties, whereas Delhaize, Ahold, Carrefour and Tengelmann did not begin to internationalize until the early seventies and Auchan, Costco and AEON in the early eighties. However, most grocery retailers entered their first foreign market around the turn of the decade at the end of the 1980s after the fall of the Iron Curtain when the European markets became more liberalized. Some retailers did not enter their first foreign market until the nineties, such as Tesco.

Today, many of the well-known retailers worldwide realize a significant proportion of sales from international operations (Swoboda, Foscht and Pennemann 2009). As Table A-1 indicates by descending order of total sales in 2011, this is the case for such leading grocery retailers as Wal-Mart, Carrefour and Metro, for leading non-food retailers such as Inditex and H&M in the fashion sector and Groupe Aedo and Kingfisher in the DIY sector. Thus, most leading retailers from the food sector are highly internationalized, as are leading retailers in the non-food sector, including electronic and fashion retailers as the largest representatives, but with only approximately one quarter of the sales achieved by the grocery sector. However, it is not just the largest retailers that operate in numerous foreign countries, but also smaller retailers, such as OBI, Douglas and Decathlon, operate in almost a dozen foreign countries. These observations agree with the recent report from Deloitte, which posits that 147 of the top 250 retailers have entered foreign countries, which is almost 60% of internationalized retailers (Deloitte 2011).

Food sector	Total sales in EUR		No. of countries		Foreign sales ratio	Non-food sector	Total sales in EUR		No. of countries		Foreign sales ratio
	1992	2011	1992	2011	2011		2000	2011	2000	2011	2011
Walmart (US)	36.0	333.0	2	28	26.1	M-Markt/ Saturn (DE)	7,6	20,8[2]	9	16[2]	56.3[2]
Carrefour (FR)	34.0	92.0	5	32	61.3	Expert (CH)	8,0	19.0	16	22	99.0
Tesco (GB)	11.0	72.0	1	13	33.0	Euronics (NL)	n.a.	15,1[2]	n.a.	29	95.6
Metro Group (DE)	40.0	67.0[2]	10	33[2]	61.2[2]	Hennes&Mauritz (SE)	4,0	14,3	13	43	92.5
Costco (US)	12.0	65.0	3	9	27.9	GroupeAdeo (FR)	5,6[1]	12,8[2]	8[1]	12	54.5
Schwarz Group (DE)	6.0	60.0[2]	2	28[2]	56.8	Inditex (ES)	4,0	12,5[2]	10	79	72.0[2]
Rewe Group (DE)	19.0	53.0[2]	1	16[2]	31.3[2]	Kingfisher (GB)	11,4[1]	12,3	9[1]	8	58.0
Aldi (DE)	16.0	51.0[2]	7	19	57.9[2]	Marks&Spencer(GB)	7,2	11,5	17	42	10.3
Seven&I (JP)	n.a.	44.0[2]	n.a.	16	30.6	Intersport (CH)	5,8	10,1[2]	25	40	64.7
Auchan (FR)	12.0	43.0[2]	2	12	54.0[2]	Obi (DE)	5,3[1]	6,7	10[1]	13	44.0[2]
E.Leclerc (FR)	17.0	31.0[2]	1	9[2]	7.4	Decathlon (FR)	2,5	6,0[2]	10	17	46.7
Ahold (NL)	11.0	30.0[2]	4	11[2]	74.0	Douglas (DE)	1,1	3,4	8	18	33.2
Casino (FR)	9.0	29.0[2]	2	8	45.4	Sephora (FR)	0,9	2,3[2]	8	25	59.2
Delhaize (BE)	2.0	21.0	1	11	77.0	Body Shop (GB/ FR)	0,8	1,3[2]	20	62	61.4

[1] Data 2003; [2] Data of 2010; n.a. = not applicable.

Table A-1: Total Sales of the Worldwide Largest Food and Non-food Retailers in 2011

Source: Own creation.

The historical developments presented refer to retail sales activities across borders. However, retail internationalization can generally be divided into two groups: on the one hand, the internationalization of sourcing operations, which is the supply of products from foreign countries to the retailer's country of operation, and, on the other hand, the internationalization of sales operations, which covers distribution of products to the foreign countries in which the retailer operates. This thesis focuses on the latter, which is the most important part of the retail business, because the distribution of products justifies the economic existence of retailing firms. Thus, the internationalization of retailing activities is defined according to Dawson (1994) as being all retail activities that encompass the selling of products and operating of stores in more than one country by foreign direct investments or different kinds of shared operation modes.

Retailers have to be investigated in particular as this sector is distinct from the manufacturing sector and, therefore, so are the decisions within the internationalization process. Accordingly, Burt and Carralero-Encinas (2000) emphasize that the applicability of established theories from the manufacturing sector is limited, and Dawson (1994) actually warns against transferring findings from the manufacturing sector. Hence, in contrast to manufacturers, the most important business activity of retailers is the distribution of manufactured products to the end-customers that justifies the retailers' existence (Rosenbloom 1991). Thus, the location of production and consumption cannot be separated, and retailers are forced to provide their services close to their customers (Blomstermo, Sharma and Sallis 2006). Based on this main characteristic, the following distinct differences concerning the internationalization of retailing emerge with regard to marketing, management and financial aspects:

- First, due to the culturally specific nature of the retail business (Vida, Reardon and Fairhurst 2000), retailers have to cope with end-customers in highly different cultural environments (Bianchi and Ostale 2006). For instance, Burt, Johansson and Thelander (2011) mention the example of the Swedish retail giant IKEA, which had to offer an assembly and delivery service because Chinese customers were not familiar with assembling their furniture by themselves.

- Second, besides coping with end-customers in culturally different markets, retailers are also challenged by the management of other stakeholder groups, such as employees, suppliers, governments and local competitors (Bianchi and Ostale 2006). For example, Wong and Hendry (1997) show from the example of Japanese retailers that the implementation of a structured employment system leads to dissatisfaction among local employees in Hong Kong. Hence, by employing expatriate managers from the home country and new retail technologies, local employees become deskilled and finally feel underutilized.

- Third, due to the need to be close to the end-customers, retailers are forced to establish a comprehensive store network with a high spatial dispersion of store units in foreign markets (Dawson 1994; Huang and Sternquist 2007; Leknes and Carr 2004). Thus, retailers require a large amount of capital to finance their internationalization efforts. For example, Bianchi and Ostale (2006) report that Carrefour, as one of the leading international grocery retailers, operates more than 9,000 stores abroad.

According to Swoboda, Foscht and Pennemann (2009), retail internationalization is facing two distinct challenges within the internationalization process: the first is going abroad and the second is being international. As far as going abroad is concerned, the choice of market entry mode is one of the cornerstones in the concept of market entry strategies (Tse, Pan and Au 1997) because it has significant performance implications (Brouthers 2002; Brouthers, Brouthers and Werner 2003; Gielens and Dekimpe 2001) and is difficult to change once a mode has been established (Pedersen, Petersen and Benito 2002). As far as being international is concerned, transfer of the retail format and its successful implementation are of paramount importance. Accordingly, Helfferich, Hinfelaar and Kasper (1997, p. 297) state that the "transfer of a retail format from one country to another country, or the management of a different retail format abroad, can be seen as the key feature of international retailing". However, despite a long research tradition (Swoboda, Zentes and Elsner 2009) and the paramount importance of retail internationalization as outlined above, previous studies are mainly based on small-N research designs such as case study investigations. Hence, the current research status is still fairly narrow as only a few studies address how decisions are actually made and how success is influenced in foreign countries, respectively. Thus, it becomes increasingly important to answer the following key questions in order to internationalize successfully and to compete against increasingly powerful firms from the respective market or even in the global arena.

(1) How do retailers choose their entry mode when going international in the area of conflict between full- and shared-controlled entry modes and how is their choice influenced by the internal and external environment?

(2) How can international retailers during the being international transfer their retail format successfully to foreign countries by standardizing or adapting the internal and external elements of their retail format?

(3) How can international retailers during the being international successfully organize and coordinate the implementation of their retail marketing program to culturally different countries?

By answering these questions, this thesis aims to shed more light on the young research field of retail internationalization. Hence, key questions on the topics of going abroad and being international are investigated, and the results provide valuable insights for researchers and retail managers because retail entry mode choice, retail format transfer and the organization and coordination of international retail activities are under-researched issues and at the same time important challenges in the growing field of retail internationalization.

2. Research Gaps and Questions

2.1. Main Decisions on Retail Internationalization

Corresponding main decisions on retail internationalization, and therefore areas of research, can be categorized into basic orientations and market-oriented decisions that result either in successful performance or in failure abroad and are moderated by internal and external context factors (Figure A-2). By focusing on market-oriented decisions, this thesis investigates market entry decisions, market operation decisions and the organization and coordination of international retail activities abroad whereas market selection has already thoroughly been investigated by Swoboda, Schwarz and Hälsig (2009).

As these areas of research have mostly been pursued in the context of manufacturing firms, retail firms have rarely been considered. The subsequent literature review emphasizes what previous studies have variously addressed by first showing a chronological table with an overview of existing studies. Thus, the respective research question, the theoretical background, the empirical background wherever possible and the core findings are described for each study to provide a substantial overview. Subsequently, the empirical and conceptual studies are described and analyzed in-depth, leading to the conclusion describing the current research status and identifying research gaps.

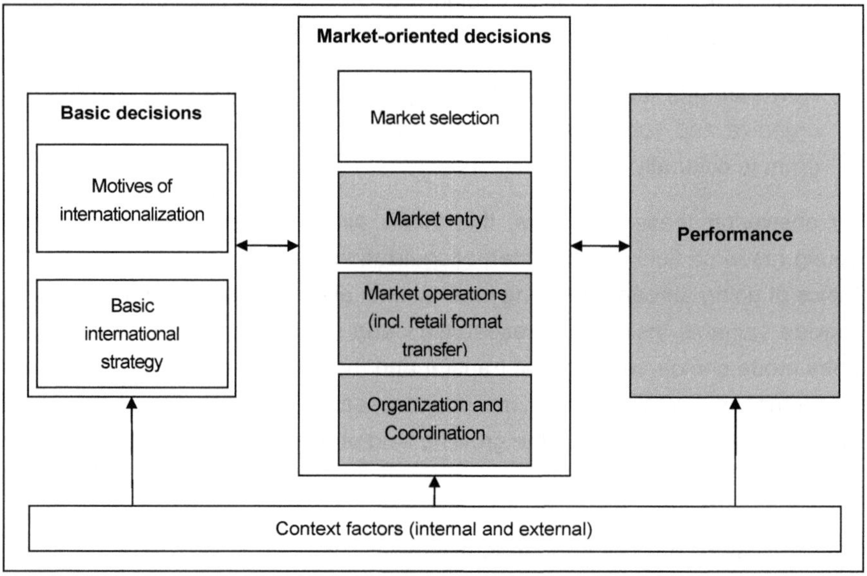

Figure A-2: Overview of Retail Internationalization Decisions
Source: Adapted from Swoboda, Zentes and Elsner (2009).

2.2. *Literature Review*

2.2.1 *Retail Market Entry Mode Choice*

Retail market entry modes are defined according to Root (1995) as the form of institutional arrangements that retailers use when entering foreign markets for the first time in order to implement their marketing strategy. Hence, these entry modes have to be distinguished from foreign operation modes, which are the modes employed beyond of the initially used entry mode, i.e., when the retailer has already been operating for a certain length of time in a foreign country (Benito, Petersen and Welch 2009). In general, retail market entry mode choice encompasses the area of conflict between the use of full- or shared-controlled modes, i.e., operating in foreign countries alone or in a partnership with others. Accordingly, the most important retail market entry modes can be ranked in descending order according to the degree of control as wholly owned subsidiaries, mergers and acquisitions, joint ventures, franchising and licensing agreements and minority stakes with various advantages and disadvantages that have been analyzed frequently in previous research (Doherty 2000; Moore, Doherty and Doyle 2010; Swoboda and Schwarz 2006). Accordingly, selected studies are reviewed in the following that address the choice between these entry modes (Table A-2).[1]

Author(s) and year	Research question	Theory/ framework	Empirical basis/ sector/ method	Core findings
			Empirical Studies	
Lu, Karpova and Fiore (2011)	Examination of fashion retail entry mode choice	Transaction cost theory, bargaining power theory, resource based view and internationalization theory	Primary and secondary data/ Italian fashion retailer in China/ case study (N=1)	- Firm-specific, country-specific and market-specific factors that influence the choice of fashion entry modes - Use of full control modes is suggested in order to be successful when asset specificity, brand equity, international experience and market potential are high - Shared-controlled modes are suggested when financial capabilities are low and host country risk, cultural distance, government restrictions and market competition are high
Evans, Mavondo and Bridson (2008), Evans, Treadgold and Mavondo (2000)	Investigation of the antecedents and performance outcomes of psychic distance	Concept of psychic distance	Primary data/ worldwide non-food retailers/ structural equation modeling (N=102)	- Entry modes used in psychically close markets: greenfield ventures (29%), acquisitions (27%) and joint ventures (21%); psychically distant markets: joint ventures (46%) and franchising (23%) - High control entry modes are favored by retailers with centralized decision-making and a large psychic distance; experience has no significant effect - High control entry modes including wholly owned subsidiaries are strategically more effective than low control entry modes - Entry modes have no significant impact on financial performance
Lessassy and Jolibert (2007)	Identification of the entry modes of international food retailers and how these are used for market penetration	Entry modes according to Root (1995)	Primary data/ international food retailers/ factor analysis, cluster analysis, analysis of variance, frequencies (N=25)	- The use of Root's (1995) generic market entry strategies, including opportunity-seeking, acquisition, franchising and joint ventures, depends on geographical and cultural distance - Use of entry mode differs depending on the availability of internal resources

– cont'd. –

[1] Studies that focus on only one of the entry modes, such as organic growth (e.g., Chaney and Gamble 2008), mergers and acquisitions (e.g., Fernie and Arnold 2002), franchising (e.g., Doherty 2007; Welch 1990), joint ventures (e.g., Palmer, Owens and de Kervenoael 2010; Suh and Howard 2009) or flagship stores (e.g., Moore, Doherty and Doyle 2010), are excluded because they do not consider the choice between different types of institutional arrangements, but only the mode choice of a single entry mode and are thus limited.

– cont'd. –

Author(s) and year	Research question	Theory/ framework	Empirical basis/ sector/ method	Core findings
			Empirical Studies	
Picot-Coupey (2006)	Examination of determinants that explain entry mode choice	Combination of internationalization theory according to Johanson and Vahlne (1977), network theory according to Welch and Welch (1996) and born-global approach according to Sharma and Blomstermo (2003)	Secondary data/ French specialized retailers/ case studies (N=6)	- Dissemination of risk, control, flexibility and resource commitment as the most important characteristics to differentiate between retail entry modes - Marketing policy meaning the concept of the marketing program, company profile including experience as well as availability of financial resources and host country market characteristics meaning market attractiveness as important determinants for characteristics of foreign entry modes - Determining factors are reinforced by motives for internationalization and relationship networks
Dawson (2001)	Impact of opportunism and strategic planning in the entry mode choice process	None	Secondary data/ Western European retailers/ case studies (N=5)	- Since the mid-1990s the strategic choice for internationalization has been removed and every large retailer is nowadays forced to internationalize - Shift from a planned entry mode choice to the leverage of opportunities
Doherty (2000)	Explanation of entry mode choice in the retail fashion sector	None	Secondary data/ UK retailers/ case studies (N=7)	- Entry mode choice is not predetermined but rather develops over time - Franchising is the predominant entry mode used in the retail fashion sector - Contrasting with previous research of Burt (1993), fashion retailers shift with increasing experience from full- to shared-controlled modes - In the course of time, entry mode choice is dependent upon historical, experiential, financial, opportunistic, strategic and company-specific factors
Doherty (1999)	Explanation of entry mode choice	Transaction cost theory, agency theory	Secondary data/ Retailers from the UK, USA and Sweden/ case studies (N=7)	- Due to a large amount of intangible assets, such as the retail format, retailers might favor internalization in order to reduce transaction costs, resulting in the use of wholly owned subsidiaries or acquisitions - Similar to franchise retailers, such as Benetton and Body Shop, master franchise agreements reduce costs for negotiating, monitoring and enforcement of contracts
			Conceptual studies	
Park and Sternquist (2008)	Strategic choices of global retailers	OLI paradigm of Dunning (1988)	Conceptual	- Wholly owned subsidiaries are used depending on ownership advantages, such as a unique retail brand concept and also unique capabilities, internalization advantages such as high contractual risks and finally the availability of resources and experience - Franchise agreements are used depending on pioneering advantages, such as rapid expansion
Huang and Sternquist (2007)	How have retailers to conform to the external and internal institutional environment by the choice of retail entry mode?	Institutional theory	Conceptual	- In countries with highly regulative constraints such as imposition governance, retailers favor the use of shared-controlled modes in contrast to host countries with inducement governments which result more in full control modes - Small cultural distance and retail market distance between home and host countries lead to full control modes - High similarities between the current and previous market entries result in use of the same market entry mode or the entry mode used most frequently in the past
Alexander and Doherty (2004)	Conceptualizing of the process determining market entry method	None	Conceptual	- Choice of retail market entry mode is dependent upon the external market environment and the internal retail environment - Both are not static but change over time
Alexander and Lockwood (1996)	Comparison of internationalization in the retailing and hotel sectors	None	Conceptual	- Management contracts as important entry modes in the context of the hotel sector - Non-food retailers favor organic growth and franchising in contrast to food retailers who prefer acquisitions and develop operations organically - Franchising is widely used in the hotel as well as in the retail sector

Table A-2: Selected Studies concerning Retail Entry Mode Choice

Source: Own creation.

One of the first empirical contributions explaining entry mode choice was provided by Doherty (1999). On the basis of transaction cost and agency theory, the author elaborates in case study-based research the circumstances under which retailers choose which entry modes. Retailers might favor full control modes if they have considerable intangible assets through their retail formats in order to protect their resources and capabilities against opportunism. Similarly, and again on the basis of case studies, Doherty (2000) explores the entry mode choice of seven UK-based fashion retailers and provides new insights by noting that entry mode choice is particularly dependent upon the internal characteristics of the firm, which also change over time. Thus, mainly historical, experiential, financial, opportunistic, strategic and firm-specific factors are responsible for the choice of retail entry mode. In a similar vein, Dawson (2001) argues that entry mode choice is determined more by the opportunities that arise in the host markets and not by a strict strategic planning process. He supports this view by considering the market entries of five Western European retailers into Poland. Picot-Coupey (2006) is one of the first authors to develop a comprehensive conceptual framework on the basis of six case studies on specialist French retailers. The conceptual framework provided states that internal firm-specific determinants as well as external host country determinants are the main influencing factors in the choice of retail entry mode. Moreover, their influence is moderated by facilitating factors including motives for internationalization and relationship networks. Lessassy and Jolibert (2007) provide one of the first contributions that investigate the choice of initial market entry modes by international food retailers and beyond this, the penetration of host markets after initial market entry. Accordingly, when penetrating the host country, it is particularly important that the resources employed suit the entry mode used. Probably one of the most distinctive contributions in retail entry mode research was provided by Evans, Mavondo and Bridson (2008) through the analysis of 102 retailers with international operations. The authors analyze the antecedents and outcomes of retail entry strategy and find evidence that a high-control entry mode is influenced by centralized decision-making and a large psychic distance, whereas extensive international experience has no significant effect. Moreover, the estimations support the assumption that high-control entry modes are strategically more effective than low-control entry modes because coordination costs are minimized. However, financial performance is not dependent upon the use of high-control entry modes, which is intuitively comprehensible because otherwise firms would be reluctant to use low-control entry modes. Finally, the most recent empirical contribution has been provided by Lu, Karpova and Fiore (2011). By analyzing the market entry of an Italian fashion retailer to China, the authors confirm the impact of different factors specific to the firm, country and market on the choice of foreign market entry mode and conclude with a conceptual framework for further investigations.

Further studies should be mentioned that provide empirical findings regarding entry mode choice, but in a more descriptive manner, in addition to other contributions. First, Alexander (1990) finds evidence that nearly half of the 80 retailers investigated prefer organic growth or acquisitions. In the context of market selection, Burt (1991) analyzes 210 international moves by European grocery retailers and confirms that the majority prefer internal growth, acquisitions and majority stakes, followed by joint ventures. Correspondingly, Burt (1993) investigates 726 investments by British retailers in foreign countries from 1960 to 1990 and suggests that retailers should start to internationalize with low resource commitment entry modes and only move to high resource commitment entry modes in the course of time. Similar to Alexander (1990), Vida (2000) shows, mainly by investigating the retail internationalization motives of 80 U.S. retailers, that wholly owned subsidiaries and majority stake joint ventures are primarily employed and are also perceived as being most important compared to minority stake joint ventures and licensing. Samiee, Yip and Luk (2004) describe eight different retail market entry modes and discuss each in the context of their use in the Chinese retail market. By investigating the internationalization process of Auchan in Russia, Roberts (2005) states that Auchan's popular hypermarket retail format operated as wholly owned subsidiary is successful in the Russian market as well. In contrast, acquisitions and joint ventures are too risky and less successful in the Russian retail market. Finally, Hutchinson, Quinn and Alexander (2006) investigate the internalization process of SME retailers and conclude from their case study-based analysis that SME retailers inherently have a limited range of entry mode choices due to their limited amount of resources. Thus, entry modes with higher resource commitment tend to be avoided, but so is franchising, which is more appropriate for large retailers with established retail brands. Instead, such entry modes as licensing or wholesaling are preferred by SME retailers.

Apart from empirical findings, important conceptual contributions have also been provided. First, Alexander and Lockwood (1996) compare the entry modes used in the hotel and retail sectors by means of examples and emphasize the importance of all entry modes in both sectors. Alexander and Doherty (2004) conceptualize the process that determines the market entry method and state that the choice of retail market entry mode is mainly dependent upon firm-specific resources and capabilities as well as environmental conditions. As the external retail environment is not static in nature, the process of entry mode choice is also subject to change over time. A similar contribution is provided by Huang and Sternquist (2007). The authors propose on the basis of institutional theory that the choice of retail entry modes has to conform to the internal and external institutional environment. Thus, as soon as constraints from the regulative host country environment arise and substantial inequalities occur between the home and the host countries, retailers might prefer shared-controlled modes in order to reduce the risk. However, when there are similarities between current and previous entry modes, retailers use the same entry mode or, in case of doubt, the entry mode used most frequently in the past. More specifically, Park and Sternquist (2008) focus on global retailers, i.e., retailers with centralized management and a standardized marketing program, and argue on the basis of the OLI paradigm (Dunning 1988) that the entry mode choice is predominantly influenced by ownership, internalization and pioneering advantages. Thus, when ownership advantages, internalization advantages and resource availability and experience, respectively, are available, it is more efficient for retailers to use wholly owned subsidiaries. In contrast, as soon as pioneering advantages exceed this, it is more beneficial to implement franchise agreements.

In conclusion, most empirical studies analyze the antecedents for choosing the most appropriate retail entry mode. It is basically assumed that retailers use shared-controlled modes as soon as uncertainties arise, and that they prefer to use full control modes as soon as there are any threats of knowledge drain. However, the current knowledge regarding retail entry mode choice suffers from two important shortcomings, resulting in a need for further research. First, the research stream is mainly characterized by descriptive empirical results provided by case study-based evaluations. Although this research method is important, it suffers from the main limitation that the results are difficult to generalize. Thus, quantitative investigations by using large sample sizes are indispensable for an in-depth exploration of entry mode choices in order to provide more sound contributions. Second, although some studies employ established theoretical frameworks, the majority of empirical contributions fail to ground their findings on common theories. This is a great disadvantage for retail entry mode research because the entry mode research stream in international business literature, in particular, is strongly based on sound theoretical underpinnings (Brouthers and Hennart 2007). Hence, new insights are needed on how retail entry modes are chosen on the basis of large databases to provide well-founded results as well as being argued on the basis of established theories.

2.2.2 Retail Format Transfer

According to Goldman (1981), retail format transfer is defined as the entity that is transferred abroad and consists of the basic parts of the external demand side on the one hand and the internal supply side on the other hand. Thus, this section is divided into two aspects: transfer of the external retail marketing program and transfer of internal retail systems and processes.

2.2.2.1 Transfer of the External Retail Marketing Program

The debate about standardization and adaptation of the marketing program is a key issue in international business literature (Schmid and Kotulla 2011) and also in the field of retail internationalization. Selected studies are reviewed therefore in the following that investigate the degree of standardization and adaptation of the retail marketing program or of individual retail marketing elements, their antecedents and outcomes (Table A-3). Studies focusing on specific retail formats, such as franchising (e.g., Kaufmann and Eroglu 1999), are excluded.

Author(s) and year	Research question	Theory/ framework	Empirical basis/ sector/ method	Core findings
			Empirical Studies	
Jonsson and Foss (2011)	Flexible replication of the retail marketing program	Replication-as-strategy according to Winter and Szulanski (2001)	Primary and secondary data/ IKEA/ 70 interviews in Russia, China and Japan from 2003-2009 + 20 interviews in Sweden/ case study	- Standardization and replicating of higher-level features of the retail format, respectively, whereas lower-level features leave room for adaptation - Adaptation is mainly influenced by local learning experience
Burt, Johansson and Thelander (2011)	Standardization of the retail marketing mix in three different countries	Standardization and adaptation debate according to Levitt (1983) and Buzzell (1968)	Primary and secondary data/ IKEA in Sweden, UK and China/ case study (N=1)	- IKEA employs a global marketing strategy with standardized products, prices, sourcing and self-assembling - However, even a global retailer is forced to adapt according to experience in the host market and to consumer culture
Gamble (2010)	Transfer of organizational practice from Japan to China	Different perspectives (e.g., industry sector, business system, agency)	Primary and secondary data/ Japanese retailers in China (N=3), local employees and expatriate managers (N=146)/ qualitative	- Japanese retailers aimed to replicate their home country's practices in China - The standardized transfer of organizational practices (i.e., human resources and customer service) from the home to the host country could create competitive advantages - For example: Standardized customer service includes welcoming the customers by bowing, which at first was unfamiliar to Chinese customers who were only used to bowing at funerals. However, this enabled Japanese retailers to distinguish themselves from local competitors, although local competitors also copied this practice in the course of time
Bianchi (2009)	Internationalization of retailers from emerging markets	None	Primary and secondary data/ Chilean retailer Falabella/ case study (N=1)	- Retailers from emerging countries that internationalize need specific resources and capabilities, including home and host country networks, innovation orientation, organizational learning, marketing knowledge and experienced management teams in order to be successful
Wigley and Chiang (2009)	Success of international retailers through adaptation	None	Primary data/ international fashion retailer per una (UK) in Taiwan/ case study (N=1)	- Adaptations are necessary for success in the retail marketing program - However, it is also important for fashion retailers to establish a consistent retail concept through a standardized brand image, product design and store layout, as well as through standardized logistics and customer relationship management
Cao and Dupuis (2009)	Core competences in retail internationalization	None	Primary and secondary data/ Managers of foreign retailers' subsidiaries in China/ grounded theory (N=18)	- Identification of basic competences including retail concept, flow management (e.g., information and financial flow), organizational capabilities and upstream-downstream relationships, as well as architectural competencies which refer to the link between basic competencies - Competence to reproduce retail concepts and integrate product services, information flows and purchasing leads to standardized policies in the host market - Competence to recognize and incorporate habits of local consumers, innovative retail concepts and combination of organizational flexibility and control leads to adapted policies in the host markets
Lowe and Wrigley (2009)	Retail innovation through adapted market entry	None	Secondary data/ UK retailer Tesco in USA/ case study (N=1)	- Tesco departs from standardized market entries by using an innovate retail format with Fresh and Easy
McKenzie and Merrilees (2008)	Transfer of retail value chains to transition economies	Retail value drivers according to Edvinsson and Malone (1997)	Primary and secondary data/ Finnish department store in Estonia and Latvia/ case study (N=1)	- Strategic market position can basically be transferred unchanged by considering department stores - Only specific adaptations are necessary, such as returns policy and sales staff training
Evans, Mavondo and Bridson (2008), Evans, Treadgold and Mavondo (2000)	Investigation of the antecedents and performance outcomes of psychic distance	Concept of psychic distance	Primary data/ Worldwide non-food retailers/ structural equation modeling (N=102)	- The higher the psychic distance, the more the retail marketing program is adapted - Decentralized decision-making and substantial international experience have no impact - Financial performance and strategic effectiveness are not influenced by adaptation of the retail marketing program

– cont'd. –

– cont'd. –

Author(s) and year	Research question	Theory/ framework	Empirical basis/ sector/ method	Core findings
			Empirical Studies	
Bianchi and Ostale (2006)	Examination of failure by different retailers' in Chile	Institutional theory	Primary and secondary data/ Home Depot, Ahold, Carrefour, J.C. Penney in Chile/ case study (N=4)	- All four retailers failed in Chile because they did not adapt to the local institutional environment and thus could not achieve legitimacy with respect to customers, competitors, suppliers, retail executives and the business community
Bianchi (2006), Bianchi and Arnold (2004)	Examination of Home Depot's failure in Chile	Institutional theory	Primary and secondary data/ Home Depot, DIY, USA and Chile/ case study (N=1)	- Home Depot failed in Chile because it did not examine the host country environment in terms of cultural and consumer habits, as well as due to inadequate management behavior, no efficient collaboration with the local partner and the suppliers network and because of appropriate preparations by competitors - Lack of adaptation leads to a lack of legitimacy in the external institutional environment
Burt et al. (2005)	Internationalization by the UK retailer through export of private labels	Different aspects of retail internationalization	Secondary data/ Boots, UK/ case study (N=1)	- As several previous internationalization attempts by Boots did not yield success, Boots started to internationalize by exporting its strong private labels abroad
Evans and Bridson (2005)	Impact of psychic distance on retail marketing program adaptation	Concept of psychic distance according to Johanson and Wiedersheim-Paul (1975)	Primary data/ non-food international retailers/ structural equation modeling (N=102)	- Great psychic distance as a result of differences in market structure, business practices and language leads to more adaptation in the retail marketing program - Differences in cultural, legal, political and economic distance show no significant effect
Burt and Sparks (2002)	Standardization of retail corporate brands across countries	None	Secondary data/ Tesco, Marks & Spencer, Sainsbury/ case studies (N=3)	- Complete standardization of retail corporate brands is not feasible due to several differences in the stakeholder structure abroad - Authors suggest building a strong local brand
McGauran (2001)	Cross-national comparison of retail selling process	Intermediary societal effects theory according to Ruberty (1994) and Lee (1993)	Primary data/ shop managers from multinational fashion retailers/ qualitative (N=27)	- Fashion stores in Paris are more engaged in the selling process by actively attracting customers, giving much professional advice and spending of a lot of time per customer in contrast to fashion stores in Dublin - Differences can be explained by differences in cultural factors, including the importance of fashion, and by differences in economic factors, including the development of capitalism
Goldman (2001)	Transferring of retail formats successfully into less developed countries	Grounded theory, concept of format transfer according to Hollander (1970) and Kacker (1988)	Primary data/ international retailers in China/ qualitative (N=27)	- Analysis of drivers of unchanged or modified format transfer: host country conditions, retailers' global position and global strategy - Format transfer process is not only influenced by economic factors such as economies of scale, but also by non-economic factors such as experience, learning and flexibility, which are at least as important - Six transfer strategies: Global niche protection strategy, opportunism strategy, format pioneering opportunity strategy, format extension, portfolio-based format extension and competitive positioning oriented strategy
Goldman (2000)	Penetration, limitation and success factors of the supermarket format in China	Modernization theory	Primary and secondary data/ foreign and local food retailers in China/ qualitative (N=n.a.)	- Local retailers in particular drive the retail modernization process in China instead of foreign retailers with international operations - Supply side factors create more difficulties in penetrating the Chinese market through the supermarket format rather than consumer behavior, government issues or local competitors
Hadjimarcou and Barnes (1998)	Effects of currency devaluation and competition from foreign retailers on retail marketing mix	None	Primary data/ US retailers in the cross-border area to Mexico/ MANOVA (N=176)	- Retailers from cross-border regions adapt their retail marketing mix to accommodate foreign customers when they have concerns about currency devaluation - In the event of strong cross-border competition, retailers do not adapt their retail marketing mix significantly to accommodate foreign customers
Danneels (1996)	Market segmentation and its influence on retail marketing mix adaptation	None	Primary data/ Belgian fashion retailers/ qualitative (N=28)	- Retailers often do not segment host country markets before market entry - Retailers use a standardized marketing mix at first and adapt to local conditions afterwards

– cont'd. –

– cont'd. –

Author(s) and year	Research question	Theory/ framework	Empirical basis/ sector/ method	Core findings
			Empirical Studies	
Segal-Horn and Davison (1992)	Standardization of retail activities in global markets	Standardization and adaptation debate according to Levitt (1983)	Secondary data/ retailers with international operations/ descriptive	- Antecedents of standardization: global market segments, global economies of scale and existence of distribution infrastructure - Some elements have to be adapted, including format, merchandise, store location and design and merchandising
Mårtenson (1987)	Standardization in culturally bound industries	Standardization and adaptation debate according to Levitt (1983) and Boddewyn, Soehl and Picard (1986)	Primary and secondary data/ IKEA, Sweden/ case study (N=1)	- In general, the retail marketing program is mostly standardized, although small adaptations are permitted regarding exact prices and local advertisements - Forces in favor of standardization come from the internal and external retail environment
			Conceptual studies	
Currah and Wrigley (2004)	Explanation of adaptations of retailing firms	Knowledge transfer management due to relational networks according to Goldman (2001)	Conceptual	- Accumulation of knowledge from outside and inside the company, as well as store-based learning (bottom-up) - Dissemination of knowledge through adaptation (top-down) - Emphasize the strategic importance of transferring process-based knowledge to adapt the retail format successfully and manage geographically dispersed knowledge
Beninati, Evans and McKinney (1997)	Adaptation of assortment to local conditions	None	Conceptual	- Due to differences in customer needs and wants across countries, retailers are forced to adapt their assortments - Assortment adaptation can be achieved by developing an assortment planning process in cooperation with employees and customers in the stores abroad for example
Brown and Burt (1992)	Conclusions of retail internationalization	Several concepts, e.g., Dunning's (1988) eclectic paradigm	Conceptual	- Standardization and adaptation debate takes place at different levels within retailing firms: brand level, format level, marketing instruments level and management systems level - The external host country environment, consisting of the customers and the marketplace, provides the main determinants for standardization/ adaptation
Kacker (1988)	Flow of retail know-how across countries for transferring the retail concept	None	Conceptual	- Retail know-how consists of technical elements, including store layout, buying and merchandise planning, selection of location, as well as managerial elements, including concepts, systems and policies - Successful transfer of retail format depends on adaptations to host country conditions (technical elements) as well as on implementing of appropriate infrastructures (managerial elements)
Goldman (1981)	How to transfer retail technology into less developed countries in the case of supermarkets	Adoption-communication perspective, geographical and technological diffusion of innovations, economic history	Conceptual	- Successful transfer of marketing technology is comprised in the response of the retail format to the supply and demand side in less developed countries

Table A-3: Selected Studies concerning the Transfer of the External Retail Marketing Program

Source: Own creation.

One of the first empirical studies was provided by Mårtenson (1987). In a case study-based research design on the Swedish retail giant IKEA, the author elaborates whether standardization is feasible in culturally bound industries. The marketing program consisting of products, prices, distribution and promotions is roughly standardized, and only exact pricing and local advertising leave room for adaptation. Also, Segal-Horn and Davison (1992) analyzes the antecedents of retail marketing program standardization on the basis of secondary data and examples in a descriptive manner. The author concludes that global market segments, global economies of scale and distribution infrastructures are necessary for standardization, while some elements of the retail marketing program have still to be adapted. On the basis of interviews with 28 Belgian fashion retailers, Danneels (1996) investigates whether retailers implement market segmentation before going abroad and how it impacts retail marketing mix adaptation. The authors find evidence that there is often no market segmentation and that the retail marketing mix is adapted afterwards in the course of time if the retailer is operating in a specific host country. In a specific context, Hadjimarcou and Barnes (1998) analyze the design of the retail marketing mix in the cross-border region of the USA and Mexico. The results indicate that the retail marketing mix is adapted to foreign customers in the case of high currency devaluation, whereas competition from foreign retailers has no significant effect on adaptation of the retail marketing mix to foreign customers.

One of the most significant contributions was provided by Goldman (2000) as well as Goldman (2001). Goldman (2000) examines the retail modernization process in China for the supermarket format. After interviewing executives from local and foreign supermarket chains, the author concludes that particularly local retailers drive the retail modernization process instead of, as mostly assumed, foreign retailers. Furthermore, in penetrating the foreign market, factors from the supply side are the main obstacles rather than consumer behavior, government restrictions or local competitors. Similarly, Goldman (2001) elaborates different format transfer strategies and their antecedents in China. The author postulates that the transfer of retail formats is influenced not only by economic, but also by noneconomic factors, it takes place over time, is characterized by an often short and nonsystematic decision-making process, and is mostly applied unchanged, although even global retailers are forced to adapt their retail format to a certain extent. McGauran (2001) focuses on a comparison of the selling process between fashion retail stores in Dublin and Paris and emphasizes cross-national differences in the selling process, although other retail marketing programs remain the same. The author argues the need for different selling processes due to differences in the economic and cultural environment. Burt and Sparks (2002) conclude from an analysis of

Tesco, Marks & Spencer and Sainsbury's that retail corporate brands cannot be standardized easily across markets due to differences in stakeholders, such as business relationships and employees, as well as due to differences in market and strategic conditions, such as positioning, image and culture. Thus, it might be valuable in specific cases to build a strong local corporate brand. An interesting case on the UK drugstore retailer Boots was provided by Burt et al. (2005). The authors show that although internationalization of the retail format failed, Boots has successfully expanded abroad by exporting its private labels.

Important contributions to the topic of retail internationalization have also been provided by Evans and Bridson (2005) as well as Evans, Mavondo and Bridson (2008). Evans and Bridson (2005) examine the influence of psychic distance on retail marketing program adaptation and confirm a positive influence if there are large differences in market structures, business practices and language. As already mentioned above, Evans, Mavondo and Bridson (2008) also investigate the antecedents and outcomes of adaptation of the retail marketing program. Their results reveal that decentralization of decision-making and considerable international experience have no significant impact on adaptation of the retail marketing program, but a large psychic distance does have an impact. However, outcome factors such as financial performance and strategic effectiveness are not influenced by adaptation of the retail marketing program. Bianchi (2006) and Bianchi and Arnold (2004) analyze the failure of Home Depot in Chile, as well as Bianchi and Ostale (2006) by three other retailers. The authors come to the conclusion that the failure was mainly due to a lack of adaptation to the local institutional environment. Thus, the importance of adaptations is emphasized by these studies due to the inherent local nature of the retail business. McKenzie and Merrilees (2008) analyze the Finnish department store Stockmann in Estonia and Latvia and come to the conclusion that the strategic market position can be transferred unchanged, whereas specific elements such as returns policy and staff training have to be adapted to the local market situation. An interesting case was provided by Lowe and Wrigley (2009) in an analysis of Tesco's market entry to the USA. Tesco developed a completely new retail format with Fresh & Easy, which is highly innovative and fully adapted to the American customer's needs and wants.

Thus, the retailer departed from its commonly used retail format and market entry methods of majority partnerships, joint ventures or acquisitions. On the basis of grounded theory, Cao and Dupuis (2009) interview 18 subsidiary managers from foreign retailers and identify several basic and architectural competencies which are necessary to reproduce a strong retail concept and conclude with propositions for further research. Additionally, the authors emphasize the importance of adaptation by acknowledging the habits of consumers in the host country. By analyzing the degree of marketing mix standardization of the UK-based fashion retailer per una in Taiwan, Wigley and Chiang (2009) also find that this factor is necessary for success. However, in order to maintain global consistency, the authors argue that it is equally important to standardize brand image, product design, store layout, logistics and customer relationship management.

As most studies investigated the internationalization of retailers from developed countries, Bianchi (2009) uses a different approach by investigating internationalization by a retailer from an emerging country. In a case study, the authors examine the essential resources and capabilities of a Chilean retailer to internationalize, and one of their conclusions states that it is important to adapt the retail marketing program to local conditions. Investigating the transfer of organizational practices of Japanese retailers to China, Gamble (2010) states that a standardized transfer of customer service can yield competitive advantages. Furthermore, human resources practices have also been transferred in a standardized form, but small adaptations, such as the introduction of seniority pay, have been implemented because the retailers have been forced to do so by the local environment. An interesting contribution was provided by Burt, Johansson and Thelander (2011), who compare the design of the retail marketing mix of IKEA in the home country (Sweden) with a psychically close market (UK) and a psychically distant market (China) in a case study-based analysis. The results reveal that there are only minor differences in retail marketing activities between the UK and Sweden, but there are considerable differences between Sweden and China. In this respect, IKEA in China departs from its well-known globalized strategy by offering local assortments, store locations closer to the city center, store layout to suit local tastes and providing an assembly service instead of the do-it-yourself concept because Chinese customers are not used to this. Most recently, an interesting concept labeled "flexible replication" was provided by Jonsson and Foss (2011). The authors note in a longitudinal case study of IKEA that higher-level features, such as fundamental values, are suitable for long-term replication, whereas lower-level features, such as pricing, need to be adapted to local conditions. The degree and type of change are therefore dependent upon local learning experience.

Additionally, some studies examine the standardization and adaptation of retail marketing programs from a consumer perspective. One of the first contributions in this respect was provided by Burt and Carralero-Encinas (2000). The authors compare the responses of 300 customers in the UK and Spain about the store image of Marks & Spencer and confirm that certain store attributes, such as customer service, are perceived similarly in both countries. However, particularly intangible factors such as store reputation are perceived less favorably in the host market. Thus, even if a standardized store image is transferred to foreign markets, it takes time for it to be accepted in the same way as in the home country. Similarly, Burt and Mavrommatis (2006) emphasize the difference between the perceived store brand image of Dia in the home (Spain) and the host market (Greece), as well as its positioning compared to competitors in the host market. Their results reveal that store brand image is perceived differently in both markets, but its positioning remains the same. Thus, they suggest that retailers should first standardize the store attributes that are necessary for building a consistent store brand image and then check whether this concept is able to establish the same positioning as in the home market. By comparing the retail store decision criteria of 1,221 customers in Western countries and in Central and Eastern European (CEE) countries, White and Absher (2007) conclude that retail store concepts should be adapted more due to differences in retail store decision criteria. Gamble (2009) examines the demand of Chinese customers by interviewing 214 local and expatriate employees of one British and two Japanese retailers. The author suggests that customers become more demanding due to the transitional change in China, so that foreign retailers have been forced to intensify their customer service and employee training compared to their home markets. Paswan, de Pineda and Ramirez (2010) investigate customers' motivation to visit small local stores or large stores of international retailers. Their results from interviewing 981 customers in Mexico reveal that small stores are favored due to their familiarity and functional benefits, such as convenience, price and merchandise compared to large retail stores. Finally, two studies are mentioned that compare the use of retail marketing elements in different countries. Fam and Yang (2006) show that outdoor promotions are less relevant in Portugal than in New Zealand as this task in usually performed by manufacturers. Corstjens, Corstjens and Lal (1995) show that grocery retailers in France compete more with prices, while retailers in the UK compete particularly with private labels.

However, before any empirical study had been conducted, Goldman (1981) and Kacker (1988) already provided conceptual analyses of the transfer of retail format. Thus, Goldman (1981) disentangles the transfer of so-called marketing technology to the supply side, such as the infrastructure conditions abroad, and to the demand side, comprising the host country market conditions. On the basis of diffusion of innovations, successful transfer depends on the standardization and adaptation of supply processes and marketing programs in response to both superior domains. In a similar vein, Kacker (1988) also conceptualizes the transfer of retail know-how by implementing managerial and technical elements of the retail concept abroad. Brown and Burt (1992) summarize from previous studies that the issue of the degree of standardization has been investigated at different levels within the retailing firm. The authors conclude that the customers abroad and the local marketplace are the main determinants for the degree of standardization. In more detail, Beninati, Evans and McKinney (1997) suggest a high degree of retail assortment adaptation due to differences in customer behavior across countries. This can be achieved by organizational improvement, such as establishment of an assortment planning process, including information from the people in the stores abroad. Finally, Currah and Wrigley (2004) refer to Goldman (2001) and emphasize that the accumulation of knowledge is realized in a bottom-up process through learning inside and outside the company, whereas the dissemination of knowledge is top-down through adaptation of the retail format. The authors conclude that transferring process-based knowledge to adapt the retail format is a key factor for success and in managing geographically dispersed knowledge.

Although some authors argue in favor of adaptation and some in favor of standardization, the overall conclusion from most contributions is the standardized transfer of the retail marketing program with enough space for adaptations to local conditions. However, there is still a lack of knowledge regarding the antecedents and outcomes of retail marketing mix standardization. For instance, one of the most distinctive contributions of Evans, Mavondo and Bridson (2008) finds no support for the impact of retail marketing strategy on financial performance and strategic effectiveness. However, it is not only of particular interest for retail managers which design of retail marketing program is most successful under which circumstances. One possible direction for further research might be the call of Goldman (2001) to disentangle the retail format into core and peripheral elements.

2.2.2.2 *Transfer of Internal Retail Systems and Processes*

As stated above, this thesis aims to investigate the internationalization of retail sales strategies instead of retail sourcing strategies. Thus, selected studies are reviewed in the following that deal with the transfer of retail background systems and processes according to Goldman (2001) as illustrated in Table A-4. Studies that investigate sourcing from overseas to the domestic market are not considered (e.g., Alpert et al. 1997; Johansson 2002; Liu and McGoldrick 1996; Lowson 2001).

Author(s) and year	Research question	Theory/ framework	Empirical basis/ sector/ method	Core findings
			Empirical Studies	
Yahagi and Kar (2009)	Transfer of business models of Seven-Eleven from the USA to Japan to China	None	Primary and secondary data/ Seven-Eleven USA, Japan, China/ case study (N=1)	- Seven-Eleven's core capability is the across-the-board continuous adaptation of all elements of the business model, ranging from retail format to procurement to supply chains - In the case of China, adaptations were not necessary so the business model implemented was mainly standardized
Coe and Lee (2006), Coe (2004)	Local responsiveness of transnational retailers	Global production network	Primary and secondary data/ Joint venture between Samsung and Tesco/ case study (N=1)	- Transnational retailers show a high level of local responsiveness through the offer of local products from local suppliers as well as through the employment of local employees with a high degree of decision autonomy for leading positions - Transnational retailers are well embedded into the host market
Coe and Hess (2005)	Impact of retail internationalization on supply network	Global production network perspective according to Henderson et al. (2002)	Primary data/ international retailers in East Asia and Eastern Europe/ qualitative (N=34)	- Restructuring of the retail supply network by the centralization of procurement, the use of standardized and established logistic systems, simplification of the supply chain by removing unnecessary intermediaries, imposition of strict contracts for local suppliers and use of own standards and certifications

– cont'd. –

– cont'd. –

Author(s) and year	Research question	Theory/ framework	Empirical basis/ sector/ method	Core findings
			Empirical Studies	
Bourlakis and Bourlakis (2001)	Logistic strategies in food retailing	None	Primary and secondary data/ Domestic and international food retailers in Greece/ case study (N=7)	- Deliberate logistic strategies meaning the establishment of warehouses of international food retailers before market entry, leads to greater efficiency compared to emergent logistic strategies of domestic retailers - International food retailers employ standardized logistic strategies in their host markets
Bengtsson, Elg and Johansson (2001)	Influence of retail internationalization on domestic retailer-supplier relationships	Network perspective according to Jarillo (1988) and resource dependent theory according to Pfeffer and Salancik (1978)	Primary data/ Swedish food retailers/ correlations (N=621)	- With the increase in international retail activities, retailers become less dependent upon domestic suppliers - However, the relationship towards small and large domestic suppliers does not become less important
Wrigley (1997a), Wrigley (1997b)	Transfer of UK-based supply chain operations	None	Primary and secondary data/ Sainsbury's (UK) market operations in the USA/ case study (N=1)	- Transfer of supply chain activities is difficult due to differences between UK and USA - Introduction of private labels and establishing of close relationships to suppliers are both uncommon in the USA and hamper implementation of the UK level of distribution control
Mathe and Dagi (1996)	The use of technology in global service business	None	Secondary data/ Wal-Mart, IKEA, Laura Ashley and Europcar/ case study (N=4)	- Back office operations are customized to support front-line operations - The degree of internationalization and success is not influenced by the sheer use of technology, but is supported - The examples of Wal-Mart and Laura Ashely show that technology has to comply with the merchandising system

Table A-4: Selected Studies concerning the Transfer of Internal Retail Systems and Processes

Source: Own creation.

Mathe and Dagi (1996) analyze empirically the impact of using back office technologies for global service business. The authors show from the example of Wal-Mart that the speed of decisions can be enhanced by using standardized technologies, including data warehouse, on-line store network, store systems and employee user tools. Moreover, through the integration of retail IT, direct connections can be established between the information systems of suppliers and store inventory. Wrigley (1997a) and Wrigley (1997b) elaborate the transfer of supply chain operations of the UK-based retailer Sainsbury to the USA. After the acquisition of Shaw and a 50% voting stock of Giant Food, Sainsbury introduced private labels in close cooperation with suppliers and therefore transferred its typically UK physical distribution and logistical techniques to the USA. However, Sainsbury had problems in transferring its UK level of distribution control, the use of IT and the third-party logistical contracting, which is typical in the UK, but not common in the USA, resulting in its market exit some years later. Bengtsson, Elg and Johansson (2001) examine how retail-supplier relationships in the domestic market are affected through the internationalization of retail activities. Their survey of 621 Swedish store managers show that although retailers become less dependent on their domestic suppliers as their internationalization activities increase, the relationships do not become less important, which is valid for both small and large suppliers. Bourlakis and Bourlakis (2001) investigate in a case study-based research design whether deliberate or emergent retail logistic strategies are more efficient. It can be concluded from their observations that deliberate retail logistic strategies, including the erection of warehouses abroad, leads to greater logistic efficiency. Thus, retailers with international operations employ a standardized retail logistic strategy in their host countries by using warehousing. Similar to Bengtsson, Elg and Johansson (2001), Coe and Hess (2005) analyze the impact of retail internationalization on international supply networks by interviewing 25 managers from large international retailers and nine managers from suppliers. The authors argue that, due to increasing international retail activities, the supply network becomes more complex and thus has to be restructured. Several arrangements are, therefore, provided to increase the efficiency of retail supply networks abroad.

Concerning the transfer of comprehensive business models, Coe and Lee (2006) and Coe (2004) analyze the use of sourcing, employees and strategic decisions. By considering the joint venture by Samsung-Tesco in South Korea, the authors conclude that the joint venture shows a high degree of local responsiveness compared to their competitors at Wal-Mart and Carrefour by offering local products from overwhelmingly local suppliers and by employing local staff, with a high degree of decision autonomy for the local managers. Finally, Yahagi and Kar (2009) analyze the business model transfer of Seven-Eleven from the USA to Japan and from Japan to China. The authors argue in a process-based view of internationalization that all elements, including retail store format, procurement and supply chain, have to be considered for a successful transfer of a complete business model. By moving from the USA to Japan, Seven-Eleven was able to suit local tastes through across-the-border continuous adaptations. However, in order to serve the Chinese market, only partial adaptations were necessary and the business model was transferred in a more standardized form.

Without directly addressing the standardization of internal processes, the following two studies are mentioned for the sake of completeness as they provided substantial insights into retail distribution systems and internal decision-making processes. Fernie (1992) compare retail distribution strategies between the UK and Continental Europe and observe that retailers employ different distribution strategies due to their different retail structures. Thus, British retailers have increased stock centralization, greater control over the supply chain and externalize their distribution to third parties compared to retailers from Continental Europe. Clarke and Rimmer (1997) show from the example of the Japanese department store retailer Daimaru that market entry to Australia was the result of initially planned behavior, but was reinforced by the coincidence that a developer of the Melbourne Central was looking for a new department store. Thus, the authors conclude that although many decisions are planned in advance, changes occur in the course of time that provide sources from which it is possible to learn.

Overall it can be concluded that retail supply networks become more complex as a result of increased internationalization of retail activities. A store business network operating abroad must be backed by extensive infrastructure, including IT, purchasing, training, logistics and finance (Coe 2004). Standardization of these internal systems and processes might be one solution, but other studies also emphasized the need for adaptations. However, the research status in this sector is still fairly narrow as it is not even known which retail systems and processes exist in the internal retail environment and to what degree these have to be adapted to the local host country conditions in order to be successful. Moreover and as already mentioned, Wigley and Chiang (2009) propose that a consistent retail concept, including brand image, product design, store layout and logistics, must be transferred abroad. Thus, it is questionable how the internal and external elements of the retail format are interrelated according to Goldman (2001). Furthermore, most studies lack a theoretical foundation on the impact that transferring a standardized or adapted retail format has on performance, which hampers the generalizability of results and the explanation of effects. Therefore, new insights are needed that demonstrate important elements of the retail format, how they are interrelated to one another and how these elements influence performance abroad.

2.2.3 Organization and Coordination of International Retail Activities

In this section, all studies are reviewed that investigate the organization and coordination of international retail activities abroad. Thus, selected studies are considered that deal with the structural dimensions of organizations, including centralization of decision-making, formalization and specialization according to Dalton et al. (1980) as illustrated in Table A-5.

Author(s) and year	Research question	Theory/ framework	Empirical basis/ sector/ method	Core findings
			Empirical Studies	
Wegner and Padula (2010)	Investigation of the governance and management of German horizontal networks	None	Primary and secondary data/ German horizontal networks of Intersport, Expert and ANWR/ case study (N=3)	- German horizontal retail networks are characterized by strongly centralized strategic decisions and thus, low participation by member companies - However, low degree of control through the network - Member companies adapt a high degree of visual standardization, which is pre-defined by the network management
Tacconelli and Wrigley (2009)	Analysis of the organizational challenges and strategic responses of international retailers in China	None	Primary and secondary data/ Management consultants, government officers (N=18), senior managers of Wal-Mart, Tesco, Carrefour (N=22)/ qualitative	- Supply chain activities are more centralized in the case of Wal-Mart and Tesco, whereas Carrefour established a decentralized organizational structure through several merchandise offices due to the highly fragmented Chinese retail market - Large cultural distance requires a large amount of retail marketing program adaptation - No general rule for standardization and adaptation of the marketing program, nor for centralization and decentralization of the organizational structure; depends rather on the fit between the external and the internal environment
Swoboda and Anderer (2008)	Systemization of the coordination of international retailing firms	System theory, network theory and contingency theory	Primary data/ Executives of European retailers (n = 60)/ frequencies and cluster analyses	- Systemization of coordination dimensions into centralization and formalization, divided into the subgroups of systemic, structural and cultural coordination - Organizational structure has no direct effect on success, unlike sole instruments of coordination
Evans, Mavondo and Bridson (2008), Evans, Treadgold and Mavondo (2000)	Investigation of the antecedents and performance outcomes of psychic distance	Concept of psychic distance	Primary data/ Worldwide non-food retailers/ structural equation modeling (N=102)	- Centralization of decision-making has no impact on the standardization and adaptation of retail strategy and the degree of perceived similarities between home and host countries (psychic distance) - However, centralization of decision-making has a significant positive impact on the choice of full control modes
Palmer (2005)	Comparison of the development of Wal-Mart International during the crossing of thresholds in the retail lifecycle	Concept of organizational life cycle according to Quinn and Cameron (1983)	Primary and secondary data/ Wal-Mart International, interviews with financial analysts, advisors and Wal-Mart executives/ qualitative (N=62)	- Organizational decisions are particularly rooted in the firm's history, but as soon as a retailer expands, pressures arise from the external institutional environment - Shift from a highly centralized organizational structure in the pre-threshold period to a more decentralized organizational structure in the post-threshold period
Verity (2005)	Examination of the transition in organization of Shell's advertising activities	Resource-based view and dynamic capability view	Primary and secondary data/ Shell gas station service/ case study (N=1)	- Successful transition from a decentralized to a centralized structure of advertising activities - More control through centralization, meaning that a structured and disciplined working process was possible as only six people were responsible for the entire international presence

– cont'd. –

– cont'd. –

Author(s) and year	Research question	Theory/ framework	Empirical basis/ sector/ method	Core findings
			Empirical Studies	
Moore, Birtwistle and Burt (2004)	Conflict and conflict resolution between headquarter and subsidiary in international fashion retailing	Agency theory and governance mechanisms according to Ghoshal and Nohria (1993)	Primary data/ international fashion retailers in UK/ case study (N=10)	- From a headquarter perspective, conflicts arise through strategic non-compliance and unauthorized decision-making - From a subsidiary perspective, conflicts arise through decision-making authority and perceptual disagreement - Possible solutions: sanctions, or collaborative methods of decision-making
Mitronen and Möller (2003)	Management of hybrid organizations according to different government mechanisms	Transaction cost economics (Williamson 1985), contractual law (McNeil 1978) and institutional theory (Powell 1987)	Primary and secondary data/ Kesko, largest retailer and hybrid organization in Finland/ case study (N=1)	- Governance mechanisms: structural and organizational solutions, managerial policies and processes and values, norms and trust - Management levels: Corporate management level, division parent company, chain management level, store management level
Arnold (2002)	Success factors of the world's leading retailers	None	Secondary data/ Ahold, Benetton, Carrefour, Home Depot, IKEA, Wal-Mart/ case study (N=6)	- Most important success factors of the world's best retailers are inspirational leadership and a motivating organizational culture through decentralized decision-making on the basis of the concept of "a company within a company" - Based on various theses, further success factors emerge, including capabilities for innovations, customer-relevant and community-relevant
Harris (2000)	Examination of organizational barriers that impede market orientation	None	Primary data/ large grocery and fashion retailers, UK/ factor and regression analysis (N=107)	- A high degree of market orientation can be achieved with a low degree of structural formalization and a low degree of centralization - Centralization leads to efficient decision-making, but impedes innovativeness and market responsiveness
			Conceptual studies	
Chang and Harrington (2000)	Optimal degree of centralization or decentralization in retail firms as multi-agents	None	Computational simulation	- Decentralization is favored as opposed to centralization when the market structure is heterogeneous, in a long-term market engagement, stable market environments and when consumers are not sensitive to store practices

Table A-5: Selected Studies concerning the Organization and Coordination of International Retail Activities

Source: Own creation.

One of the first contributions was provided by Harris (2000). The author interviews 107 store managers of large UK-based grocery and fashion retailers and concludes among other things that a high degree of centralization leads to efficient decision-making, but not to market orientation. Instead, this study confirms that the lower the degree of centralization and formalization, the higher the degree of market orientation. Arnold (2002) analyzes the success factors of the world's best retailers and comes to the conclusion that inspirational leadership and decentralized organizational structures form the basis of sustainable long-term success. By focusing rather on the balance between centralization and decentralization in a business-to-business context, Mitronen and Möller (2003) examine a hybrid organization in retailing. Based on transaction cost economics, contractual law and institutional theory, three important governance mechanisms were identified for different management levels: structural and organizational solutions, managerial policies and processes, as well as values, norms and trust. Moore, Birtwistle and Burt (2004) analyze in a case study-based research design the reasons for conflicts between headquarters and subsidiaries of international fashion retailers based in the UK. The authors conclude that the main potential for conflicts lies in the desire of subsidiary managers to respond to local conditions, whereas managers from the headquarters wish to standardize in order to gain global economies of scale. A smart solution to which both parties can agree is a collaborative decision-making process in which subsidiary managers contribute their experience and headquarter managers can further explain their strategic concepts. In contrast to Arnold (2002), Verity (2005) presents the successful transition of Shell's advertising activities from a formerly decentralized to a centralized organizational structure, but the results have to be treated with caution because, by considering gas stations, the results deal with a product that is homogenous worldwide. Palmer (2005) compares among other things the organizational structure and management processes of Wal-Mart International between a pre- and post-threshold period, i.e., the early years of international expansion vs. a more accelerated international growth phase afterwards. The pre-threshold period has been characterized by a highly centralized organization with excessive standardizations and unnecessary adaptations, resulting in considerable frustration in the local management. However, this changed in the post-threshold period as core infrastructure elements, such as sourcing and administrative functions, remained centralized, whereas all other functions were decentralized, resulting in greater autonomy of the local management.

By referring to more comprehensive observations, Evans, Mavondo and Bridson (2008) also assess the impact of centralized decision-making on psychic distance, retail strategy and retail entry strategy in their conceptualization mentioned previously. However, the investigation of 102 retailers confirms only statistical support for the latter. Thus, greater centralization of decision-making in the organizational structure leads more to the use of full control entry modes. In an investigation of 60 European retailers, Swoboda and Anderer (2008) identify the following coordination dimensions of retailing firms: systemic, structural and cultural coordination, which can also be applied to the formalization and centralization of decisions. By considering success according to these dimensions, the results show that the organizational structure itself has no direct effect on success, but the sole instruments of coordination do. Tacconelli and Wrigley (2009) analyze the strategic responses of retailers with international operations towards logistics and supply networks, real estate markets and the consumer market in China. The authors report that Wal-Mart has centralized its supply chain activities, similar to Tesco, by erecting two regional distribution centers in the northern and southern parts of China to achieve economies of scale. In contrast, Carrefour employs a decentralized structure in its supply chain due to the highly fragmented Chinese retail market. Wegner and Padula (2010) provide an interesting comparison of the organizational structure and inter-organizational governance of the German horizontal networks Intersport, Expert and ANWR. Their observation shows that strategic decisions in all three networks are made centrally and the participation of the member companies in these decisions is low, resulting in a high degree of adaptation in the strategic retail marketing program. However, the degree of control through the network is low, thus relinquishing enough autonomy to the member companies.

For the sake of completeness, further studies must be mentioned that investigate the organization and coordination of international retail activities, but only amongst other issues and in a more descriptive manner. As already mentioned, Mårtenson (1987) states further from the example of IKEA that the headquarter provides a standardized communication model to their store managers which has to be followed on the one hand, but leaves enough space for autonomous decisions on the other hand. In this respect, store managers are allowed to choose the advertising agency on their own and to develop an individual advertising campaign as long as it conforms to the guidelines from headquarters. By analyzing the transfer of a standardized employment system of a Japanese retailer to Hong Kong, Wong and Hendry (1997) report that local employees become frustrated because control was centralized to the headquarter and they felt deskilled as responsibilities were withdrawn. By investigating the internationalization of voluntary groups, Pederzoli (2008) concludes that voluntary groups are able to combine centralized functions with the autonomy of local independent retailers.

The only conceptual study in the area dealing with the organization and coordination of international retail activities was provided by Chang and Harrington

(2000). The authors provide an interesting contribution through a computational simulation of the optimum degree of decentralization and centralization, respectively. The results of the simulation indicate that decentralization is appropriate when market environments are heterogeneous but stable, consumers are less sensitive to retail store practices and the host country market engagement is laid out on a long-term horizon.

In accordance with the previous sections, international retail research regarding the organization and coordination of international retail activities, meaning the centralization of decision-making, formalization and specialization of tasks, is mainly descriptive, with the sole exception of Evans, Mavondo and Bridson (2008). From the current research status, it can be concluded that most studies argue in favor of a more decentralized organizational structure due to the culturally bound nature of the retail business. However, substantial empirical support for this notion is still missing, as even Evans, Mavondo and Bridson (2008) do not analyze the impact of centralized decision-making on retail performance. Furthermore, the idea of whether the centralization of decision-making is dependent upon the external environment is subject to question. For instance, Chang and Harrington (2000) suggest on the basis of their computational simulation that centralization of the organizational structure depends also on the stability of external conditions. Furthermore, no study known to the author investigates the degree of formalization and centralization, respectively, at the same time as the degree of standardization of the retail marketing program in the international retail context. Finally, no theoretical explanations are provided to explain the impact of rather mechanistic or organic organizational structures on performance abroad. Hence, new insights are needed on how the retail marketing program can be implemented successfully and with which organizational structure in culturally different foreign countries.

2.3. General Research Objectives

By emphasizing the increasing dynamics of retail internationalization and its differences compared to the internationalization of commonly investigated manufacturing firms, as well as by illustrating the current research status including the identification of relevant research gaps, three general research objectives of the present thesis emerge.

The general research objectives of this thesis encompass the investigation of how retailers employ specific decisions and which of them are most successful under which conditions through the replicated or adjusted use of whole strategies or strategic elements. Due to the high relevance of retail internationalization and the fairly narrow research status, new insights are provided into the drivers for strategic choices and success in increasingly distant foreign countries in order to leverage the full potential of the retailers' resources, to fulfill foreign customers' needs and to compete in the international arena.

On the one hand, the literature review above has uncovered the under-researched field of retail internationalization and has emphasized the need for more substantial insights. On the other hand, managers are particularly interested in these insights because previous research and retail management in practice have shown that retail internationalization is a double-edged sword. Accordingly, Gregory (2010) reports on the internationalization dilemma by stating on the one hand that many international retailers are highly successful, with increased sales, management experience gained and new positions in future growth markets. On the other hand, however, internationalization also suffers from high risks and costs and distracts management attention, resulting in a drain on resources, decreased profits and misdirected focus. Hence, new insights are of paramount importance to learn more about the appropriate decisions in international retailing and their successful use within the retail internationalization process. To shed more light on these complex issues, three studies have been designed that examine the following general research objectives:

- The first objective is to examine the role of institutionalized entry modes that develop over time and their boundary conditions from the external and internal environment for the choice of foreign retail market entry mode.
- The second objective attempts to disentangle the successful transfer of the retail format by standardizing or adapting various elements of the retail format including internal elements, which are invisible to the end-customers, and external elements, which are visible to the end-customers.
- The third objective also aims to analyze the success of retailers in foreign countries, but by elaborating how the retail marketing program can be suc-

cessfully implemented by means of an appropriate organizational structure, under consideration of culturally different markets.

These three general research objectives are addressed and evaluated in Chapter E by referring to each of the three studies. Each study in turn analyzes its general research objective in-depth by referring to detailed research questions. The next section provides a brief overview of the three studies, introducing the research focus, the gap in the literature including the detailed research questions, the conceptual framework, the empirical analysis and the contribution of each study.

3. Structure of and Contributions by the Studies

3.1. Study 1 – Retail Market Entry Mode Choice

According to the first general research objective, study one of this thesis investigates the choice of retail entry modes, which are defined as an organizational arrangement that makes possible the entry of a firm's resources to a foreign country (Root 1995). This decision is of paramount importance because it drives performance (Brouthers 2002; Brouthers, Brouthers and Werner 2003) and is difficult to change once established (Pedersen, Petersen and Benito 2002; Swoboda, Olejnik and Morschett 2011). Several studies have been conducted in the manufacturing context, based on various theories on more than 200 antecedents, as the most recent literature reviews indicate (Brouthers and Hennart 2007; Canabal and White 2008; Morschett, Schramm-Klein and Swoboda 2010). In this context, most studies from previous research assume that each entry mode choice follows the firm's deliberate efforts to enhance its competiveness, efficiency and control over critical resources (Brouthers, Brouthers and Werner 2008). However, Anderson and Gatignon (1986) have already stated that only a few firms actually demonstrate this behavior, whereas other firms rely on past decisions. To analyze how retail firms choose entry modes in response to such past decisions, the present study focuses on the role of an institutionalized entry mode in a subsequent entry mode choice. Thus, this study addresses the gap between the entry mode actually chosen and the entry mode that has been used predominantly in the past.

In general, the literature rarely views entry mode choice as depending upon past decisions (Benito, Petersen and Welch 2009). Although the research status of retail entry mode choice is still fairly narrow, as the literature review above indicates, the relevance of past decisions on subsequent entry mode choice is undisputed for service firms (Sanchez-Peinado, Pla-Barber and Hébert 2007). In general, however, only a few studies analyze this specific phenomenon empirically in further detail. In particular, little is known about whether an institutionalized entry mode influences a retailer's subsequent entry mode choice over time, in dependence upon boundary conditions from external pressures and internal capabilities. This is important because it can be assumed that retailers do not use only a few modes of entry, but revert mostly to entry modes that have been used predominantly in the past. Hence, the following research questions will be examined in further detail:

- To what extent can entry modes that have been used predominantly in the past predict a subsequent entry mode choice?
- By assuming opposing effects, this study asks additionally: how do external regulative and normative pressures in a host country and internal capabilities of retailers moderate the impact of institutionalized entry modes on subsequent entry mode choices?

The conceptual framework of study one is threefold. First, it is assumed that market entry mode choice is mainly influenced by the entry mode that has been used predominantly in the past. Such entry modes are understood as being institutionalized entry modes, i.e., full- and shared-controlled entry modes that have been employed as taken for granted in the course of time. Hence, this study refers to institutional theory, which argues that if a certain action is justified, it becomes an approach that is taken for granted with an increasing frequency of adoption (Zucker 1977). Second, it is assumed that retailers are forced to depart from their institutionalized actions when huge differences arise between home and host country regarding the political and cultural environment. Hence, it is again argued on the basis of institutional theory that retailers depart from their institutionalized entry mode due to pressures from the external institutional environment. Third, it is assumed that the use of an institutionalized entry mode can also be reinforced through firm-specific capabilities. Thus, this study refers additionally to the resource-based view (RBV) by arguing that accumulated international knowledge, including international experience and internationalization speed, facilitates the use of an institutionalized entry mode. In conclusion, institutional theory and the RBV are combined as requested by Meyer et al. (2009) and Brouthers, Brouthers and Werner (2008) and serve, therefore, as the theoretical underpinning of this study.

For empirical analysis of the conceptual framework derived, including the institutionalized entry mode that develops over time, a longitudinal data set was established based on secondary data from publicly available databases. Thus, market entries by the world's 30 leading grocery retailers were recorded in the time period from 1960 to 2007. This approach ensures that the analysis of inter-temporal variations is enabled and that data are available which are contemporaneously documented accurately and objectively. To test the proposed relationships, a binary logistic regression analysis was carried out due to the dichotomous nature of the dependent variable, which also allows investigation of the moderating effects of the boundary conditions from the external and internal environment.

By responding to the above mentioned research questions, this study contributes to the international business literature and, in particular, to the young research field of retail internationalization by overcoming the shortcomings of previous research. From a methodological perspective, the study provides profound insights for the first time on how retail entry modes are actually chosen by investigating more than 300 market entries. Furthermore, this study responds to the request by previous researchers to investigate the market entry mode choice over the course of time (e.g., Benito, Petersen and Welch 2009; Brouthers and Hennart 2007; Canabal and White 2008). From a theoretical perspective, this study combines institutional theory with the RBV and therefore provides a sound theoretical underpinning for the relationships analyzed. As a result, internal and external regulative and normative institutions are combined in a new manner. Furthermore, the relationships between internal and external institutional pressures in entry mode choices are analyzed in the retail context, as suggested in the conceptual study of Huang and Sternquist (2007). The results provide a more realistic view of how retail entry modes are actually chosen by confirming that retail entry mode choice is influenced more by institutionalized entry modes over time rather than by deliberate and conscious decisions that lead to the use several different entry modes depending on the respective situation, as was commonly assumed in previous research.

3.2. *Study 2 – Retail Format Transfer*

According to the second general research objective, study two of this thesis focuses on successful transfer of the retail format known from the retailers' home market. Thus, the retail format is understood as the elements of retail value chain activities that encompass the internal processes invisible to end-customers on the one hand, i.e., marketing and supply chain processes, and the external marketing program visible to end-customers on the other hand. Previous research has shown that retailers transfer these elements in a standardized way with regard to the home market or in an adapted way to the local host country environment (Goldman 2001; Jonsson and Foss 2011). This issue is of particular interest for research and practice because the right balance between costs savings achieved by standardization and benefits of local responsiveness achieved by adaptation provides both competitive advantages for retailers (Douglas and Wind 1987). Moreover, the wrong decision about the degree of standardization leads to a waste of resources and increases the possibility of market failure (Goldman 2001).

The issue of standardization and adaptation has been discussed by scholars for more than 50 years in more than 300 research contributions (Schmid and Kotulla 2011). However, despite the long-lasting debate and distinctive differences between retailers and manufacturers (Dawson 1994; Grönroos 1997), the successful transfer of processes and marketing offers has been neglected, as the above literature review indicates. First, little is known about the degree of standardization of retail format elements, how these elements are interrelated with each other and how these elements are associated with performance in a country. But with increasing retail internationalization, these decisions gain relevance because retailers have complex systems of inter- and intra-firm relational networks on the one hand that require standardization of processes to achieve greater efficiency of operations (Manrodt and Vitasek 2004; Wrigley, Coe and Currah 2005). On the other hand, retailers are forced to adapt their offers in order to fulfill customer needs due to their inherently high level of territorial embeddedness and local aspects of consumption (Dawson 2007). Second, although previous research suggests that certain retail format elements have to be distinguished into core and peripheral elements (Carman and Langeard 1980; Kaufmann and Eroglu 1999), no study known to the author has yet investigated which elements of the retail format belong to the group of core and which to the group of peripheral elements and how these elements influence successful retail format transfer. In conclusion, the following research questions emerge:

- Whether and which process and marketing program elements are standardized or adapted and how both internal processes and visible offers interact?
- By assuming that processes and marketing programs include more or less standardized core and peripheral elements, the relationship between them and towards performance might vary, generating the following questions: whether and how the degree of standardization of marketing program elements, as well as of marketing and supply chain processes, determines retailers' performance in a foreign country?

The conceptual framework of study two is twofold. First, it is assumed on the basis of the flexible format replication (FFR) approach according to Jonsson and Foss (2011) that the standardization degree and associations between process and program elements are positively associated by distinguishing between core and peripheral elements. Hence, it is argued that internal processes facilitate the standardization of marketing programs and therefore form the basis for global efficiency (Griffith, Chandra and Ryans 2003). Second, it is assumed on the basis of the profit maximization theory (PMT) (Samiee and Roth 1992) that the standardization of internal core and peripheral processes is associated with higher performance in a foreign country as is the standardization of core marketing program elements because these elements of the retail format serve as the template that is implemented in the same way in all foreign countries. In contrast, however, for peripheral marketing program elements, PMT suggests adjusting the visible offers according to the characteristics of the specific host country because these are able to drive local sales.

In order to analyze the proposed relationships, a dataset has been created using in-depth, face-to-face interviews with 126 executives at the headquarters of 102 retail firms from German-speaking countries, namely Austria, Germany and Switzerland, to assure a culturally homogenous sample and to avoid measurement invariance problems. The retailers were selected systematically by ensuring that each retailer operates abroad in at least two foreign countries. Before the interviews, extensive pre-tests were conducted with retail experts and retail managers in executive management seminars in order to create a standardized questionnaire, which was needed to disentangle and measure the elements of the retail format empirically. In order to test the hypotheses derived, structural equation modeling on the basis of the partial least squares (PLS) approach was applied as this enables an examination of causal interferences and is particularly suitable for small sample sizes (Henseler, Ringle and Sinkovics 2009).

By responding to the above mentioned research questions and in response to the research gaps revealed in the literature review, this study contributes to how the retail format can be transferred abroad successfully, argued on the basis of sound theoretical frameworks such as the FFR approach and the PMT, and validated with a comprehensive dataset for generating substantial and generalizable insights. Hence, this study responds to Goldman's (2001) call to investigate the elements of the know-how part as well as of the offering part of the retail format, but excludes retail culture, which can be considered as the implicit and informal part of the retail format and is therefore difficult to influence. Furthermore, this study builds on Jonsson and Foss (2011) by addressing two different levels of standardization, i.e., core and peripheral elements of the retail format, with more or less adaptation due to market-based learning. The results contribute to the current research status by demonstrating that the issue of transferring the retail format largely unchanged or adapted must be considered with more differentiation by distinguishing between internal and external elements, as well as between core and peripheral elements of the retail format. Hence, important suggestions can be drawn for retail managers.

3.3. Study 3 – Organization and Coordination of International Retail Activities

According to the third general research objective, study three of this thesis focuses on successful implementation of the retail marketing program, i.e., the use of standardized or adapted marketing-mix characteristics in foreign countries, by coordinating activities, i.e., by employing a mechanistic or an organic organizational structure (Sine, Mitsuhashi and Kirsch 2006) in psychically close and psychically distant countries. Both management of the external marketing program and its coordination by the organizational structure are among the most important and challenging decisions in the domain of international marketing because of increased global competition as well as increasingly dispersed activities around the world (Martinez and Jarillo 1989; Theodosiou and Leonidou 2003). The latter is particularly the case for retailers with international operations that are characterized by dispersed store units because the retailers' production location is usually in the host country, with important implications for management of the retail marketing program and its coordination through the organizational structure.

Despite the long research tradition, the results are still indecisive (Theodosiou and Leonidou 2003; Vorhies and Morgan 2003) and investigations in the retail context are widely lacking, as indicated by the above literature review, particularly for the organization of retail activities abroad (Burt and Carralero-Encinas 2000). However, according to Bartlett and Ghoshal's (1989) superior transnational strategy, it can be assumed that retailers have to be efficient by integrating activities and at the same time be locally responsible by adjusting activities according to the host country conditions. The question here is how retailers realize such a strategy by implementing which marketing program with which organizational structure. Furthermore, previous research has shown that both decisions depend on whether they are used in psychically close or psychically distant countries (Chang and Harrington 2000; Özsomer, Bodur and Cavusgil 1991). Hence, the following detailed research questions emerge:

- Is it more promising to apply a standardized marketing program to realize economies of scale implemented by an organic organizational structure to achieve local responsiveness or an adapted marketing program implemented by a mechanistic organizational structure?
- How are the marketing program and the organizational structure influenced in psychically close and psychically distant countries?

The conceptual framework of this study is twofold. It is first assumed for psychically close countries that retailers are most successful if they use a standardized marketing program with a formalized and decentralized organizational structure. It is therefore argued on the basis of the profit maximization theory (PMT) that this approach is more beneficial because a standardized marketing program is suitable in these countries and ensures economies of scale, whereas the structural empowerment of foreign entities, i.e., by the formalized decentralization of decision-making according to Mintzberg (1979), ensures that the firm can respond to the local host country conditions. Second, for psychically distant countries, it is assumed in contrast that retailers are most successful by applying an adapted marketing program with a less formalized and centralized organizational structure. Again, it is argued on the basis of the PMT that this strategy is more beneficial because an adapted marketing program is particularly suitable in psychically distant countries and ensures that the firm can respond to the local host country conditions, whereas no structural empowerment of foreign entities, i.e., informal centralization of decision-making, ensures economies of scale and reduces risk in psychically distant countries.

In order to test the proposed relationships, the same sample was used as in study two. Thus, the dataset includes the responses from 126 interviews by 102 retail firms from the aforementioned German-speaking countries. The average retailer in this sample is characterized as having total sales of 5,772 m €, 25,507 employees, a foreign sales share of 41.6%, 19.1 operating countries and has been operating internationally for 23.7 years, resulting in a representative sample of large European retail firms with international operations. Again, structural equation modeling on the basis of the PLS approach has been applied as this enables a comprehensive investigation of the moderating effect of psychically close and psychically distant countries and is particularly suitable for small sample sizes.

By addressing the above mentioned research questions and in response to the research gaps revealed in the literature review, this study contributes to successful implementation of the retail marketing program through the organizational structure in different foreign markets under consideration of a sound theoretical framework of the PMT and a substantial empirical database. Thus, this study responds to the call of Quester and Conduit (1996) to investigate the efficiency of marketing strategy and organizational structure. Furthermore, from a methodological perspective, the established approach of Evans and Mavondo (2002) by distinguishing between psychically close and psychically distant countries could be confirmed. The results contribute to the current research status by confirming empirically the assumption of the case-study based analysis of Jonsson and Foss (2011) that successful retailers use a template for their international expansion and adjust their concept due to local learning through a decentralized organizational structure, at least in psychically close markets. In conclusion, important implications can be drawn for managers.

4. Further Remarks

All three studies in the context of retailers with international operations explore the above mentioned research questions regarding the internationalization of retailing, encompassing the going and being international. In the following, each study is organized as follows:

- Introduction,
- theoretical background and conceptual framework,
- hypotheses development,
- empirical study, including sample design, measurement, method and results,
- discussion and conclusions, as well as limitations and directions for further research.

This structure is fixed no matter how each research question is explored. Furthermore, the structure is also independent of the methods applied, such as binary logistic regression on the basis of secondary data in study one or structural equation modeling on the basis of primary data in studies two and three. However, all research questions are explored on the bases of a suitable theoretical foundation, such as the institutional theory and the RBV in study one, the FFR and the PMT in study two as well as the PMT in study three.

All theories used are rooted in traditional management research. The institutional theory was established by Meyer and Rowan (1977) and further developed by DiMaggio and Powell (1983), Zucker (1983), North (1990) and Scott (1995), and claims that institutions from the external and internal environment impose isomorphic pressure to which organizations respond to gain legitimacy. Hence, the theory explains how organizations behave as social actors embedded in their own internal and external environment. The RBV was introduced by Wernerfelt (1984) and provides the perspective that strategic options emerge from the firms' internal resources. Accordingly, resources represent core capabilities that offer the potential for a unique advantage over competitors, whereas the external environment with its opportunities and threats is the same for every firm (Barney 1991; Priem and Butler 2001). Hence, the theory explains that when firms possess considerable capabilities, they behave accordingly in their strategic decisions in order to establish sustainable competitive advantages. The FFR approach is based on the contributions of Winter and Szulanski (2001) as well as of Jonsson and Foss (2011) and postulates that the replication of concepts is the dominant organizational form because the exploitation of existing know-how is ensured. However, this replicable template has to leave enough space to adjust certain elements according to the local host country conditions. Hence, this theoretical approach helps explain how to transfer a certain business formula abroad. Finally, the PMT was introduced by Samiee and Roth (1992) and posits that the main goal of a firm can be achieved by realizing economies of scale or through the benefits of market segmentation. As soon as the economies of scale exceed the benefits of market segmentation or vice versa, integration or adjustment of activities to the local host country conditions might be more profitable. Hence, the theory explains which strategic or organizational arrangement pays off under different conditions.

After exploring the detailed research questions in the following by means of the three studies presented in chapters B, C and D, the research and managerial implications of all three studies are summarized in chapter E in response to the general research questions. Finally, points of contact are addressed for further research in all three studies.

B. Study 1 – Effects of Institutionalized Entry Modes on Entry Mode Choices

1. Introduction

The choice of a foreign market entry mode, i.e., an institutional arrangement that makes possible the entry of firm resources into a foreign country (Root 1987), is known as a crucial decision because this choice drives performance (Brouthers 2002; Brouthers, Brouthers and Werner 2003) and is difficult to change once established (Pedersen, Petersen and Benito 2002; Swoboda, Olejnik and Morschett 2011). Consequently, foreign entry mode choices are intensively analyzed based on various theories on more than 200 antecedents (for reviews, see Brouthers and Hennart 2007; Canabal and White 2008; Morschett, Schramm-Klein and Swoboda 2010) and often based on the assumption that each choice follows the deliberate efforts of firms to enhance their competiveness, efficiency and control over critical resources (Brouthers, Brouthers and Werner 2008). However, Anderson and Gatignon (1986) have already stated that relatively few firms actually behave like this, as other firms rely instead on past decisions. To analyze how firms choose entry modes in response to past decisions, this study focuses on the role of institutionalized entry modes in subsequent entry mode choices. Thus, this study addresses the gap between a predicted entry mode choice and the actual entry modes that have predominantly been used in the past (Brouthers and Hennart 2007).

Previous studies have frequently investigated the effects of past decisions on future strategic behaviors (e.g., Amburgey and Miner 1992). Also the relevance of past decisions on subsequent entry mode choices is undisputed, as these decisions have even been included as control variable in cross-sectional studies but with mixed results (Sanchez-Peinado, Pla-Barber and Hébert 2007). However, only few studies empirically analyze this specific phenomenon in detail. Two studies analyze the relevance of past mode decisions for repeated entries by referring to mode inertia based on institutional theory regarding the same host country (Yiu and Makino 2002) and across different host countries (Lu 2002), and three studies refer to organizational learning based on transaction cost theory (Chang and Rosenzweig 2001) and the resource-based view (RBV) (Padmanabhan and Cho 1999; Sanchez-Peinado,

Pla-Barber and Hébert 2007). Benito, Petersen and Welch (2009) acknowledge both mode inertia and mode learning as major evolutionary concepts related to entry modes in addition to a third type known as mode dynamics, which refer to changes in foreign operation modes in a host country (e.g., Swoboda, Olejnik and Morschett 2011). However, although mode learning refers to the deliberate efforts of firms, including past experiences, Anderson and Gatignon (1986) argue beyond this by assuming that entry mode choices are also made without deliberate or conscious evaluations because habitual behavior tends to supersede the conscious awareness of decision makers (Grewal and Dharwadkar 2002; Oliver 1996). Thus far, an institutional theory that posits internal isomorphic pressures and leads managers to follow institutionalized decisions has been analyzed across different host countries only by Lu (2002). Because the interdependencies of past decisions with the external and internal environments are neglected, two research gaps emerge.

There is a lack of empirical research whether institutionalized entry modes, i.e., full- and shared-controlled entry modes that have been employed as taken for granted in the course of time, are able to predict subsequent entry mode choices and, in particular, how contingently stable this relationship is over time. Institutional theory provides an appropriate theoretical basis for the investigation of both topics because this theory is able to explain the relevance of internal isomorphic pressure and its dependence upon external isomorphic pressure, i.e., pressures from regulative and normative institutions in a host country. Thus, the relationship between institutionalized entry modes and subsequent entry mode choices may be weakened as the external institutional environment forces firms to adapt their entry modes (institutional duality), whereas the relationship may be reinforced as a firm's internal capabilities enable the application of an institutionalized mode. Both scenarios are relevant to subsequent entry mode choices and require detailed analyses. Therefore, a combination of theories is necessary because institutional theory assists in explaining the influence of internal and external isomorphic pressures on entry mode choice and thus explains institutional duality from a socially justified perspective while neglecting the economically justified perspective that is addressed by capabilities that are based on the RBV.

Prior studies primarily investigate manufacturing firms. In contrast, this study argues that service firms are distinctive, and their specific characteristics have not yet been sufficiently addressed in entry mode research (Canabal and White 2008). Specifically, the retail sector is distinctive because of the need to be locally adapted to a host country and to establish a store network abroad (Swoboda, Zentes and Elsner 2009). More importantly, the entry mode choice seems to be particularly relevant for retailers because of their relatively high dependence on the external environment in a host country and because of their typically high resource needs with respect to the expansion of store networks abroad. Consequently, institutional theory is particularly relevant in this context (Huang and Sternquist 2007) and for investigating the relationship between institutionalized entry modes and subsequent mode choice as well as its influence through external and internal factors.

In sum, the aim of this study is to analyze the following research question: to what extent can entry modes that have predominantly been used in the past predict a subsequent entry mode choice? Assuming opposing effects, this study addresses an additional question: how do external regulative and normative pressures in a host country and the internal capabilities of firms moderate the relationship between past entry modes and future entry mode choices?

By responding to these questions, this study contributes to the international business literature, especially with respect to institutional theory and service industries. From a methodological perspective, this study responds to calls for the use of panel data in entry mode research to obtain a better understanding of entry mode choices over time (Andersen 1997; Asmussen, Benito and Petersen 2009; Benito, Petersen and Welch 2009; Canabal and White 2008). From a theoretical perspective, this study responds to the call of Meyer et al. (2009) and Lu (2002) to investigate the extent to which internal institutions influence variations in entry mode choices. According to Huang and Sternquist (2007), the relationships between internal and external institutional pressures in entry mode choices in retail are analyzed. Therefore, internal and external regulative and normative institutions are combined in a new manner. That is, the internal pressures that are antecedences of subsequent entry mode choices and external pressures that moderate this relationship (institutional duality). Furthermore, this study combines institutional theory with the RBV by analyzing how firm-specific capabilities moderate the relationship between institutionalized entry modes and subsequent entry mode choices. The observations in this study may assist in providing a more realistic view of how managers reach actual entry mode decisions by emphasizing that retail entry mode choices are actually influenced by institutionalized entry modes over time rather than the result of deliberate and conscious decisions, as was commonly assumed in previous research, e.g., studies that were based on transaction cost analyses (e.g., Zhao, Luo and Suh 2004).

The study begins with a review of the institutional theory literature on entry mode research because this theory represents the theoretical foundation. Subsequently, a set of hypotheses will be deduced and tested empirically using panel data for 309 market entries of the world-leading retailers for the period from 1960 to 2007. The results are presented and discussed subsequently as well as the limitations of this study.

2. Literature on Institutional Theory in Entry Mode Choice

Prior research on institutional predictions of entry mode choice is sparse and distinctive from research that pertains to the choice of the most efficient entry mode, which often only investigates the external institutional environment. However, the literature on institutional theory regarding foreign entry mode choices has been reviewed by focusing on four aspects: 1) the role of internal institutional pressures, 2) the role of external institutional pressures, 3) the correspondence of internal and external institutional pressures and 4) studies that combine institutional theory and the RBV.

Huang and Sternquist (2007) discuss conceptually and Lu (2002) demonstrates empirically that the frequency of adoption of an entry mode in previous market entries increases the propensity to use the same entry mode in subsequent market entries. In particular, Lu (2002) shows that intra-organizational mimetic behavior within multinational enterprises (MNEs) has a stronger influence on entry mode choices than inter-organizational mimic behavior. Furthermore, Yiu and Makino (2002) support the use of the same institutionalized mode by MNE but for sequential market entries into the same host country.

The authors underline the influence of the entry modes that were most frequently used in the past for subsequent mode choices and thus emphasize internal institutional pressures, i.e., historical norms that lead to institutional persistence in the entry mode choice.

Many studies discuss the relevance of external institutional pressures by addressing selected norms and regulations as antecedents of entry mode choices. The importance of these antecedents is demonstrated by Xu, Pan and Beamish (2004) with respect to regulative and normative distance, by Meyer and Nguyen (2005) with respect to variations in economic institutional factors, by Uhlenbruck et al. (2006) with respect to the pervasiveness of corrupt governments, by Estrin, Baghdasaryan and Meyer (2009) with respect to institutional distance and finally by Xia, Tan and Tan (2008) and Chan and Makino (2007) with respect to inter-organizational mimic behavior and within host countries. Similarly, some studies combine transaction cost analysis (TCA) and external institutional pressures, such as country risk, legal restrictions and the level of intellectual property protection (Delios and Beamish 1999), progress in institutional reforms (Meyer 2001), legal restrictions (Brouthers 2002), political constraints, corruption and cultural and linguistic distance (Demirbag, Glaister and Tatoglu 2007). The main contribution of most of these studies is the finding that regulative and normative pressures in host countries force firms to choose entry modes with lower levels of resource commitment.

Conceptually, Xu and Shenkar (2002) and Huang and Sternquist (2007) question how internal and external institutions correspond with one another to explain entry mode choices (institutional duality). However, only a few studies empirically investigate internal and external institutions, and these studies usually consider institutions to be direct antecedents. For example, such studies consider entry mode choice in one country (e.g., past entry modes and cultural distance (Chang and Rosenzweig 2001) as well as regulatory institutions (Yiu and Makino 2002)) and in different countries (e.g., internal cognitive structures and regulative risk and cultural distance (Chen et al. 2009)) as well as entry mode change (internal isomorphic pressures and governmental regulations (Puck, Holtbruegge and Mohr 2009)). Indirect relationships between internal and external institutions are only empirically investigated by Estrin, Baghdasaryan and Meyer (2009), who support a converted U-relationship for the influence of institutional distance on mode choices, and Schwens, Eiche and Kabst (2011), who show the moderating effects of having an informal institutional distance and formal institutional risk on the entry mode choices of SMEs in a TCA-based model. In conclusion, studies that investigate the direct effects simultaneously provide similar results, which indicate that internal institutional isomorphism results in entry mode persistence, and external institutional pressures result in entry modes with lower resource commitment levels.

On the basis of the RBV, some studies address various antecedents, primarily those with direct effects rather than moderating effects, of entry mode choice. For example, Mutinelli and Piscitello (1998) argue that international knowledge is an important capability of MNE and show that the accumulation of knowledge increases the probability of establishing full control modes. Three studies combine institutional theory with the RBV. Oliver (1997) conceptualizes how capabilities are embedded into the internal and external institutional environments. Brouthers, Brouthers and Werner (2008) show empirically that when institutional distances regarding social norm, legal and country risk decrease, firms with low levels of specific resources shift from shared- to full control modes. Finally, Meyer et al. (2009) show that, for strong local institutions, acquisitions and joint ventures are favored over greenfield modes when a foreign entrant has a high need for intangible resources. In conclusion, this research indicates the importance of extending the RBV with institutional reasoning that employs external institutions as the antecedents or moderators of entry mode choices.

3. Theoretical Foundation

Scholars have examined entry mode decisions from different angles, such as TCA, the OLI paradigm, internationalization theory, the RBV and institutional theory (Brouthers and Hennart 2007; Canabal and White 2008). With regard to the research questions outlined above, two research streams are analyzed: 1) studies that consider how institutionalized entry modes determine subsequent entry mode choices and 2) studies that analyze the effects of external and internal determinants on this relationship. Thus, this study focuses on institutional theory and the RBV. The use of both theories broadens the arguments regarding the procedural character of entry mode choices (Kostova 1999; Penrose 1995) and thus overcomes the main limitation of the most frequently employed TCA in entry mode research (Jones and Coviello 2005; Williamson 1985). Institutional theory is employed to determine the effects of institutionalized entry modes on entry mode choice and the influence of external institutional pressures. The RBV is employed to determine the effects of internal firm-specific capabilities because these capabilities are not considered by the socially justified institutional theory (Oliver 1997).

Institutional theory considers organizations to be social actors who are embedded in their own internal and external environment consisting of structures, standards and practices that have been established in the past and by other social actors, organizations and institutions (DiMaggio and Powell 1983; Meyer and Rowan 1977). These institutions impose isomorphic pressure to which organizations respond to gain legitimacy. According to Scott (1995), there are three factors related to the institutional pressures to which an organization responds to strive for legitimacy: internal cognitive pressures, external regulative pressures and external normative pressures. Firms that do not respond to these pressures assume the risk of failure abroad (Brouthers and Hennart 2007). Specifically, *internal cognitive pressures* are related to the imprinting concept of Stinchcombe (1965), i.e., if a certain action is justified, then it becomes an approach that is taken for granted with an increasing frequency of adoption (Zucker 1977). Hence, institutionalized actions, such as institutionalized entry modes, are characteristically uniform and resistant to change, even in future entry mode choices. *External regulative pressures* refer to the establishment, monitoring and enforcement of formal rules, such as political-legal requirements, whereas *external normative pressures* refer to informal norms, values and beliefs, such as cultural distance. It is evident from a sociological (DiMaggio and Powell 1983) and an economical perspective (North 1990) that such external pressures influence organizational decisions because the institutional environment varies among countries. Thus, institutional duality can be assumed because decision makers may employ institutionalized actions, such as entry modes, that were predominantly used in the past to gain internal legitimacy but may depart from this practice with regard to external regulative and normative pressures.

The RBV allows for the consideration of internal firm-specific capabilities and their effect on the propensity to choose an institutionalized entry mode. Therefore, the RBV assumes that a strategy choice depends on a firm's resources and capabilities that emerge over time (Madhok 1997). With regard to the reasoning of the RBV (Barney 1991; Penrose 1995), scholars generally assume that the choice of a foreign market entry mode depends on whether a firm's own capabilities can be exploited abroad or whether the foreign markets themselves serve as sources for the acquisition and development of new resources (Brouthers and Hennart 2007; Ekeledo and Sivakumar 2004). It is assumed that firm-specific capabilities represent input factors for strategy development and implementation (Amit and Schoemaker 1993). Consequently, the emergence of firm-specific capabilities may enable firms to realize a specific strategy and, therefore, an institutionalized entry mode. As capabilities such as international knowledge are crucial for MNEs (Mutinelli and Piscitello 1998), it is assumed that international knowledge that is accumulated over time may reinforce the use of organizational routines and, therefore, that of institutionalized entry modes.

4. Conceptual Framework and Hypotheses Development

In this section, the hypotheses proposed by this study are deduced. The conceptual model summarizes the set of relationships examined in this study (Figure B-1). It is proposed that the choice of market entry modes primarily depends on the institutionalized entry mode with regard to the organizational imprinting effect in contrast with mode dynamics and mode learning. Moreover, it is argued that this behavior changes in response to the external environment because regulative and normative pressures force firms to adjust their institutionalized entry mode within a country. In turn, it is argued that this behavior is reinforced by firm-specific capabilities because accumulated international knowledge, including international experience and internationalization speed, facilitates the employment of an institutionalized entry mode.

Subsequently, each relationship is discussed from a theoretical perspective, and empirical evidence for the assumptions is also provided in the retail context.

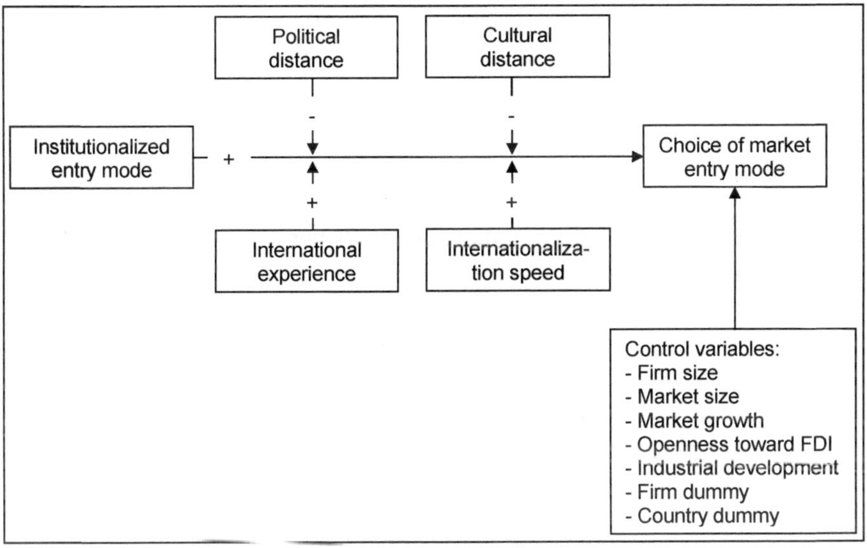

Figure B-1: Conceptual Framework
Source: Own creation.

4.1. Institutionalized Entry Mode and Subsequent Entry Mode Choice

Various concepts pertaining to the evolution of entry modes are first introduced to explain the relevance of institutionalized entry modes for subsequent entry mode choices. Accordingly, Benito, Petersen and Welch (2009) distinguish between the concepts of mode learning and mode inertia by considering the choice of the initial entry mode and the concept of mode dynamics by considering the choice of foreign operation modes. Studies that refer to mode learning through experiences, routines or competencies use resource-based reasoning to argue that the chosen entry modes are those for which the highest amount of resources, such as knowledge, has been accumulated (Padmanabhan and Cho 1999) or use transaction-cost reasoning to argue that the chosen entry modes are those for which the lowest amount of transaction costs, such as opportunity costs, has been acquired (Chang and Rosenzweig 2001). However, previous research has shown that habitual behavior can supersede the conscious awareness of decision makers (Grewal and Dharwadkar 2002; Oliver 1996). Thus, it is assumed in this study that entry mode decisions are based on constraints based on cognitive mindsets rather than deliberate and conscious evaluations that are formed by habits and inertia to conform to previously established modes. This results in the use of an existing entry mode rather than the pursuit of alternative modes. Furthermore, decisions become with an increasing frequency of adoption a taken for granted approach in the course of time. Thus, institutional theory suggests that firms may use existing institutionalized entry modes in subsequent entry mode choices. Such institutionalized behavior exists "when managers [...] justify actions with the claim that 'we have always done it this way', 'everybody does it this way' or 'that's just the way things are done around here'" (Oliver 1997, pp. 699–700). According to Lu (2002), this organizational imprinting phenomenon is understood as intra-organizational mimic behavior and can, therefore, be described as institutionalized entry modes.

Few of the reviewed studies provide evidence that MNEs use entry modes that have frequently been used in the past in the same host country which underlines the influence of historical norms that lead to institutional persistence (Yiu and Makino 2002). Lu (2002) supports this behavior of manufacturing firms across countries for initial market entries by referring to the concept of intra-organizational mimic behavior, whereas Sanchez-Peinado, Pla-Barber and Hébert (2007) find no support in the context of capital-intensive service firms. However, with respect to the retail context, Huang and Sternquist (2007) argue that institutionalized retail entry modes may influence subsequent entry mode choices because global retailers, such as The Body Shop or Wal-Mart, tend to favor the same shared- or full control entry modes for subsequent market entries.

Hypothesis 1: Institutionalized entry modes enhance the propensity to use the same market entry mode in subsequent initial market entries across countries.

4.2. Moderating Effects of the External Institutional Environment

Institutional theory suggests that external regulative and normative pressures may influence the relationship between institutionalized entry modes and the subsequent choices regarding entry modes. Such external pressures are especially important for international retailers, who are particularly exposed to various regulative pressures, e.g., political-legal requirements, and normative pressures, e.g., culture-specific customer behavior, because of their local presence with store networks abroad (Bianchi and Ostale 2006). Because retailers evaluate external environments prior to market entry, the regulative and normative distances between the home and host markets may be particularly relevant (Kostova and Zaheer 1999). Consequently, retailers may maintain an entry mode that was predominantly used in the past until regulative and normative distances force them to depart from such an entry mode. Accordingly, this study focuses on the political and cultural distance.

4.2.1 Political Distance

The regulative environment refers "to establish the right to do business in the new market" (Yiu and Makino 2002, p. 670). Firms are therefore forced to conform to the regulative environment, so it can be assumed that greater differences of this environment between the host and home country make it more difficult for firms to transfer strategic routines abroad because such behavior could lead to conflicts (Kostova 1999). Thus, as firms are forced to conform to political pressures, a large political difference may force them to choose entry modes other than institutionalized entry modes. In contrast, a small political distance enables firms to choose an institutionalized entry mode because this mode is legitimate from a regulative perspective.

The literature in the review supports the moderating role of political distance but not in the context of institutionalized entry modes (e.g., Brouthers, Brouthers and Werner 2008; Meyer and Nguyen 2005). Xu and Shenkar (2002) and Xu, Pan and Beamish (2004) show that as political distance increases, firms choose shared-controlled modes to reduce the risk of institutional conflicts, whereas Kostova and Roth (2002) show that with an increasing political distance, firms choose greenfield investments as it facilitates the transfer of business practices. Thus, in both contexts, legitimacy is secured in a local environment if firms depart from their institutionalized modes, i.e., a full control mode in the first context and a shared-controlled mode in the second context. Consequently, increasing political distance moderates the relationship between institutionalized entry modes and subsequent entry mode choices. The moderating effect is also indicated by Schwens and Kabst (2009), who show that the higher the political uncertainty the higher the probability that the entry mode will be changed for a second market entry. Also in the retail context, in which political distance is particularly important because retailers must conform to regulations that include land planning, pricing and store opening hours (Huang and Sternquist 2007), retailers are forced to employ entry modes with greater resource commitments as local governments aim to attract foreign direct investments (FDI) in their country (Grewal and Dharwadkar 2002; Huang and Sternquist 2007) whereas other retailers, such as the UK retail giant Tesco, were forced to engage in joint ventures with local partners when entering China and Thailand (Samiee, Yip and Luk 2004). In conclusion, it is assumed that different retailers with various institutionalized entry modes depart from their institutionalized entry modes in their host countries with greater political distance to conform to the regulative environment.

Hypothesis 2: The impact of an institutionalized entry mode on the choice of subsequent entry modes will be weaker with a greater political distance between the host and home countries.

4.2.2 Cultural Distance

In contrast to the political distance, the cultural distance between a host country and a home country refers to the normative institutional environment to which firms have also to conform by coping with the established local expectations of each respective society (Yiu and Makino 2002). According to institutional theory, a high level of cultural distance makes it difficult for MNEs to transfer strategic routines abroad. Thus, as firms are forced to conform to cultural pressures, a high level of cultural distance may force them to choose an entry mode other than the institutionalized entry mode. In contrast, a lower level of cultural distance makes it more likely that a firm will choose an institutionalized entry mode because this mode is legitimate from a cultural perspective.

The reviewed literature shows that even in meta-analyses (Morschett, Schramm-Klein and Swoboda 2010; Tihanyi, Griffith and Russell 2005), cultural distance shows ambiguous direct effects on entry mode choice so that it is suggested to consider cultural distance as a moderating effect. Xu and Shenkar (2002) and Xu, Pan and Beamish (2004) show that with increasing cultural distance, firms choose shared-controlled modes because when less ownership is employed, local branches are perceived as less “foreign”, whereas Estrin, Baghdasaryan and Meyer (2009) show that with an increasing cultural distance, firms choose full control modes because these modes are less concerned from difficulties in management collaborations due to different norms, values and beliefs in organizational cultures and management styles. Thus, in both contexts, legitimacy is secured in a local environment if firms depart from their institutionalized mode, i.e., a full control mode in the first context and a shared-controlled mode in the second context. Consequently, increasing cultural distance moderates the relationship between institutionalized entry modes and entry mode choices. Also in the retail context, in which cultural distance is of particular importance because of the need for retailers to conform to several stakeholders in foreign markets (Bianchi and Ostale 2006), retailers are forced to employ shared-controlled modes to prevent market failure through missing adaptations (El-Amir and Burt 2008), whereas other retailers are forced to employ full control modes due to highly perceived retail brand equities within a host country society (Lu, Karpova and Fiore 2011). In conclusion, it is assumed that different retailers with various institutionalized entry modes depart from these modes to conform to the normative environment, especially in host countries with a high level of cultural distance.

Hypothesis 3: The impact of an institutionalized entry mode on the choice of subsequent entry modes will be weaker with a greater cultural distance between the host and home countries.

4.3. Moderating Effects of Internal Capabilities

The RBV highlights international knowledge as an important capability of MNEs (Newbert 2007) that may influence the relationship between institutionalized entry modes and subsequent entry mode choices. However, firms accumulate international knowledge as soon as the first country has been entered (Erramilli 1991) and also through the number of country entries within a specific period of time (Oviatt and McDougall 2005; Wagner 2004). Thus, both international experience and internationalization speed may reinforce the employment of an institutionalized entry mode.

4.3.1 International Experience

The process of learning through international experience can be described as "the legacy of firm's own history" (Colombo 1995, p. 5). With regard to the RBV, firm-specific capabilities, i.e., international experience, arise through learning processes over time so that the use of an institutionalized entry mode is facilitated in the case of a high level of international experience. Thus, benefits can be increased through accumulated experience and legitimacy can be secured due to the facilitated use of an institutionalized entry mode. In contrast, a low level of international experience causes uncertainty and results in intensive evaluations of the external environment (Haunschild and Miner 1997). Thus, as benefits cannot be increased and legitimacy cannot be secured due to missing international experience, the preference for the use of an institutionalized entry mode may be reduced.

Padmanabhan and Cho (1999) show that organizational routines, which are established through prior experience with a mode, facilitate the use of the same mode in subsequent market entries (for an alliance context, see Madhok 1998) and thus reduce costs and enhance benefits through knowledge transfer (Sambharya 1996). Moreover, for manufacturing firms, Lu (2002) supports the moderating role of country experience on the relationship between intra-organizational mimic behavior and entry mode choices in the same country. Consequently, it is assumed in this study that an increasing amount of international experience reinforces the influence of institutionalized entry modes on the choice of subsequent entry modes. In the retail context for instance, Alexander and Quinn (2002) present the case of Marks & Spencer, which, as the result of internal learning processes (several country openings, exits and re-entries), was able to conclude that franchising is their preferred entry mode abroad, although this mode is not used in their home country. Accordingly, it is likewise assumed that because of increased international experience, the use of an institutionalized entry mode in subsequent market entries is reinforced over time.

Hypothesis 4: The impact of an institutionalized entry mode on the choice of subsequent entry modes will be stronger with a larger amount of international experience.

4.3.2 Internationalization Speed

In contrast to international experience, internationalization speed refers to the number of foreign markets that have been entered over time and encompasses the country scope, i.e., how rapidly foreign market entries are accumulated within a specific period of time (Vermeulen and Barkema 2002). With regard to the RBV, firm-specific capabilities, i.e., the ability to internationalize within a short period of time, emerge through learning processes over time and lead to economies of scale by multiplying a business concept and facilitating the use of an institutionalized entry mode to ensure that legitimacy is secured. Consequently, a high internationalization speed reinforces the use of institutionalized entry modes. In contrast, a low internationalization speed may limit the realization of economies of scale by multiplying the retail format and the securing of legitimacy so that the preference for an institutionalized entry mode may be reduced.

Previous studies show that a high internationalization speed increases the difficulty with which firms adopt new business model configurations (e.g., Hannan and Freeman 1984) and hampers the employment of new organizational routines (Nelson and Winter 2008). Consequently, it is more beneficial to employ an institutionalized entry mode if a firm enters many countries in a short period of time. In the retail context, Carruthers (2003) reports that the fashion retailer Zara has entered 30 countries within only two years by applying the same format transfer strategies, and Swoboda, Zentes and Elsner (2009) report that the German retail giant Metro Group realizes a high internationalization speed using preferred entry modes and formats. Thus, it is hypothesized in this study that a higher internationalization speed makes it more advantageous to employ an institutionalized entry mode in subsequent market entries.

Hypothesis 5: The impact of an institutionalized entry mode on the choice of subsequent entry modes will be greater with a higher internationalization speed.

5. Empirical Study

5.1. Data Set

For the testing of the hypotheses, a panel data set based on secondary data has been employed to analyze causal interferences over time and to ensure the availability of data that are accurately, objectively and contemporaneously documented. A sample of grocery retailers was chosen for analysis because of the ability to control multilevel sectoral influences that can occur if retailers from further sectors are considered (Brouthers and Hennart 2007; Davis, Desai and Francis 2000) and because the grocery sector is the largest retail sector that attracts different consumer segments and encompasses the broadest range of food and non-food products in contrast with specialized retailers. Data pertaining to the individual foreign market entries of the 30 world-leading retailers were collected because smaller grocery retailers (e.g., those with world rankings of 31 to 50) are either less internationalized or not internationalized at all. Within this group of 30 world-leading retailers, the retailers with less than one percent of foreign sales (e.g., Kroger, Target and Walgreens) and those with only one foreign market (e.g., Sears, Safeway and Woolworth) were excluded. This procedure resulted in 309 country entries of 18 retailers in 82 countries between 1960 and 2007, so that this sample represents the market entries of all internationally operating grocery retailers (Table B-1). Thus, the subjects of analysis are the 309 individual market entries of grocery retailers, which are defined as the first instance in which a retailer operates a local store-based business in a host country from which it was previously absent.

Rank in world according to sales	Retail firm	Founding year	Start of internationalization (first market entry)	Country of origin	Total sales in bn $	No. of served foreign markets in 2007	Foreign sales ratio in %	Number of initial foreign market entries
20	AEON	1950	1984	Japan	40	3	5	4
23	Ahold	1887	1976	Netherland	33	8	65	29
13	Aldi	1960	1967	Germany	51	17	41	17
12	Auchan	1961	1981	France	51	11	50	18
2	Carrefour	1959	1973	France	110	31	56	44
21	Casino	1898	1993	France	37	10	32	15
5	Costco	1983	1984	USA	71	7	22	7
29	Delhaize	1867	1970	Belgium	24	7	77	12
19	Edeka	1907	1989	Germany	40	1	5	7
17	Intermarché	1969	1988	France	44	8	10	9
15	Leclerc	1949	1992	France	46	5	6	5
3	Metro Group	1964	1968	Germany	86	32	61	32
9	Rewe	1927	1991	Germany	61	14	29	15
6	Schwarz Group	1930	1989	Germany	69	22	49	22
22	Spar	1932	1947	Netherland	37	33	56	34
25	Tengelmann	1893	1972	Germany	30	14	42	19
4	Tesco	1924	1993	UK	85	13	27	15
1	Walmart	1962	1991	USA	342	16	25	18

Excluded with foreign sales less than 1% such as Kroger (Rank 7), Target (8), Walgreens (11), CVS (14), Supervalu (26), Wesfarmers (27), Sainsbury (28), Migros (30) or only one foreign market such as Sears (16), Safeway (18), Woolworths (24), specific history of expansion Seven&I (10).

Table B-1: The World Leading Grocery Retailers in 2007

Source: Planet Retail (2008).

The data for all of the variables were collected at the time of market entry because Brouthers and Hennart (2007) state that the most effective method for investigating entry mode decisions is at the time when such decisions are being made. Thus, entry mode decisions are analyzed when they actually occur rather than retrospectively, as in cross-sectional research designs. Firm data, such as the number of employees, were obtained from annual reports, and the year of market entry and the entry mode choices were obtained from the Planet Retail database, which belongs to the leading retail intelligence provider, which covers data on the corporate level across 211 markets (Planet Retail 2011a). Country data were collected from publicly available databases including the World Bank, the Globe study, the Macro Data Guide, Nationmaster and the United Nations World Urbanization Prospects.

5.2. Measurement of Variables

5.2.1 Dependent Variable

As in this study, most contributions in entry mode research acknowledge control as a crucial factor (e.g., Ekeledo and Sivakumar 2004) and, therefore, analyze the choice between full- and shared-controlled entry modes to assure the comparability of the results (Canabal and White 2008). Table B-2 indicates that a full control mode (coded by 1) is composed of wholly owned subsidiaries and acquisitions, in contrast with shared-controlled modes (coded by 0), such as joint ventures, franchise and licenses and minority stakes (Herrmann and Datta 2002; Tan, Erramilli and Liang 2001). As shown in the results section, the results are stable even when acquisitions and franchising/ licensing are excluded from the estimations, as it could be argued that acquisitions do not belong to any entry mode choice and that franchising and licensing are entry modes with no control factors. The distribution of the observed entry modes shows 213 full- and 96 shared-controlled modes, which is according to previous studies in the service sector (e.g., Sanchez-Peinado, Pla-Barber and Hébert 2007).

5.2.2 Independent Variables

The *institutionalized entry mode*, i.e., the entry mode that has predominantly been used in the past, has been measured for the retail sector, as suggested by Huang and Sternquist (2007) and as applied by Lu (2002) and Yiu and Makino (2002) for manufacturers, according to the ratio of the number of full control modes to the total number of entry modes used for the same company in its host countries (Table B-2).

No.	Variable	Description	Scale	Item characteristic	Sources
Dependent variable					
1	Entry mode	Shared- vs. full control modes	Dichotomous	0/1	Canabal and White (2008)
Predictor variable					
2	Institutionalized entry mode	Percentage of previous market entries that were full control modes	Continuous	0 - 1	Huang and Sternquist (2007); Lu (2002); Yiu and Makino (2002)
Moderating variables					
3	Political distance	POLCONV	Continuous	0 - 1	Henisz (2000)
4	Cultural distance	Distance in Globe dimensions between home and host country according to Kogut and Singh (1988)	Continuous	0 - ∞	Estrin, Baghdasaryan and Meyer (2009); House et al. (2007)
5	International experience	Number of years since the first market entry	Continuous	0 - ∞	Blomstermo, Sharma and Sallis (2006); Brouthers (2002)
6	Internationalization speed	Number of market entries divided by the number of international experience	Continuous	0 - ∞	Chan, Finnegan and Sternquist (2011); Vermeulen and Barkema (2002)
Control variables					
7	Firm size	Number of employees per 10,000	Continuous	0 - ∞	Brouthers, Brouthers and Werner (2008); Erramilli and Rao (1993)
8	Market size	Host country GDP per 10 bn	Continuous	0 - ∞	Barkema and Vermeulen (1998)
9	Market growth	Percentage annual development of GDP	Continuous	± ∞	Barkema and Vermeulen (1998); Herrmann and Datta (2002)
10	Openness toward FDI	Ratio of FDI over GDP	Continuous	0 - ∞	Contractor and Kundu (1998); Johnson and Tellis (2008)
11	Industrial development	Percentage of urbanization	Continuous	0 - 1	Alon and McKee (1999)
12	Corporate dummy	No corporate vs. corporate of investigation	Dichotomous	0/1	Beck, Brüderl and Woywode (2008); Vermeulen and Barkema (2001)
13	Country dummy	No country vs. country of investigation	Dichotomous	0/1	Beck, Brüderl and Woywode (2008); Vermeulen and Barkema (2001)

Table B-2: Measurement of Variables
Source: Own creation.

Political distance was measured by employing the political constraint index (POLCONV) of Henisz (2000), which is one of the most comprehensive measures for the political environment (Jiménez 2010). To calculate the index value for each country annually from 1960 to 2007, the independent institutional actors with veto power are considered (García-Canal and Guillén 2008). The index ranges from 0, which denotes governments with no veto power by other institutions, such as dictatorships, to 1, which denotes governments in which several institutions have veto powers, such as democracies. To measure the political distance for each market entry, the political constraint values of the home and host country were subtracted from one another, as suggested by Berry, Guillén and Zhou (2010).

The *cultural distance* between the home and host countries was measured according to the Euclidian distance of the dimensions of the Globe study (House et al. 2007; Kogut and Singh 1988) because these dimensions are focused solely on cultural aspects, as suggested by institutional theory. According to Schwens, Eiche and Kabst (2011), this study employs the "practice" indices because these values are particularly suitable for analyzing the influence of culture in an organizational context rather than in a societal context. Moreover, it is particularly important for grocery retail firms to measure the distance between the home and host countries because retailers conduct their market entry decisions mostly centrally in their headquarters instead of by the entities abroad (Håkanson and Ambos 2010; Swoboda, Zentes and Elsner 2009).

International experience is measured by the number of years between the first foreign market entry and the observed market entry (e.g., Blomstermo, Sharma and Sallis 2006; Brouthers 2002). As this study investigates entry mode choice as part of the overall internationalization strategy, this measurement of international experience is more appropriate (Erramilli 1991) because it refers to how international business operations can be used, developed and transferred from one market to another (Johanson and Vahlne 2003).

Finally, *internationalization speed* was measured according to Vermeulen and Barkema (2002), and Chan, Finnegan and Sternquist (2011) in the retail context, based on the average number of market entries per year. Therefore, the number of foreign markets in which a retailer operates was divided by the number of years that the retailer has operated abroad and thus indicates how rapidly foreign market entries are accumulated in a certain period of time which is differently from the scope of international experience (Erramilli 1991). In conclusion, higher computed values indicate a greater number of markets entered per year.

5.2.3 Control Variables

This study controls for the effects of firm size, market size, market growth, openness toward FDI, industrial development and firm and country dummy variables. However, further home country factors were not considered because such factors are already incorporated into the distant measures of political and cultural distance, and their inclusion would lead to only a marginal improvement in explanatory power (Brouthers and Hennart 2007). Firm size was controlled for because this factor is considered as a critical resource, particularly for the entry mode choices of retail firms, and is measured according to Brouthers, Brouthers and Werner (2008) using the total number of employees. Market size was controlled for using the amount of the host country's GDP (Barkema and Vermeulen 1998) because it is an important indicator of market attractiveness (Henisz and Delios 2001). Similarly, previous studies have shown an important effect of market growth on entry mode choices (e.g., Agarwal and Ramaswami 1992). Thus, the results are controlled by market growth through measuring with the percentage of GDP development (Barkema and Vermeulen 1998; Herrmann and Datta 2002). According to Contractor and Kundu (1998) and Johnson and Tellis (2008), the influence of openness toward FDI, which indicates whether host countries appreciate FDI by computing the ratio of FDI to GDP, has been controlled. Previous research has also shown that entry mode choices are influenced by the degree of industrial development, which is measured by the percentage of urbanization (Alon 2006). Therefore, this effect has also been controlled. To exclude any biases through unobserved firm heterogeneity, Beck, Brüderl and Woywode (2008) and Snijders and Bosker (1999) recommend the inclusion of fixed effects. Thus, according to Vermeulen and Barkema (2001), firm dummy variables have been included to control for any higher-order effects due to the 18 retailers that were investigated. The same procedure was used with four countries that had more than ten observed market entries.

5.3. Method

A binary logistic regression analysis was performed, which is the method used most often for investigating the choice of market entry modes (Canabal and White 2008). Before the analysis was conducted, a separate outlier diagnostic was conducted to avoid biases in the analysis that could result from extreme values. Eight observations were excluded because they exceeded the cut-off points of 3.0, which represents the standardized residuals, and 1.0, which represents the Cook's distance (Cohen et al. 2003). Furthermore, all of the variables were z-standardized prior to the analysis to avoid multicollinearity in models with comprehensive interaction effects (Aiken and West 1991; Brouthers and Brouthers 2003). As illustrated by Table B-3, all of the correlations are below the recommended threshold of 0.7 (Anderson, Sweeney and Williams 2010). Furthermore, the variance inflation factors (VIFs) were calculated and all values are lower than the recommended threshold of 10 (Diamantopoulos and Winklhofer 2001), and the standard error of each independent variable is below 0.8 (Menard 2002). Hence, multicollinearity is not a serious problem in this study.[2]

2 To show that multicollinearity is also not a serious problem when the firm dummy variables are incorporated, the correlation matrix has additionally been calculated including all firm dummy variables as illustrated in Table Appendix-1 in the appendix.

Variables	1	2	3	4	5	6	7	8	9	10	11	12	13	14	15
Mean value	0.690	0.699	0.173	2.336	18.410	0.733	18.240	44.548	0.036	0.059	0.642				
Standard deviation (std)	0.463	0.296	0.239	1.412	13.991	0.356	28.598	106.754	0.039	0.283	18.033				
Minimum	0	0.000	0.000	0.000	0.000	0.170	0.230	0.240	-0.131	0.000	0.000				
Maximum	1	1.000	0.850	10.780	58.000	2.000	200.000	1,007.590	0.129	3.210	3.210				
Variance inflation factor (VIF)	-	1.949	1.148	1.285	1.771	1.369	1.297	1.079	1.095	1.050	1.126	1.085	1.531	2.815	1.366
Standard error	-	0.428	0.174	0.318	0.255	0.259	0.190	0.375	0.196	0.480	0.189	0.215	0.399	0.441	0.353
1 Entry mode	-														
2 Institutionalized entry mode	0.669**	-													
3 Political distance	-0.048	-0.039	-												
4 Cultural distance	0.117*	0.074	0.108†	-											
5 International experience	0.070	0.172**	0.046	0.374**	-										
6 Internationalization speed	-0.111†	-0.123*	0.062	-0.139*	-0.409**	-									
7 Firm size	-0.149**	-0.287**	0.131*	-0.052	0.074	0.172**	-								
8 Market size	0.102†	0.025	-0.075	-0.211**	-0.115*	0.018	0.028	-							
9 Market growth	0.012	-0.026	0.216**	-0.079	0.020	-0.004	0.064	-0.064	-						
10 Openness toward FDI	0.062	0.043	-0.069	-0.062	0.069	-0.109	-0.015	-0.059	0.020	-					
11 Industrial development	0.028	0.068	-0.231**	-0.092	-0.113*	-0.010	-0.123*	0.116*	-0.121*	0.116*	-				
12 Institutionalized entry mode x Political distance	-0.066	-0.049	-0.067	0.065	0.008	-0.109†	-0.165**	-0.005	-0.039	-0.015	0.074	-			
13 Institutionalized entry mode x Cultural distance	-0.144*	-0.262**	0.059	-0.060	-0.027	0.129*	0.160**	-0.036	0.111†	0.011	-0.016	0.062	-		
14 Institutionalized entry mode x International experience	-0.301**	-0.546**	0.003	-0.023	0.207**	-0.053	0.105†	-0.040	0.114*	0.001	-0.097†	0.058	0.518**	-	
15 Institutionalized entry mode x Internationalization speed	0.126*	0.012*	-0.077	0.101†	-0.043	-0.183**	-0.138	-0.023	-0.089	-0.028	0.007	0.150**	-0.148*	-0.386**	-

N = 301. Two-tailed Pearson correlations. † $p < 0.10$, * $p < 0.05$, ** $p < 0.01$, *** $p < 0.001$.

Table B-3: Descriptive Statistics, Test of Multicollinearity and Correlation Matrix

Source: Own creation.

5.4. Results

5.4.1 Model Fit

Table B-4 illustrates the results of models 1 to 6, which incorporate stepwise the interaction terms to demonstrate the stability of effects. The overall model fit of the final model 6 is reasonably high with a Nagelkerke's R^2 value of 0.658. Thus, the data demonstrate a good fit with the proposed conceptual framework, and 84.7% of the observations are correctly classified. With regard to the asymmetric size of the full- and shared-controlled modes, this value must be compared with the proportional chance criterion (PCC) value, which is 57.2%. Thus, the classification rate of model 6 is 25% higher than the PCC, which is required to indicate good predictive power (Hair et al. 2010).

Model 2 is compared with Model 6 to demonstrate the increase in the explanatory power caused by the moderating effects. The test provided by Aiken and West (1991) to compare different degrees of Nagelkerke's R^2 shows that the Nagelkerke's R^2 values of 0.624 for Model 2 and 0.658 for Model 6 differ significantly at $p < 0.001$ with a f-value of 7.133. In conclusion, the explanatory power is substantially enhanced by the moderating effects.

Furthermore, rival models, including 1) a model without the acquisition mode and 2) a model without franchising/ licensing-type agreements, have been estimated. Nagelkerke's R^2 increases to 0.710 and 0.740, respectively, and the main effect of an institutionalized entry mode on the choice of subsequent entry modes and the moderating effect of all constructs remain highly significant, as indicated below. Thus, the stability of the present solution may be acknowledged.[3]

3 For robustness purposes, a binary probit analysis has additionally been carried out on the basis of Generalized Estimating Equations according to Liang and Zeger (1986). However, the results in Table Appendix-2 in the appendix show the same results.

	Dependent variable: Full control mode = 1											
	Model 1		***Model 2***		***Model 3***		***Model 4***		***Model 5***		***Model 6***	
Measures	Beta	Exp(B)	Beta	Exp(B)	Beta	Exp(B)	Beta	Exp(B)	Beta	Exp(B)	Beta	Exp(B)
Independent variable												
Institutionalized entry mode	2.227***	(9.270)	2.565***	(13.004)	2.679***	(14.568)	2.677***	(14.545)	2.847***	(17.240)	3.191***	(24.311)
Moderator variables												
Political distance			-0.052ns	(0.949)	-0.159ns	(0.853)	-0.160ns	(0.852)	-0.140ns	(0.870)	-0.098ns	(0.907)
Cultural distance			0.901**	(2.463)	0.972**	(2.642)	0.975**	(2.652)	0.985**	(2.677)	0.975**	(2.650)
International experience			-0.624**	(0.536)	-0.640**	(0.527)	-0.640**	(0.527)	-0.772**	(0.462)	-0.705**	(0.494)
Internationalization speed			-0.314ns	(0.731)	-0.324ns	(0.723)	-0.324ns	(0.723)	-0.276ns	(0.759)	-0.101ns	(0.904)
Interaction terms												
Institutionalized entry mode x Political distance					-0.411*	(0.663)	-0.411*	(0.663)	-0.395*	(0.674)	-0.477*	(0.620)
Institutionalized entry mode x Cultural distance							0.012ns	(1.012)	-0.292ns	(0.747)	-0.357ns	(0.700)
Institutionalized entry mode x International experience									0.644†	(1.904)	0.996*	(2.707)
Institutionalized entry mode x Internationalization speed											0.905**	(2.471)
Controls												
Firm size	0.226ns	(1.254)	0.409*	(1.505)	0.391*	(1.478)	0.389*	(1.476)	0.418*	(1.518)	0.590**	(1.803)
Market size	0.693*	(1.999)	0.789*	(2.201)	0.834*	(2.302)	0.832*	(2.299)	0.831*	(2.296)	0.929*	(2.531)
Market growth	0.114ns	(1.121)	0.167ns	(1.182)	0.137ns	(1.147)	0.137ns	(1.147)	0.141ns	(1.151)	0.110ns	(1.116)
Openness toward FDI	0.399ns	(1.490)	0.480ns	(1.616)	0.474ns	(1.606)	0.473ns	(1.605)	0.524ns	(1.689)	0.519ns	(1.680)
Industrial development	-0.094ns	(0.910)	-0.064ns	(0.938)	-0.030ns	(0.970)	-0.031ns	(0.970)	-0.025ns	(0.975)	0.034ns	(1.034)
Constant term	1.161 ***	(3.195)	1.349***	(3.853)	1.363***	(3.910)	1.365***	(3.914)	1.319***	(3.740)	1.332***	(3.787)
Model indices												
N	301		301		301		301		301		301	
Model chi-square	159.2***		175.9***		179.5***		179.5***		182.3***		189.3***	
Cox & Snell R^2	0.411		0.443		0.449		0.449		0.454		0.467	
Nagelkerke's R^2	0.579		0.624		0.633		0.633		0.640		0.658	
Correct classification	83.1%		85.0%		84.7%		84.4%		85.0%		84.7%	

† $p < 0.10$, * $p < 0.05$, ** $p < 0.01$, *** $p < 0.001$, ns = not significant.

Table B-4: Results of Hierarchical Logistic Regression Analysis

Source: Own creation.

5.4.2 Main Effect

According to hypothesis 1, it is suggested by the organizational imprinting effect that the more often an entry mode has been used in the past the higher the propensity to use the same entry mode in subsequent market entries. The positive coefficient is highly significant (Exp(B)=24.311; $p < 0.001$) and strongly supports this hypothesis, as shown by the high odds ratio. Thus, entry mode choices are particularly dependent on the entry modes that have been frequently used in the past.

5.4.3 Moderating Effects

In hypothesis 2, it is assumed that the aforementioned relationship will be negatively influenced by a great amount of political distance between the host and home countries because retailers must conform to local conditions. The negative coefficient (Exp(B)=0.620; $p < 0.05$) suggests that retailers do adapt their institutionalized entry modes in countries with a great amount of political distance. However, because of the nonlinear relationship in the logistic regression, it is recommended to visualize the moderating effects to facilitate their interpretation. Thus, the moderating effect of political distance is shown in visual form in Figure B-2, according to the approach of Jaccard (2001), by computing one standard deviation above and below the mean of the moderating variable. As illustrated, in host countries with a great amount of political distance, retailers that predominantly used a full control mode in the past are less likely to use a full control mode than are countries with less political distance and retailers that predominantly used a shared-controlled mode in the past shift toward the use of full control modes. Thus, it can be concluded for the case of a large political distance that retailers depart from their institutionalized entry mode. However, although the coefficient is significant, the odds ratio indicates a smaller effect than that observed for the other interaction terms.

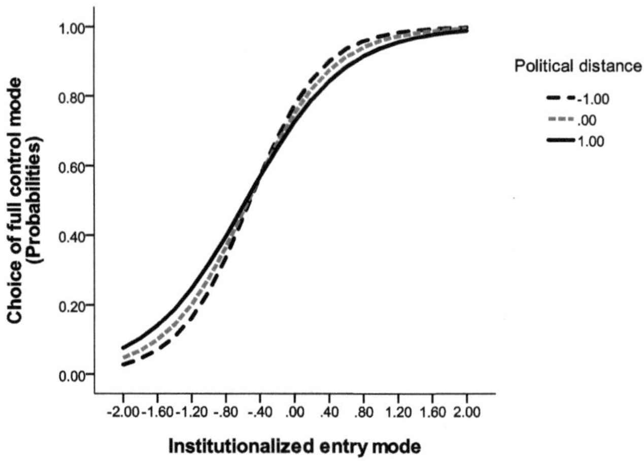

Figure B-2: The Moderating Effect of Political Distance
Source: Own creation.

In hypothesis 3, it is assumed that a retailer tends to depart from the institutionalized entry mode when the cultural distance between the host and home countries is large. It is argued that strategic routines are less easily employed in culturally distant markets because a greater amount of cultural distance results in a greater need to conform to local conditions. The negative beta coefficient in Table B-4 is in the expected direction but is not significant. Thus, hypothesis 3 is rejected. Three reasons could explain this result. First, this study only employs the cultural distance measure of the Globe study. Second, cultural distance has already been shown to have ambiguous effects in previous meta-analytic research contributions on entry mode choice. Third, retail entry mode choices with respect to institutionalized entry modes may be less strongly affected by cultural distance than is suggested by previous research.

Based on the RBV, it is assumed that as firm-specific capabilities are developed over time, organizational routines become reinforced. Therefore, hypothesis 4 posits that greater international experience results in a greater propensity to employ the same entry mode that has predominantly been used in the past. The positive coefficient in Table B-4 is strongly significant (Exp(B)=2.707; $p < 0.05$), as the comparably high odds ratio indicates. Thus, hypothesis 4 is supported. Figure B-3 shows that when there is a high level of international experience, retailers with a predominantly used full control mode are more likely to use a full control mode than in the case of low international experience. The opposite pattern is also true for shared-controlled modes.

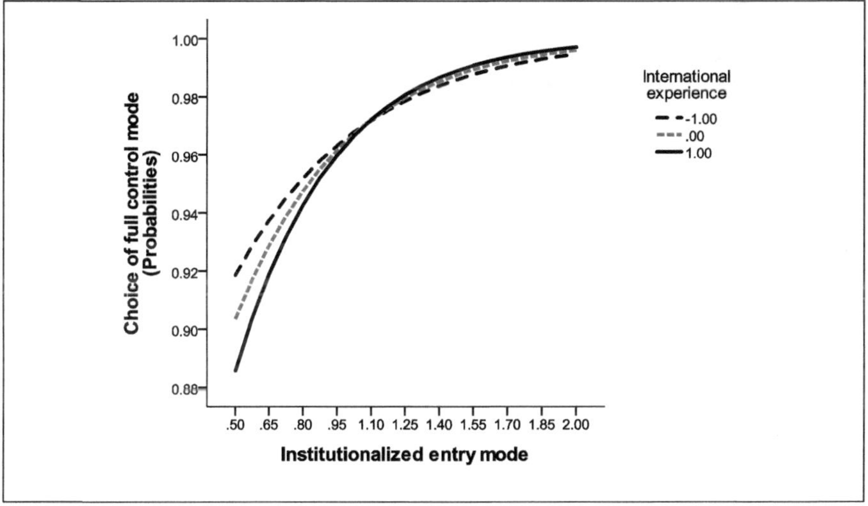

Figure B-3: The Moderating Effect of International Experience
Source: Own creation.

Hypothesis 5 states that internationalization speed reinforces the propensity to employ an institutionalized entry mode. Thus, it is assumed that firms that internationalize rapidly follow a strategic routine. The results in Table B-4 support this assumption (Exp(B)=2.471; $p < 0.01$). Figure B-4 shows that a retailer with high internationalization speed who has predominantly used a full control mode in the past favors the continued use of a full control mode. The opposite pattern holds also for shared-controlled modes. Furthermore, the high odds ratio indicates that the moderating effect of internationalization speed is particularly strong. Thus, retail firms that began to internationalize early and enter many markets within a short period of time tend to use institutionalized entry modes.

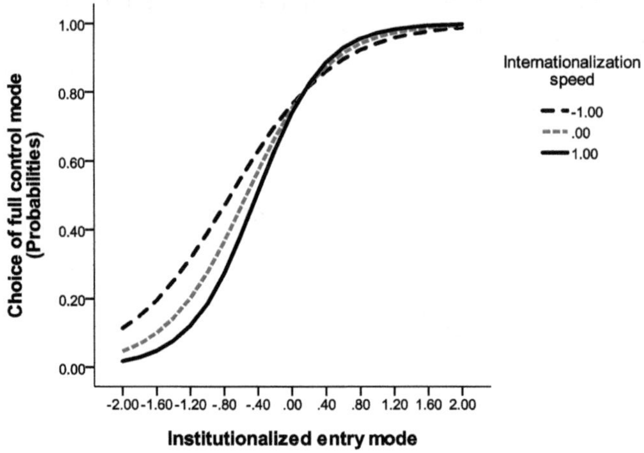

Figure B-4: The Moderating Effect of Internationalization Speed
Source: Own creation.

5.4.4 Control Variables.

According to previous observations of market entry mode choices, firm size and market size are significantly and positively linked with the choice of a full control mode. The effects of openness toward FDI, market growth and industrial development are not significant. For controlling of changes through the observed 18 retailers, three out of 17 firm dummies (not shown in Table B-4) were significant, and the results remained unchanged when the firm dummy variables were omitted, whereas the four country dummy variables do not show any significant effect.[4]

6. Discussion

This study examines the influence of an institutionalized entry mode on the choice of a subsequent entry mode and, therefore, not on the choice of the

[4] Due to shortcomings of the firm dummy approach, the results have also been checked by a binary logistic regression based on Generalized Estimating Equations Liang and Zeger (1986). The results remain nearly the same as illustrated in Table Appendix-3 in the appendix.

most efficient entry mode (Sarkar and Cavusgil 1996). Furthermore, the moderating effects of the external institutional environment and of firm-specific capabilities are analyzed in the context of international retailers because retailers are strongly dependent on the external institutional environment, given their local business and the intangible capabilities within the internationalization process. Such a specific context can be considered as strength of this study because this context addresses a seldom-investigated part of the service sector, or it can be viewed as a weakness because the generalization may be limited. However, this under-researched area regarding the effects of institutionalized entry modes is relevant because entry mode choices are known to be critical decisions with respect to international expansion. With respect to institutional theory, the results strongly support the argument that past decisions influence subsequent entry mode choices. Moreover, external institutional factors, i.e., political and cultural distance, force firms to adjust their institutionalized entry modes. Empirically, regulatory pressures have a negative moderating effect on the relationship between the institutionalized entry mode and subsequent mode choices. With respect to the RBV, internal capabilities, such as international experience and internationalization speed, reinforce this behavior. These observations provide two major research implications and conclusions for managers.

6.1. Research Implications

With respect to the first research question concerning the extent of the effect of institutionalized entry modes on subsequent entry mode choices, the results underline the strong influence of institutionalized entry modes on subsequent entry mode choices over time. Thus, according to Huang and Sternquist (2007), it can be concluded that institutionalized entry modes provide a useful explanation for the dynamics of entry mode choices in different countries in the retail context. Furthermore, in response to the works of Canabal and White (2008) and Brouthers and Hennart (2007), this study uses a panel approach to provide a more realistic view about how entry modes are actually chosen and to emphasize the choice of an entry mode as a dynamic process. This study extends the studies on entry mode choice that are typically static in nature (Andersen 1997) and provides new insights with respect to those studies that focus only on external institutional pressures and disregard internal institutional pressures. The results support three previous studies regarding sequential market entries into a single host country (Chang and Rosenzweig 2001; Yiu and Makino 2002) and market entries into different host countries (Lu 2002). Finally, especially in retail, institutions are more than simply background conditions but they represent 'the rules of the game', as North (1990) states, and are especially able to impose pressure on the choice of the foreign market entry modes (Meyer and Peng 2005). Moreover, the applied measurement of intra-organizational behavior over time highlights the inherent nature as a process of actions that becomes taken for granted over the course of time. However, further studies that investigate the formation of institutionalized entry modes are important because institutionalized entry modes may be influenced by both institutional pressures and mode learning (Benito, Petersen and Welch 2009) and thus strategic decisions. Hence, this study calls for research about the antecedences and differences of entry mode evolution, e.g., mode inertia and mode learning.

With respect to the second research question concerning the moderating role of external institutional pressures and the internal capabilities of the relationship between institutionalized entry modes and subsequent mode choices, the results show that firms depart from their institutionalized entry modes in politically distant countries. Thus, this study finds evidence of institutional duality meaning that subsidiaries abroad encounter dual pressures (Rosenzweig and Singh 1991). Foreign branches must respond to pressures within an organization and to local institutional pressures in a host country. The results of this study emphasize the existence of particularly strong pressures from inside of a firm with respect to entry mode choice, whereas pressures from the external institutional environment counter this effect. However, this study includes only two specific regulative and normative variables. These two variables could be enhanced by considering further proxy variables for the regulative and normative institutional environment that may have different effects. In contrast, with increasing international experience and internationalization speed, the use of an institutionalized entry mode is reinforced. Thus, the compatibility of the RBV and institutional theory is evident as the increase in intangible resources leads to an efficient use of institutionalized entry modes and the securing of internal legitimacy. Both of these conclusions are discussed below.

First, this research is one of the first studies that combine all three institutional pressures to which an organization must respond to strive for legitimacy. The results show that external institutional pressures decrease the influence of internal institutional pressures. Firms employ rather institutionalized entry modes within politically close countries but depart from this behavior in countries with antagonistic environments. However, although the results do not confirm the moderating role of cultural distance, they do show a tendency in this direction and may thus provide the basis of a promising area of further research (e.g., based on different or specific cultural measures in the retail context Huang and Sternquist 2007). Although the effect of entry mode choice on performance was not considered in this study, Brouthers (2002) has shown that the entry modes that are suggested by theories perform better than the entry modes that do not correspond with theoretical underpinnings. Similarly, it could also be assumed that an institutionalized entry mode that is adjusted according to the external and internal environments would be more successful than an entry mode that is not legitimatized and not consistent with internal capabilities. Thus, research regarding the performance effects of institutional duality may be promising.

Regarding the RBV, the results underline that international experience and internationalization speed reinforce the institutional behavior of firms with respect to their entry mode choice, which suggests the compatibility of both theories. Therefore, international experience and internationalization speed lead to the use of the same entry mode rather than, for example, an efficiency-driven variation of modes. Thus, international experience and internationalization speed facilitate the use of organizational routines to ensure that economies of scale can be realized and can even assist in overcoming external institutional barriers (Schwens, Eiche and Kabst 2011). However, in this study, only the higher magnitudes of international experience and internationalization speed support such an implication. Thus, this interrelationship may be a promising field for further research.

6.2. *Managerial Implications*

This study also provides managerial implications by highlighting the view of expansion managers with regard to entry mode choices in retail firms and the role of the moderating effects.

Expansion managers in MNC are clearly aware of their institutionalized entry modes. These managers conform to internal isomorphic pressures to ensure that the complex process of entry mode choice occurs through a decision-making heuristic that is an 'efficiency-satisfying' solution rather than an 'efficiency-maximizing' solution because time and effort have been saved (Simon 1959). These managers may acknowledge that an institutionalized entry mode may be the most efficient international expansion strategy. However, it is questionable whether managers will actually select new country markets on that basis. In this case, consequences arise. Specific entry modes may determine the functions, steps and criteria that are applied in country selection models, which may be standardized and, therefore, more efficient. However, managers must ask themselves whether they will select the most promising countries or the countries that are the most promising for their specific institutionalized entry mode. This difference is important because those who select the latter may have disadvantages compared with their competitors who select the most attractive markets first and then choose the most efficient entry mode. Thus, managers must understand that entry modes determine long-term foreign performance (Gielens and Dekimpe 2007) and that entry mode choice and market selection are two distinctive decision processes that drive international performance.

Huang and Sternquist (2007) conclude that retailers must identify institutional pressures to understand their different magnitudes and to strategically manage the institutional environment. However, such management is probably not feasible in practice. This study indicates a few factors that significantly lead to reconsideration with respect to institutionalized entry modes. For example, regulatory institutions are observable prior to mode decisions and could be easily included in market selection models, whereas normative institutions may be less easily evaluated prior to decisions. Furthermore, the relevance of such factors and of the institutionalized mode might depend on firms' internationalization speed, flexibility or different reasons for entering a country (e.g., a new market with high potential vs. peripheral countries). Thus, managers need a broad understanding of the interdependencies among the challenges of international expansion, e.g., challenges related to the questions of which market to select, how to enter a market and how to serve a market.

6.3. Limitations and Further Research

Finally, some concluding remarks concerning the limitations of this study are offered, and some avenues for further research are suggested. First, the generalization of the results may be limited because only grocery retailers were analyzed. In other words, results that pertain to specialized non-food retailers or firms from other industries may differ from those obtained in this study. However, as examples of other industries, Zara, H&M, The Body Shop, Sephora and Starbucks seem to use institutionalized entry modes, as stated by Huang and Sternquist (2007). Second, although full and shared-controlled modes have been distinguished, a more fine-grained comparison may provide different insights, for example, with regard to addressing different equity holdings in WOS or franchising/ licensing contracts that are particularly important in non-food retailing and will enable multinomial regression analysis but are not provided by Planet Retail. Third, the results might be dominated by a few retailers with many foreign entries (e.g., Carrefour) even though the firm dummy variable does not indicate any important significant effect. However, although multi-level analyses may be appropriate, the data do not allow such analyses in this study. Furthermore, the host country-related variables were measured with respect to the year of market entry, which could be questioned because grocery retailers must establish new value chains in new host markets, and this process requires time. Hence, the market entry decision process could begin one or two years prior to entry or could occur during the year of entry, which cannot generally be estimated. Finally, cultural distance was measured with the Globe dimensions for one specific point in time and only between the home and host country, but cultural distance may actually change over time (e.g., Shenkar 2001).

Thus, further research may address these limitations and questions that extend beyond this study, such as those related to the performance of institutionalized entry modes, the effect of management changes on institutionalized entry modes or inter-organizational mimic behavior, which also influences entry mode choices (Lu 2002). With respect to performance, one could argue that an institutionalized entry mode is legitimatized by the internal and external environment, but one could also question whether an institutionalized entry mode represents antiquated structures that render the implementation of an institutionalized entry mode as less successful.

C. Study 2 – Transferring the Retail Format Successfully into Foreign Countries

1. Introduction

Retailers have been aggressively internationalizing for two decades, first into psychically close countries and then into distant countries, primarily based on format elements familiar in the home markets. Goldman (2001) has already demonstrated that few retailers transfer formats and thus combinations of visible marketing offers and retail know-how (i.e., processes and firm culture according to Hollander 1970; Kacker 1988) unchanged, whereas most retailers adapt various format elements. Recent studies confirm this finding. Even global firms such as IKEA vary their market offers in response to market-based learning (Jonsson and Foss 2011). These standardization and adaptation decisions have been thoroughly analyzed (for a recent review see Schmid and Kotulla 2011). But, with the increasing internationalization of retail, such decisions have increased in relevance, although little is known regarding which standardized or adapted format elements are associated with performance in a host country. This knowledge is crucial. Retailers as distributors design offers to attract local customers into their stores and are devoted to establishing efficient processes. The two decisions are interrelated. Marketing processes (e.g., promotion planning) and supply chain processes (e.g., purchasing procedures) determine the design of market offers and drive efficiency. Thus, retailers may adapt offers and processes by establishing new assortments and new supply chains in a host country. In contrast, retailers may also build on the know-how parts of their retail format to design offers and processes abroad. Hence, to determine how retailers can successfully design their formats abroad, this study investigates the relationships between marketing programs that attract customers and two important types of processes—marketing and supply chain processes—that determine retailer efficiency and the design of market offers. Marketing processes are defined as the employed sales-related procedures, systems and regulations (Griffith, Hu and Ryans 2000; Walters 1986), whereas supply chain processes are defined as the employed purchase and logistics procedures, systems and regulations (Bourlakis and Bourlakis 2001; Swoboda, Foscht and Cliquet 2008). This study suggests particularly that successful retailers transfer more standardized core elements and more adapted peripheral elements of their formats.

Although scholars increasingly analyze international retailers (a recent review is provided by Swoboda, Zentes and Elsner 2009), the literature rarely focuses on retail format transfer. The latter is of undisputed relevance for competitive position and success in host countries, but only few studies address processes and performance empirically. By analyzing format transfer elements, Goldman (2001) shows that retailers standardize their offers and processes differently but frequently do not adjust the know-how part. However, the author judges all of the elements as equally important. Goldman (2000) shows that Chinese and foreign supermarkets differ in terms of their internal processes but not with regard to their offers. Also Jonsson and Foss (2011) emphasize the existence of differently designed format elements. The authors demonstrate that global retailers allow marketing elements to vary across countries, whereas higher-level features (e.g., processes) are replicated in a uniform manner. Thus, the design of core and peripheral retail format elements varies. Furthermore, small-N research examines processes and offers but primarily analyzes the latter (e.g., Bianchi and Ostale 2006; Currah and Wrigley 2004). Similarly, numerous studies address single marketing program elements, including assortments, prices and promotions and conclude mostly that adaptations to the local environment drive performance in a country. Finally, few studies investigate how the standardization of processes determines offers and performance (e.g., Chandra, Griffith and Ryans 2002; Chung 2003; Griffith, Chandra and Ryans 2003; Townsend et al. 2004) but address only marketing processes in the manufacturing context. Thus, two research gaps emerge.

Prior studies are inconclusive regarding the degree of standardization of particular format elements but indicate that retailer know-how parts and thus processes provide the foundation for foreign expansion. This finding is conclusive because standardizing internal processes and adapting visible offers determines retailer efficiency and local sales (Chandra, Griffith and Ryans 2002). However, we argue that more standardized core elements of a format can be found among processes and offers as less standardized peripheral elements. Hence, process and marketing program elements, identified as fundamental and replicable features for an ideal target application such as the foreign expansion (Winter and Szulanski 2001), may form the basis for retail format transfer, whereas other elements are permitted to vary locally. This view of more standardized and more adapted elements enhances our understanding of the relationship between processes and programs. For these reasons, we analyze whether and which elements of internal processes and visible offers are more or less standardized abroad and how they interact.

There is a dearth of empirical findings about the interactions between retailer processes, marketing program elements and performance in foreign countries. It is possible that the performance effects of equally standardized or adapted marketing and supply chain processes and marketing programs might be equal, as both are consistent with a global or multinational strategy among retailers. However, the associations of these factors with performance in a country might also be different because marketing programs in particular are visible to customers and must therefore be adapted to attract customers to local stores and to enhance local sales in contrast to internal processes. However, marketing programs may include both more standardized and more adapted elements with fundamentally different associations with performance. Such scenarios are relevant to studies of format transfer and should be analyzed in more detail with respect to retailer performance abroad.

In sum, this study aims to analyze the research question: whether and which process and marketing program elements are standardized or adapted and how both processes and offers interact? In assuming that processes and programs include more or less standardized core and peripheral elements, we assume that the relationship between them and their relationship with performance will vary. Thus, we ask: whether and how the degree of standardization of marketing program elements and marketing and supply chain processes determine retailer performance in a foreign country? The degree of standardization is defined as the extent to which activities are similar abroad compared to the home market (Cavusgil, Zou and Naidu 1993; Zou and Cavusgil 2002).

In investigating these questions, this study contributes to the international marketing literature and particularly to the emerging field of retail internationalization. From a theoretical perspective, we respond to Goldman's (2001) call to investigate both the important know-how and the offering part associated with a retail format transfer strategy. We focus on processes because retail culture is shown to be strongly standardized in most cases and because, for instance, important supply chain processes generate a significant portion of total retail costs (Einarsson 2008; Mentzer, Min and Zacharia 2000). Thus, we follow Walters (1986) and Ganesan et al. (2009) by analyzing the effects of various standardized marketing and supply chain processes. Finally, we build on Jonsson and Foss (2011) by addressing core and peripheral elements of retail formats and their greater or lesser standardization due to market-based learning. Our findings may show managers which elements of a format must be more standardized or adapted, which are interrelated and depend on each other and, finally, whether and how their degree of standardization is associated with performance in foreign countries.

The remainder of the study is structured as follows. We derive our hypotheses and test them using in-depth, face-to-face interviews with 126 executives at the headquarters of 102 internationally operating retail chains. We differentiate between operations in psychically close and distant countries to ensure robustness. After presenting the results, we discuss implications and avenues for further research.

2. Theoretical Foundation and Conceptual Framework

Scholars have examined format transfer from different perspectives, including grounded theory, the integration-responsiveness (I-R) framework and the replication-as-strategy approach. To address our research questions, we analyze two research streams: 1) studies that consider which process and program elements are standardized or adapted and how those elements interact and 2) studies that analyze the performance effects of those designs. Thus, we focus on the learning-based flexible format replication approach (FFR) and on profit maximization theory (PMT) (Jonsson and Foss 2011; Samiee and Roth 1992). Using both theories broadens the existing arguments concerning format transfers, especially for aggressively internationalizing retailers that primarily transfer known format elements from home to host countries. Accordingly, we employ FFR to determine the degree of standardization and the associations between process and program elements. Our argument that there are more standardized core elements and fewer standardized peripheral elements allows us to draw advanced conclusions concerning the relationships between processes and programs as well as their associations with performance. We employ PMT to determine the general associations of internal processes and visible offers with performance. Hence, our theoretical framework proposes that the degree of standardization of processes is related to that of marketing programs and that both are associated with performance in a country (Figure C-1). The framework suggests particularly that the relationships between core and peripheral elements and performance are different.

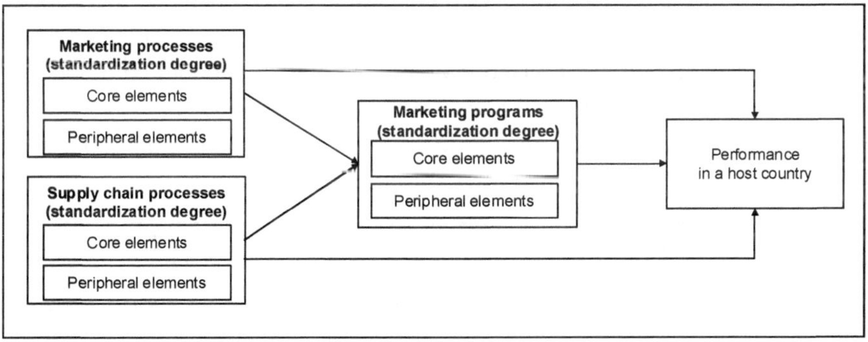

Figure C-1: Conceptual Model
Source: Own creation.

FFR illuminates the design of format transfers by highlighting the identification of core and peripheral elements and the motivation for standardizing or changing these elements that arise from market-based learning. Winter and Szulanski (2001) argue that organizations identify core business elements by defining an information set, i.e., a "full and correct specification of the fundamental, replicable features of a business model and its ideal target application" (Jonsson and Foss 2011, p. 1081). Such core elements build important values and lead to routines, i.e., features that are replicated unchanged. They allow for large-scale replications, rapid leveraging, knowledge transfer and not fully for competitors visible and imitable routines (Jensen and Szulanski 2007, 2008; Winter and Szulanski 2001). Consequently, retailers may strategically define routines for international expansion, e.g., preferred store types or store layouts. In addition to a systematic evaluation, Jonsson and Foss (2011) find that core and peripheral elements are designed in accordance with market-based learning by retailers, which is particularly important for internationalization into heterogeneous environments. Considering path-dependent learning processes in a specific host country and across various host countries, the authors conclude that retailers allow frequent variations in peripheral format elements (e.g., assortments) but seldom change core elements (e.g., procedures) and alter their whole business model only over an extensive period of time. We utilize FFR to draw two conclusions. First, FFR provides a valuable theoretical justification for the existence of core and peripheral format elements (supporting past classifications of Carman and Langeard (1980),Kaufmann and Eroglu (1999) and Cao and Dupuis (2009)), whose design is based on strategic evaluations by firms and market-based learning. Scholars agree that core and peripheral elements are difficult to identify but include demand- and supply-side factors and therefore offers, processes and firm culture (Goldman 2001). For illustration purposes, Table C-1 presents possible examples.

	Marketing program	Marketing processes	Supply chain processes
Core elements	- Retail brand - Store type - Store layout and store design - Store location	- Procedures of market and trend analysis - Category development processes - Procedures of store location planning - Identification of target groups - Procedures and systems for CRM	- Purchasing systems/procedures (e.g., direct store, central) - Relationships with key suppliers - Logistics and warehouse systems - ERP/IRP systems - Facility planning processes (location and design of logistics facilities)
Peripheral elements	- Assortment - Price - Private labels - Sales promotion and POS marketing - Service - Hours of operation - Standard operating sales procedures (incl. personnel planning in stores)	- Processes of category composition - Cost and price calculation procedures - Processes of sales planning and monitoring - Processes of customer service - Processes of promotion planning - Complaint management procedures	- Distribution logistics for stores - Warehouse management - Cross-docking procedures - Store logistics processes - Logistics of disposal - Personnel recruitment processes

Table C-1: Possible Core and Peripheral Program and Process Elements in Retailing
Source: Own creation.

Second, although FFR refers to global firms that adapt their format elements locally after standardized entry into countries, we see no reason why multinational retailers should not behave similarly. These retailers may implement routines before entry or, as a result of market-based learning, may later search for standardizable elements that they can use to gain advantage across countries. More importantly, FFR provides foundational theoretical reasoning regarding the relationships between more or less standardized process and program elements and suggests conclusions regarding the associations between retail format elements and performance: the relationships between both standardized core elements and adapted peripheral elements and performance are positive.

PMT provides a general understanding of the degree to which the standardization of processes and marketing programs is related to performance. PMT postulates that a firm's main goal is to maximize profits and that this goal can be reached by keeping costs low (e.g., via high purchase volumes or low purchase prices) and sales high (e.g., via higher prices or higher sales volumes) (Samiee and Roth 1992). We utilize PMT to examine how the degree of standardization of processes and offers relates to performance (see Schmid and Kotulla (2011) for a detailed contingency perspective). PMT provides advanced theoretical reasoning even if retailer format transfers are affected by a common trade-off between globalization and localization in which the standardization of elements determines the retailer's global performance but not necessarily its country-specific performance. In general, the standardization of processes across countries enables most retailers to achieve economies of scale, which, in turn, reduce costs and enhances profits if sales remain constant. Thus, standardized processes used in both the home and the host country will reduce costs because the local entity will be able to benefit from previously established systems and procedures that improve performance also in the respective host country. Adapting offers in a country enables most retailers to address local customer needs, which in turn enhance local sales so that profits will increase if costs are held constant or exceeded through the increase of sales. Thus, adapted marketing programs will increase sales and performance in a country because, for example, local customer needs are addressed. However, those general conclusions must be considered in conjunction with the idea of standardizing core elements or adapting peripheral elements of retail formats.

3. Literature Review and Hypotheses Development

In this section, the hypotheses proposed in this study are deducted. We provide an overview of past studies in the two research streams mentioned: 1) the interaction between process and program elements of retailers and 2) the association of these elements with performance. Moreover, we discuss the proposed relationships based on theoretical arguments and empirical evidence.

3.1. Relationships between Processes and Marketing Program Elements

In accordance with the high importance of marketing and supply chain processes for retailers (landed costs represent the highest total costs Einarsson 2008; Mentzer, Min and Zacharia 2000), past studies have underlined the relationships between the design of processes and visible offers. For example, Christopher, Lowson and Peck (2004) and Tokatli (2007) report that market and trend analysis and store layout development are important marketing processes and represent the first decisions made by Zara, one of the world's leading fashion retailers, regarding the design of market offers. Furthermore, in the case of the British retail giant Tesco and in general, it is reported that supply chain processes determine market offers, for example, excellent assortments or prices due to excellent sourcing (Ganesan et al. 2009) or logistic (Lynch, Keller and Ozment 2000; Schramm-Klein and Morschett 2006). Consequently, there are strong indications that processes play a determining role in the design of market offers in general and in particular, when scholars refer to advantageous relationships, for example, between promotion planning and promotion offers or between logistic processes and out of stock products, etc. by arguing with low-cost computing and the availability of retail-related data (Bourlakis and Bourlakis 2001; Griffith, Chandra and Ryans 2003).

However, the literature is inconclusive regarding the degree of standardization of specific retail format elements and especially regarding the relationships between various elements, but indicates the preference of firms for unchanged processes and adapted offers. Primarily for manufacturers, it has been argued that processes and offers are similarly standardized or adapted based on global or multinational strategy. In contrast, Chandra, Griffith and Ryans (2002) and Manrodt and Vitasek (2004) assume that MNCs benefit from implementing standardized processes across countries and adapted marketing programs in a specific country. Standardized supply chain processes in retail have also been addressed. The literature shows that these processes determine offers (e.g., Bourlakis and Bourlakis 2001; Currah and Wrigley 2004; Tacconelli and Wrigley 2009). This finding is consistent with the PMT reasoning regarding the standardization of internal processes due to MNC efficiency (e.g., economies of scale and coordination advantages) and the adaptation of visible offers based on MNC local sales. Goldman (2000) emphasizes the tendency of retailers to standardize internal processes. However, the author also notes that retailers may differentiate between core and peripheral elements when evaluating internal processes and visible offers and standardize therefore not generally, for example, supply chain processes. Instead, retailers may prefer to standardize core supply chain process elements, whereas other elements may be permitted to vary across countries. Thus, to advance our understanding about international retail format transfer, we must analyze the relationships between core and peripheral types of processes and marketing program elements. Three relationships must be addressed: 1) those between core processes and core marketing programs, 2) those between core processes and peripheral marketing programs and 3) those between peripheral processes and peripheral marketing programs. In all of these relationships, we assume that retailers' core elements are more standardized than their peripheral elements.

3.1.1 Core Processes and Core Marketing Programs

Theoretically, the core elements of a retail format may be mostly replicated unchanged due to advantages such as large-scale effects, rapid leveraging and widespread know-how etc. (e.g., Jensen and Szulanski 2007; Winter and Szulanski 2001), and adaptations in response to market-based learning may be slow (Jonsson and Foss 2011). Core elements are standardized across countries among global retailers, whereas also most multinational retailers may aim to standardize those elements before or after entry due to market-based learning. Accordingly, such elements may be part of the retail chain or corporate related. Scholars show that store format elements that are familiar to the parent firm and new in the host country are the most successful (Gielens and Dekimpe 2001). Consequently, most retailers may attempt to standardize core processes and core marketing program elements across countries to achieve competitive advantage. Thus, a positive relationship between the degree of standardization of core processes and core marketing program elements is expected. The literature partly provides empirical support for this conclusion.

Past studies indicate that standardized core marketing processes such as store layout development or procedures of store location planning are positively related to standardized store layouts or store locations across countries. The above mentioned examples of Zara and Tesco highlight this behavior, as does Hernandez and Bennison (2000), which discusses store location planning and choice based on know-how and cost advantage. Jonsson and Foss (2011) show this behavior for store layout, arguing that the degree of standardization of the store layout abroad is directly influenced through related processes. Furthermore, standardized supply chain processes such as purchasing and logistics procedures are known to be positively related to store type or store location. For example, discounters and hypermarkets have characteristic purchase and logistics procedures (concentrated/ tight vs. dispersed/ decentralized). More generally, studies indicate that standardized supply chain processes serve as a platform for retailer offers (e.g., Bourlakis and Bourlakis 2001; Currah and Wrigley 2004; Tacconelli and Wrigley 2009).

Based on this reasoning, it can be hypothesized that most retailers will standardize core processes and core marketing program elements due to advantages such as large-scale operations, know-how in the host country and advantages across countries. Thus, a higher degree of standardization of core processes should be positively related to that of core marketing program elements. We conclude that:

Hypothesis 1: The higher (a) the degree of standardization of core marketing processes and (b) the degree of standardization of core supply chain processes, the higher the standardization of core marketing program elements.

3.1.2 Core Processes and Peripheral Marketing Programs

If the core processes of a retail format are mostly transferred unchanged, the question is how they are related to peripheral, less adapted marketing program elements that are defined as low-level and to product-related features such as assortment, price and promotion. One must address the possibility that some retailers consider processes to be the template for their retail format and therefore to be a foundation for internationalization, determining their peripheral local offers on this basis. The established processes thus determine more flexible offers (Kaufmann and Eroglu 1999). In addition, it is possible that previously adapted core processes (e.g., those put in place after the acquisition of a competitor abroad) will eventually be standardized (e.g., by assuming economies of scale in purchasing across countries or due to market-based learning). Theoretically, in both cases, a positive relationship between core processes and peripheral marketing program elements can be expected. Core processes build a platform but also a boundary condition for the design of marketing program elements such that a positive relationship between them can be inferred.

The literature addresses the relationship between core processes and marketing programs but does not employ empirical analysis for this purpose. For example, it is reported that marketing processes—such as excellent standardized market analysis or the development of store layouts or customer relationship systems—determine the design of assortments adapted to local customer needs at Tesco (Coe and Lee 2006). Furthermore, standardized marketing processes are used to design assortments and prices across countries, as in the case of Zara (Tokatli 2007). It is also reported that retailers with specific purchasing, logistics or supply chains leave supply chain processes unchanged in entering new countries because supply chain processes comprise the core template of their format strategy (e.g., this would be the case for Zara or IKEA). Accordingly, Wal-Mart attempted to implement process know-how after entry by M&A (e.g., in Germany, United Kingdom and Japan) because its purchasing and logistics systems are Wal-Mart's competencies (Colla and Dupuis 2002).

In summary, we conclude based on theoretical reasoning that most retailers will standardize core processes and that those processes determine the design of the peripheral marketing program elements. Thus, we hypothesize the following:

Hypothesis 2: The higher (a) the degree of standardization of core marketing processes and (b) the degree of standardization of core supply chain processes, the higher the standardization of peripheral marketing program elements.

3.1.3 Peripheral Processes and Peripheral Marketing Programs

Theoretically, peripheral retail format elements represent the 'flexible' aspect of the FFR approach for responding to the idiosyncrasies of the host country. These elements can be adjusted more rapidly overtime based on market-based learning (Jonsson and Foss 2011), and most retailers aim to increase local sales by addressing local customer needs (Goldman 2001). Consequently, most international retailers adapt more intensively peripheral elements of retail formats. Even global firms such as McDonalds, KFC or Gucci are increasingly adapting their assortments, prices or promotions in foreign countries (Schuiling and Kapferer 2004). These product-related offers likely include local assortment or promotion planning in addition to local supply and logistics processes. Thus, a positive relationship between standardization within peripheral processes and peripheral marketing program elements can be expected. In contrast, it can also be assumed that the adaptation of peripheral processes is determined according to the adaptation of peripheral offers. However, based on the FFR approach, we consider internal processes to be the foundation for designing the retail format abroad.

The literature addresses the relationships between processes and offers differently, but it addresses empirically only single marketing processes. For example, it is reported that the process of promotion and sales planning standardization determines the standardization of promotional offers and daily prices (Chandra, Griffith and Ryans 2002, 2003) and that adapted processes of category and sales planning generate locally adapted assortments, e.g., in Vietnam by the Metro-Group or in China by Carrefour (Colla and Dupuis 2002; Metro Group AG 2011). Regarding supply chain processes, it is obvious that retailers harmonize local purchasing and distribution logistics with local product offers. Thus, it is reported that retailers with standardized peripheral supply chain processes are able to offer standardized assortments (Johansson 2002; Quintens, Pauwels and Matthyssens 2006). Conversely, it is reported that firms such as the Metro-Group and Carrefour increasingly utilize local suppliers and logistics to address customer needs with locally adapted assortments.

Hence, it can be hypothesized that the degree of standardization of peripheral processes and that of marketing program elements are correlated because a high (low) degree of standardization of peripheral processes will co-occur with a high (low) degree of standardization of peripheral marketing program elements. Thus, we formulate the following hypothesis:

Hypothesis 3: The higher (a) the degree of standardization of peripheral marketing processes and (b) the degree of standardization of peripheral supply chain processes, the higher the standardization of peripheral marketing program elements.

3.2. Relationships between Processes, Marketing Program Elements and Performance

Seven empirical studies investigate the performance of international retailers by focusing on antecedents of performance such as psychic distance (Evans and Mavondo 2002; Evans, Mavondo and Bridson 2008), the timing and mode of entry (Gielens and Dekimpe 2001; Gielens et al. 2008), advertising (Fam and Yang 2006) and the degree of internationalization (Assaf et al. 2012; Etgar and Rachman-Moore 2008). Small-N research concerning retail format transfer emphasizes the relevance of adapted format elements, e.g., assortments and prices (Bianchi 2006; Currah and Wrigley 2004), to performance. Such research considers mostly successful multinational retailers rather than global retailers. However, a vast body of research addresses marketing programs and performance relationships in the manufacturing context (see Schmid and Kotulla (2011) for a recent review) whereas the degree of standardization of important retail processes is rarely observed (e.g., Coe and Lee 2006; Colla and Dupuis 2002). To shed light upon whether and how standardized vs. adapted processes and marketing program elements determine performance, we explore the role of core and peripheral elements in retailer performance in a foreign country. Thus, two issues are of interest.

We know that for most retail firms, adapted peripheral marketing programs are viewed as determinants of performance in a country, but we do not know how core elements interact with firm performance in a country. This question is of interest because the standardization of core marketing program elements determines global performance but may not determine retailer performance within a specific country. Consequently, we do not know the relative importance of core and peripheral marketing instruments for firm performance in a country.

We also know from research on manufacturing firms that performance is positively related to marketing processes in general (Townsend et al. 2004) and to the standardization of marketing processes in particular (Chung 2003; Walters 1986). However, we do not know whether this fact holds true for retail firms. We do know that retail supply chain processes determine retailer performance because previous research confirms this relationship for elements such as supply chain information and management (e.g., Barratt and Oke 2007; Green, Whitten and Inman 2008), sourcing and purchase networks (e.g., Ganesan et al. 2009; Seevers, Skinner and Dahlstrom 2010) and logistics processes (e.g., Lynch, Keller and Ozment 2000; Schramm-Klein and Morschett 2006). However, it is still unclear whether and how the standardization or adaptation of such processes in general and that of core and peripheral process elements in particular is related to performance in a country. Theoretically, it can be assumed that internal processes may be rather standardized due to advantages such as economies of scale or easier coordination (e.g., Griffith, Chandra and Ryans 2003). This behavior may also lead to cost or coordination savings at first across countries and afterwards in a specific country.

It is important to examine both, 1) the relationships between the degree of standardization of marketing program elements and performance and 2) the relationships between the degree of standardization of processes and performance.

3.2.1 Marketing Programs and Performance

Based on PMT, it can generally be assumed that the adaptation of retail marketing programs increases sales in a host country by fulfilling local customer needs, for example, through local market segmentation (de Mooij and Hofstede 2002). However, the FFR approach indicates that firms may aim to standardize strategic core elements of the retail format, whereas peripheral elements are permitted to vary due to idiosyncrasies of the host country. Also beyond the group of global firms, successful multinational retailers may generally employ established routines in expanding abroad (e.g., store types) or may strive to harmonize their routines and format after adaptation (e.g., after market entry through acquisition or a joint venture). Consequently, there are compelling reasons to employ standardized core and adapted peripheral elements in successful retail firms. We recognize that the degree of standardization of core and peripheral offers in a country may depend on other boundary conditions such as institutional issues, local or global pressures or the fit between offers and the local environment (Schmid and Kotulla 2011). However, we conclude that more positive performance effects accrue from the unchanged transfer of core marketing program elements and adapted peripheral marketing program elements.

The existing literature addresses often peripheral elements but seldom addresses the relevance of core marketing program elements to performance. The latter is addressed for global retailers. Those replicators use elements such as store type, store layout, store brands or even store locations as platforms. Such companies include service retailers such as KFC, category killers such as IKEA and hard discounters such as Aldi (Burt, Johansson and Thelander 2011; Jonsson and Foss 2011). Also other retailers tend to standardize core elements such as stores type, store layout and store location and to adapt assortments, prices and promotion to the local setting, for example, when considering Auchan in Russia, Aldi in Australia and Tesco in China. Further studies provide mostly implicit evidence of the high relevance of routines to success. For example, timing has empirically been shown to be a core factor in the success of international retailers (e.g., Gielens and Dekimpe 2001), particularly if certain format elements are standardized to make it possible for a firm to quickly enter numerous countries. In contrast, there are various studies addressing the effectiveness of adapted peripheral elements. Management studies emphasize the relevance of adapted assortments, prices and promotions as a main driver of success or failure in foreign countries (e.g., Bianchi and Ostale 2006; Fam and Yang 2006; Gielens and Dekimpe 2001; Mårtenson 1987; Wigley and Chiang 2009). In addition, several consumer studies emphasize the relevance of local perceptions of local adapted assortment qualities and prices as core values for consumers' retail patronage (see, e.g., Pan and Zinkhan 2006 for a review).

According to this reasoning, it can be hypothesized that successful retailers in a foreign country standardize core marketing program elements while adapting peripheral marketing program elements. Foreign retailers rely on the advantages of the core offers and will not change them, but they will adapt peripheral offers to local customer needs. Thus, we hypothesize the following:

Hypothese 4: The higher (a) the degree of standardization of core marketing program elements and (b) the higher the degree of adaptation of peripheral marketing program elements, the higher the performance in a foreign country.

3.2.2 Processes and Performance

Based on PMT, it can also be concluded that the standardization of internal processes generates advantages through economies of scale and reduces coordination costs across countries. Because the primary function of retailers is to distribute products, retailers are forced to standardize their internal marketing and supply chain processes by avoiding duplications and redundancies to be efficient. Furthermore, because internal processes are not visible to the end-customer, they offer greater potential for standardization. However, the differentiation between core and peripheral processes is advantageous. Because core elements of marketing and supply chain processes are transferred rather unaltered, it can be assumed that this high level of standardization will be positively related to performance in a country because they may represent the retailers' efficient routines and determine the design of offers as it has been previously concluded. Performance assumptions concerning adapted peripheral processes are more difficult to make. The PMT suggests that standardization will be positively related to performance because retailers that standardize peripheral processes will be more successful in a country because the local entity will be able to benefit from established procedures, which will reduce operation costs, thus resulting in increased profits.

The literature is inconclusive concerning performance effects, especially those of retailers' marketing processes. Only Rogers, Ghauri and George (2005) address marketing process standardization and performance in the retail context and demonstrate that the success of Tesco is based on the transfer of unaltered marketing processes which are sometimes transferred several years after entry, as was the case for customer relationship management systems in Thailand. However, for manufacturers, Walters (1986) and Sorenson and Wiechmann (1975) acknowledge that the standardization of marketing processes drives performance, and based on empirical data, Akaah (1991) confirms this relationship in contrast to Chung (2003) and Townsend et al. (2004). Thus, the previous results are inconclusive. The literature concerning supply chain processes emphasizes their importance for retail performance (e.g., Schramm-Klein and Morschett 2006; Wigley and Chiang 2009) because faster and more reliable delivery results in better product availability and a better competitive position in the host country (Tacconelli and Wrigley 2009). However, a positive relationship between the degree of standardization of supply chain processes and performance is addressed by examples only in the case of fashion retailers (Brun et al. 2008) and grocery retailers (Wrigley 1997a, 1997b).

Thus, we conclude carefully based on the aforementioned theoretical reasoning that more standardized core marketing and supply chain processes will positively influence performance in a country, whereas the same conclusion for peripheral processes is based only on the general assumption that the standardization of internal processes is advantageous. Thus, we hypothesize the following:

Hypothesis 5: The higher (a) the degree of standardization of core marketing processes, (b) of peripheral marketing processes, (c) of core supply-chain processes and (d) of peripheral supply-chain processes the higher the performance in a country.

4. Empirical Study

4.1. Sample Design

In-depth face-to-face interviews have been conducted among international retailers from Austria, Germany and Switzerland. This focus has been chosen because it ensures a culturally homogeneous sample and because including firms from other countries will enhance generalizability, although issues with measurement invariance may also result (Hult et al. 2008). To develop the sample, each firm was selected from the commercial Hoppenstedt database (e.g., Schilke and Goerzen 2010) from section G52, "Retail trade, except of motor vehicles and motorcycles". This procedure yielded 758 retail chains. Retailers without international sales in at least two countries were excluded, and we contacted national retail associations to ensure that no international retailer was missing. This process yielded a potential sample of 193 firms.

CEOs were informed personally about the study, and an interview was requested at the retailer's headquarters first by postal mail and then by electronic mail and via telephone calls two weeks later. A total of 65 retailers refused to participate in the study because they do not provide any information to third parties. Other retailers did not respond to mails and telephone calls. However, 126 managers (53% CEOs/ heads of chains, 47% expansion managers) from 102 retail chains were available for interviews at their headquarters in the year 2010. Thus, we enjoyed a high response rate of 53% (Evans, Mavondo and Bridson 2008), possibly because of the convenience of the interviews for the respondents and the high interest in retail internationalization. The average retailer in the sample has total sales of 5,772 m Euro, 25,508 employees, a share of foreign sales of 41.6%, 19.1 operating countries and 23.7 years of international experience (Table C-2). These statistics indicate that these large retail firms are similar to internationally operating retail firms from other countries.

Each interview lasted approximately 120 minutes. We asked the respondents to evaluate the situation in two countries in which they had operated for at least five years. This time period was chosen to ensure market-based learning after market entry and based on the pre-test conclusions. Furthermore, the aforementioned country selection is necessary to ensure similar areas of analysis and because we assume that no country exists that has more than 100 operating foreign retailers to control for possible effects of the external environment. Following the procedure used by Evans and Mavondo (2002), we asked the respondents to select one psychically close and one psychically distant country, i.e., countries with business and cultural environments similar to and different from those of the home country. The choices were evaluated using ten business and cultural distance items (Evans and Mavondo 2002). High mean value differences between the two country groups (p < .001) and no differences within the country groups were reported for each item. The close-country group primarily includes Western European countries, whereas the distant-country group primarily includes Eastern European and Asian countries (Table C-2). Thus, we acknowledge this procedure as the best available and most appropriate way of ensuring similar areas of analysis and strengthening the robustness of the results (similar to O'Grady and Lane 1996). We have not formulated hypotheses regarding country group differences because of a weak theoretical and empirical basis for those differences concerning the analyzed relationships.

	Mean value	Std	Close country[1]		Distant country	
Number of total sales in m €	5,772	10,371	Western Europe	85.3%	Eastern Europe	46.1%
Sales abroad in %	41.6	25.9	Eastern Europe	11.8%	Asia	31.4%
Number of employees	25,508	56,268	Other	2.9%	Americas	17.6%
Employees abroad in %	40.4	25.9			Other	4.9%
Number of operating countries	19.1	23.5	**Entry modes**			
International experience in years	23.7	17.1	WOS	62.8%	WOS	54.9%
Country experience in close countries in years	19.5	14.1	Franchising	16.7%	Franchising	22.5%
Country experience in distant countries in years	10.9	5.2	M&A	13.7%	M&A	11.8%
Retail sector	39.2% food		Joint Venture	3.9%	Joint Venture	5.9%
	60.8% non-food		Other	2.9%	Other	4.9%

N=102; Country of origin: German = 80.4%, Austria = 11.8%, Switzerland = 7.8%.

[1] Please choose two different countries to evaluate in which your company operates for at least five or more years: one psychically close country (with similar legal, political, economic, business and cultural environment compared to your home country) and a psychically distant country. The country selection has been controlled according to Evans and Mavondo (2002) by using ten business and cultural dimensions; all mean value differences are significant at a p<.001 level (two-sided).

Table C-2: Sample Distribution

Source: Own creation.

4.2. Measurement of Variables

We first considered general aspects, using five-point scales to examine the hierarchy of effects and the visual design. The questions were adapted from previous studies but we had also to develop appropriate scales for our specific context and thus conducted comprehensive pre-tests as part of the scale development process, as will be described below (Table C-3).

Performance in a country is understood according to Hult et al. (2008) and we had to rely on self-reports because most retailers are not obligated to communicate their performance data in general and are especially not required to do so for specific countries. To measure performance, we followed Evans and Mavondo (2002), who refer to Cavusgil and Zou (1994) and measured performance in a country by using three financial performance indicators for each country (sales development, return on investment and market share) on a five-point Likert-type scale (1 declining/ constant, 2 increase of up to 10%, 3 increase of 11-20%, 4 increase of 21-30%, 5 increase of more than 30%) and a strategic effectiveness indicator (degree of satisfaction from 1, very unsatisfied, to 5, very satisfied with the overall development in a country). Because the strategic effectiveness indicator does not fulfill the requirements for factor loadings and indicator reliability, it has been excluded from further analysis so that financial performance represents the performance measure in this study.

Because there is no consistent measurement of marketing and supply chain processes or of retail marketing programs, we developed a list of items for each construct from prior studies (e.g., Goldman 2001; Mulhern 1997; Quintens, Pauwels and Matthyssens 2006; Srivastava, Shervani and Fahey 1999; Swoboda, Foscht and Cliquet 2008) and assessed them in several pre-tests. Three retail CEOs were asked in in-depth interviews to list retail marketing program and process indicators that are relevant for the international expansion of their retail chains and to evaluate several well-known international retailers that we had previously evaluated based on the literature and official firm databases. The results were discussed afterwards. Moreover, two executive workshops on retail internationalization (with seven and eight international senior executives, respectively) were used to identify important transferred marketing programs and process elements and to evaluate the managers' own retail chains as well as their competitors based on these indicators. After we had eliminated the items with inconclusive results from the last pre-test, six items were chosen for use in measuring the degree of standardization of the retail marketing program and each eight items were selected as a means of measuring marketing processes and supply chain processes (Table C-3). The degree of standardization for each item was measured reflectively on a semantic differential scale from 1 (fully adapted) to 5 (fully standardized) when compared to its equivalent in the home market (similar to, e.g., Baalbaki and Malhotra 1995; Cavusgil, Zou and Naidu 1993; Zou and Cavusgil 2002). To extract more or less standardized elements of the retail format, a factor analysis was executed for each construct. Remarkably, a two-factor solution was identified for each marketing and supply chain process and for the retail marketing program, which were identical for the two country groups. We acknowledge that these elements are more or less standardized but categorize the more standardized factors as the core elements and the more adapted factors as the peripheral elements based on the FFR approach. For example, the retail marketing program includes core elements such as store types, store locations and store layouts and peripheral elements such as assortments, prices and sales promotions. Similarly, marketing and supply chain processes include more standardized core elements (e.g., procedure of market analysis or purchasing) and less standardized peripheral elements (e.g., processes of category composition or daily supply processes).

We controlled for variables that might have an influence on performance: retail sector, measured binary (0=food retailers and 1=non-food retailers according to Swoboda, Elsner and Morschett 2012), retail firm size measured by the number of employees (e.g., Xu, Cavusgil and White 2006) and the geographic scope of the operations as measured by the number of countries of operation (e.g., Cavusgil and Zou 1994). Furthermore, we controlled for the retailer's country experience (i.e., its number of years in operation in the evaluated country) because significant experience may influence retailer performance. We also controlled for the employed retail entry mode because the chosen institutional arrangement (Root 1987) may determine performance. Therefore, we used entry mode dummy variables for each of the five entry modes (Table C-2) because performance might be influenced by the possibility of standardizing market offers such as by employing franchising as an entry mode or if there is no option of standardization by employing joint venture as an entry mode. To present a more rigorous test of our hypotheses and to better indicate the results, only the models with significant dummy variables (here, acquisitions) are reported in the following. Finally, we controlled our results for possible effects of five retail formats (e.g., hypermarkets, specialty stores) but without any significant effects so that those factors are excluded from further analyses.

	Mean values MV	EFA (> .50)	ItTC (>.50)	KMO (X^2) (>.50)	Factor-loading PLS	Indicator reliability (>.30)	AVE (>.50)	Composite reliability (>.60)	Cronbach's alpha (> .60/.70)	Mean values MV	MV[1] diff.[3]	EFA (> .50)	ItTC (>.50)	KMO (X^2) (>.50)	Factor-loading PLS	Indicator reliability (>.30)	AVE (>.50)	Composite reliability (>.60)	Cronbach's alpha (> .60/.70)
	Close countries									Distant countries									
Core marketing processes[1]																			
Procedures of market and trend analyses	3.77	.802	.490		.528	.379				3.51	ns	.784	.521		.664	.440			
Procedures of store location planning	3.94	.844	.634		.768	.590	.533	.817	.743	3.65	*	.823	.568		.794	.631	.544	.826	.727
Procedures of store layout development	3.89	.745	.566		.770	593				3.84	ns	.612	.539		.699	.489			
Procedures and systems of CRM	3.81	.532	.529	.768 (316.93)	.820	.672				3.70	ns	.719	.545	.767 (262.95)	.784	.614			
Peripheral marketing processes																			
Processes of category composition	3.32	.661	.501		.779	.607				3.03	*	.677	.513		.793	.629			
Processes of sales planning and monitoring	3.10	.862	.730		.861	.741	.646	.879	.822	3.09	ns	.845	.696		.828	.686	.636	.875	.817
Processes of customer service	2.98	.887	.744		.845	.713				2.91	ns	.880	.734		.822	.676			
Processes of promotion planning	2.96	.774	.614		.722	.521				2.69	*	.799	.629		.743	.552			
Core supply chain processes[1]																			
Purchasing processes	4.03	.793	.531		.743	.553				3.93	ns	.847	.565		.609	.371			
IRP systems	4.28	.950	.596		.802	.643	.605	.859	.793	4.09	ns	.945	.637		.865	.749	.626	.868	.792
Logistic processes	4.05	.751	.656		.816	.666				3.81	ns	.707	.712		.825	.680			
ERP systems	4.29	.947	.732	.804 (532.40)	.746	.557				4.11	ns	.948	.755	.791 (539.64)	.838	.702			
Peripheral supply chain processes																			
Short-term supply processes	3.79	.775	.656		.827	.685				3.42	*	.707	.595		.777	.604			
Purchasing logistics	3.71	.902	.788		.884	.781	.717	.910	.869	3.55	ns	.905	.726		.851	.724	.673	.891	.838
Internal logistics processes	3.78	.818	.737		.850	.722				3.34	*	.794	.720		.847	.717			
Distribution logistics for stores	3.35	.849	.720		.826	.682				3.04	*	.814	.662		.804	.647			
Core marketing elements[1]																			
Store type	4.27	.890	.701		.872	.760	.686	.867	.771	4.12	ns	.862	.532		.663	.439	.581	.804	.679
Store location	3.77	.809	.535		.771	.595				3.48	†	.857	.542		.753	.567			
Store layout	3.81	.773	.558	.714 (152.02)	.839	704				3.59	ns	.561	.497	.689 (116.44)	.858	.736			
Peripheral marketing elements																			
Assortment	3.49	.833	.541		.848	.720	.585	.808	.664	3.16	*	.822	.545		.836	.700	.594	.814	.696
Sales Promotion	3.42	.779	.527		.740	.548				3.12	*	.726	.535		.735	.540			
Price	3.07	.663	.482		.699	.488				2.75	†	.717	.505		.736	.542			
Performance[2]																			
Sales development	2.66	.903	.805		.887	.786				2.87	ns	.891	.801		.842	.709			
Return on investment	2.58	.850	.718	.812 (200.23)	.849	.721	.792	.919	.873	2.72	ns	.889	.797	.833 (254.47)	.927	.859	.816	.930	.893
Market share	2.38	.865	.742		.932	.869				2.69	*	.900	.813		.938	.881			
Strategic effectiveness (satisfaction)[4]	3.50	.764	.610		.384	.148				3.57	ns	.865	.762		.450	.203			

[1] How strongly does your company adapt or standardize the following [elements] in country [...] in comparison to the home market? (Please estimate as follows: 1 totally adapted to 5 totally standardized.)
[2] How successful was your company in country [...] on average over the past three years? (Please estimate as follows: 1 Declining/constant, 2 Increase of up to 10%, 3 Increase of 11-20%, 4 Increase of 21-30%, 5 Increase of more than 30%).
How satisfied are you with the overall development? (1 very unsatisfied to 5 very satisfied).
[3] Two-sided test of significance between close and distant countries: *p<.05, †p < .10, ns=not significant. [4] Excluded.

Table C-3: Measurement of Variables

Source: Own creation.

4.3. *Methodological Approach*

The methodical approach includes three steps: the measurements are tested for reliability and validity, possible biases are checked and the method of hypotheses testing is addressed.

In examining *reliability*, we initially ensured that any corrected item-to-total correlation would not fall below .500. To assess the constructs' reliability, we computed the coefficient alpha and composite reliability. In every case, these values exceeded the recommended thresholds of .70 and .60, respectively (Table C-3) (Nunally and Bernstein 1978; Peterson 1994). The average variance extracted (AVE) was above .500 for each of the latent variables. With regard to *validity*, we assessed face validity in the pre-tests. Indicating the degree of construct validity, Table C-4 illustrates the convergent validity of the items as proven by the AVE values, which were above .500, as well as their discriminant validity as proven by all of the squared correlations, which were lower than the corresponding AVE values (Fornell and Larcker 1981). Additionally, the variance inflation factors (VIF) were calculated, and all values were lower than the recommended threshold of 10 (Diamantopoulos and Winklhofer 2001). Hence, we conclude that multicollinearity was not a serious problem for either country group in this study.

		Squared latent variable correlation											
	AVE	1	2	3	4	5	6	7	8	9	10	11	12
VIF		1.473	1.581	1.035	1.847	1.357	1.037	1.060	1.400	1.213	1.284	1.345	1.072
AVE		.533	.646	.605	.717	.686	.585	.792	1.000	1.000	1.000	1.000	1.000
1 Core marketing processes	.544	-	.315	.315	.357	.294	.200	.001	.107	.000	.016	.038	.032
2 Peripheral marketing processes	.636	.184	-	.374	.518	.189	.413	.000	.171	.000	.070	.082	.040
3 Core supply chain processes	.626	.264	.241	-	.567	.174	.334	.001	.091	.000	.016	.008	.009
4 Peripheral supply chain processes	.673	.225	.452	.530	-	.394	.425	.011	.154	.000	.020	.059	.097
5 Core marketing elements	.581	.173	.099	.114	.199	-	.175	.029	.132	.000	.038	.018	.048
6 Peripheral marketing elements	594	.186	.262	.293	.277	.175	-	.006	.147	.035	.025	.016	.009
7 Performance	.816	.025	.002	.020	.022	.064	.002	-	.005	.012	.003	.049	.041
8 Retail sector	1.000	.021	.158	.022	.117	.042	.058	.001	-	.000	.114	.134	.014
9 Country experience (log)	1.000	.023	.000	.012	.000	.018	.056	.000	.000	-	.059	.113	.000
10 Firm size (log)	1.000	.000	.073	.001	.008	.004	.009	.001	.114	.000	-	.008	.016
11 Geographical scope (log)	1.000	.002	.054	.002	.024	.011	.002	.003	.134	.000	.008	-	.000
12 Entry mode dummy[1]	1.000	.001	.021	.005	.002	.000	.000	.019	.002	.000	.049	.000	-

Close countries above (distant countries below) the diagonal; Discriminant validity: Squared correlation < AVE. [1] M&A vs. others.

Table C-4: Discriminant Validity

Source: Own creation.

The probability of *non-response bias* is assumed to be limited based on a comparison of the results for early versus late respondents (Armstrong and Overton 1977). Furthermore, secondary data were gathered regarding the firms' total sales and employees abroad to compare the respondents with the non-respondents whenever such information was available. Again, we found no significant differences. The two respondent groups, CEOs/ heads of chains and expansion managers, were not different with respect to their correlations or mean values for performance. We addressed *common method bias* a priori using an appropriate questionnaire design and a posteriori using Harman's single-factor test (Podsakoff et al. 2003). Because no single factor emerged and because the first factor accounts for only 26.8% of the total variance explained, we can assume that common method bias is limited within this study. Our efforts to control *for single response bias* with a second respondent in each firm yielded 24 second respondents (mostly expansion managers) who were also interviewed personally. However, a comparison of the responses between the two groups revealed high correlations and insignificant mean value differences for all measures. Given that we personally interviewed each senior executive, we can additionally assume that single response bias might be lower in the present dataset (Kumar, Stern and Anderson 1993).

To test the hypotheses, we employed the partial least squares (PLS) approach despite the shortcomings of this method, e.g., a lack of indicators for estimating global goodness of model fit (Hulland 1999) but acknowledge also the appropriateness of this approach given the present sample size (Chin, Marcolin and Newsted 2003; Reinartz, Haenlein and Henseler 2009).

4.4. Results

The descriptive results indicate that the mean values for more standardized core process and program elements are higher than those for peripheral process and program elements (Table C-3). This finding supports Goldman's (2001) supposition that these elements are designed differently and that core and peripheral elements exist at different levels of the retailer value chain. Furthermore, process and program elements are more standardized in psychically close than psychically distant countries, whereas peripheral elements are often significantly different. Retailers respond to uncertain environments in distant countries via greater adaptation, especially with regard to peripheral format elements. Finally, performance levels are higher in psychically distant countries in accordance to the psychic distance paradox (O'Grady and Lane 1996).

To test the hypothesized relationships, several models were calculated. Models 4a and 4b (psychically close and distant countries) are relevant for the hypothesis tests (Table C-5).

The data support *hypothesis 1a/b* in both groups of countries, in which a positive relationship between the degrees of standardization of core processes (marketing and supply chain) and core marketing programs is assumed (close: $\beta = .451$, $p<.001$ and $\beta = .166$, $p<.01$; distant: $\beta = .334$, $p<.001$ and $\beta = .168$, $p<.01$). Consequently, retailers tend to design core elements consistently in host and home countries, especially marketing processes and programs.

Hypothesis 2 and 3 propose that the degree of standardization of core marketing and supply chain processes (H2a/b) and that of peripheral marketing and supply chain processes (H3a/b) are positively related to that of peripheral marketing program elements (assortment, promotion and price). The results support the relationship, but are partly different in both country-groups. H2b and H3a are fully supported (close: $\beta = .147$, $p<.01$, $\beta = .343$, $p<.001$; distant: $\beta = .316$, $p<.001$, $\beta = .247$, $p<.001$), whereas H2a is supported in psychically distant and H3b in psychically close countries ($\beta = .128$, $p<.01$; $\beta = .297$, $p<.001$). This finding may be explained intuitively. For example, standardized core marketing processes (e.g., market research, location planning) might not inspire adapted assortments or prices due to saturation in psychically close Western countries (H2a). In turn, adapted peripheral logistics/ purchasing may not be related to assortments/ prices in psychically distant countries (H3b) due to the dynamism of transition and emerging economies, where efficient supply chains are difficult to establish.

The data support *hypotheses 4a/b* in both country groups, in which a positive relationship between the degree of standardization of core marketing programs and the degree of adaptation of peripheral marketing programs is assumed to be related to performance (close: $\beta = .244$, $p<.001$ and $\beta = -.202$, $p<.05$; distant: $\beta = .273$, $p<.001$ and $\beta = -.134$, $p<.05$). Thus, internationally successful retailers standardize their core marketing program elements (store type, location and layout) and adapt peripheral marketing program elements (assortment, promotion and prices) to attain success in psychically close and distant countries.

Finally, *hypothesis 5* assumes that the standardization of marketing and supply chain processes has a positive effect on performance because those processes are not visible to end-customers and are therefore particularly suitable for standardization. Models 2a/b show the positive and significant relationships that exist between performance and all processes, whereas the final models 4a/b do not show significant effects of processes on performance for psychically close or distant countries. The only exception is core marketing processes in psychic close countries that might underline the growing direct performance relationship of these elements in saturated markets. However, this finding is remarkable because these processes have previously been found to have no significant effect on offers. In conclusion, the Sobel approximations confirm that the standardization of most marketing and supply processes have a significant indirect effect on performance through the standardization of marketing program elements (close: f-value CMP = 3.029**, f-value PMP = 2.301*, f-value CSCP = 2.069*, f-value PSCP = 2.149*; distant: f-value CMP = 3.735***, f-value PMP = 1.797†, f-value CSCP = 2.574*; Sobel 1987). Thus, the design of marketing programs mediates even fully the effects of processes on performance in psychically close and distant countries.

With respect to the control variables, we should note that geographical scope has a positive impact on performance in psychically close countries, whereas M&A as an entry mode has a negative (positive) impact on performance in close (distant) countries which is both unsurprisingly in the line of past literature. M&A are known as a less successful entry mode for retailers in Western countries (e.g., Burt and Limmack 2001) but might be suitable in distant countries because they allow a firm to acquire local knowledge (Morosini, Shane and Singh 1998). Furthermore, especially country experience exhibits a positive, significant effect on performance in psychically distant countries, which emphasizes the need for market-based learning in those countries.

	Close countries				Distant countries			
	Model 1a	***Model 2a***	***Model 3a***	***Model 4a***	***Model 1b***	***Model 2b***	***Model 3b***	***Model 4b***
	Beta t-value	Beta t-value	Beta t-value	Beta t-value	Beta t-value	Beta t-value	Beta t-value	Beta t-value
Core processes and core marketing elements (1)								
H1a: Core marketing processes → 1			.426 8.040***	.451 7.311***			.333 7.042***	.334 5.773***
H1b: Core supply chain processes → 1			.194 3.385***	.166 2.663**			.169 3.380***	.168 3.122**
Processes and peripheral marketing elements (2)								
H2a: Core marketing processes → 2			-.013 0.386ns	-.004 0.123ns			.126 3.308***	.128 2.813**
H2b: Core supply chain processes → 2			.161 2.762**	.147 2.639**			.325 6.671***	.316 4.449***
H3a: Peripheral marketing processes → 2			.363 6.131***	.343 5.653***			.245 5.631***	.247 4.717***
H3b: Peripheral supply chain processes → 2			.269 4.425***	.297 4.793***			.057 1.203ns	.064 1.189ns
Marketing elements and performance (3)								
H4a: Core marketing program elements → 3			.199 4.200***	.244 4.207***			.313 8.471***	.273 4.231***
H4b: Peripheral marketing program elements → 3			-.201 3.355***	-.202 2.371*			-.073 1.659†	-.134 2.088*
Processes and performance (3)								
H5a: Core marketing processes → 3		.206 2.295*		-.212 2.574*		.168 2.333*		.062 1.107ns
H5b: Peripheral marketing processes → 3		.175 1.875†		-.005 0.070ns		.144 1.706†		-.094 1.459ns
H5c: Core supply chain processes → 3		.164 2.744**		-.021 0.496ns		.192 2.721**		.122 1.486ns
H5d: Peripheral supply chain processes → 3		.133 1.739†		.126 1.371ns		.136 1.643†		.050 0.857ns
Controls								
Retail sector	-.012 0.402ns	-.002 0.079ns	-.007 0.222ns	-.001 0.040ns	-.017 0.384ns	-.070 1.430ns	-.087 1.768†	-.093 1.513ns
Country experience (log)	.007 0.238ns	.041 1.254ns	-.042 0.950ns	-.066 1.437ns	.056 1.563ns	.094 2.536*	.097 2.523*	.094 2.144*
Firm size (log)	.062 1.610ns	.063 1.634ns	.076 1.627ns	.078 1.583ns	-.077 1.578ns	-.128 2.398*	-.085 1.839†	-.114 1.871†
Geographical scope (log)	.219 4.984***	.140 3.163**	.229 4.074***	.244 3.624***	.063 1.645†	.104 2.295*	.061 1.608ns	.087 1.565ns
Entry mode dummy	-.211 4.681***	-.180 4.487***	-.191 3.377***	-.183 3.870***	.166 3.483***	.163 4.082***	.136 3.725**	.137 3.120**
R^2 Performance	9.5%	15.0%	13.8%	16.6%	3.2%	9.0%	10.6%	12.5%
Core marketing program elements			31.2%	31.4%			19.8%	19.9%
Peripheral marketing program elements			50.3%	49.8%			39.1%	39.0%

***p<.001, **p<.01, *p<.05, †p<.10, ns=not significant; standardized beta coefficient are illustrated.

Table C-5: Results

Source Own creation.

The overall quality of the models is satisfactory. The Stone-Geisser criterion Q^2 for assessing prediction relevance yields positive values (close: .110; distant: .084) (Fornell and Bookstein 1982). The effect sizes for the paths as well as the R^2-values (16.6% and 12.5%) are satisfactory because they are consistent with previous studies (e.g., Birkinshaw, Morrison and Hulland 1995; Peña-Vinces, Cepeda-Carrión and Chin 2012) and because unchanged or adapted format elements are just one of many performance drivers (e.g., Haugland 2010; Lin and Hsieh 2010). The f^2 values are satisfactory and account for core marketing program elements .067 and .101 and for peripheral elements .070 and .025. Finally, a rival model was calculated based on the assumption that international retailers may first decide about their marketing programs and subsequently choose the processes that result in performance. However, the results indicate lower total effects that drop from 13.8% to 12.1% in psychically close countries and from 10.7% to 7.6% in psychically distant countries because of a missing direct influence of processes on performance and therefore imply that marketing program elements have insignificant indirect effects on performance. A second rival model was tested based on the idea that the design of marketing program elements might be determined by past retailer performance. However, as the previously estimated explained variance is not exceeding for psychically close and distant countries, our framework is supported from an empirical perspective.

5. Discussion

5.1. Core Results

This study examines which elements of the retail format are transferred unchanged or adapted abroad and whether and which internal processes (marketing and supply chain processes) and visible offers interact with retailer performance in a country. This under-researched area is especially relevant for the majority of those retailers that are increasingly shifting their attention to promising foreign markets and transfer elements of their format known from their home markets but face challenges in adapting offers and in standardizing important processes in a way that help them to win local customers and to be efficient. This issue is also relevant because past studies do not conclusively indicate which program and process elements of a retailer's format, and therefore of the value chain, should be transferred unchanged or adjusted (Alexander 2008; Goldman 2001) and whether and how those elements in general and core and peripheral elements in particular drive performance abroad (Colla and Dupuis 2002; Jonsson and Foss 2011). Therefore, our study was governed by an attempt to identify the processes that are of paramount importance for retailer efficiency and the design of local offers. Our study was also guided by the aim of investigating more or less standardized core and peripheral format elements.

With respect to FFR and PMT, we find two kinds of marketing program elements that determine a firm's performance in a host country: the unchanged transfer of format types, store locations and store layouts (core elements) and the adapted transfer of assortments, promotions and prices (peripheral elements). Important retail processes are indirectly related to performance through the degree of standardization of marketing programs. Finally, retailers treat format transfer hierarchically, meaning that some peripheral elements are allowed to vary more across countries in response to the local environment and market-based learning, whereas other core elements are more standardized. However, core elements are identified simultaneously in the retail offers and processes and therefore across the whole retail format. Remarkably, the results are stable in psychically close and distant countries, and retailers standardize format elements more often than expected in some previous studies, i.e., only a few elements are strongly adapted. These observations yield two major theoretical implications and suggestions for managers.

5.2. *Theoretical Implications*

With respect to our first research question regarding whether and which process and marketing program elements are standardized or adapted and how both processes and offers interact, our results show that offers and processes are designed differently but in relation to one another. We will now discuss two conclusions in further detail.

This study proposes a conceptualization of how marketing and supply chain processes are related to marketing programs that enhance retailer performance. We respond to the calls for investigations of important processes because market analyses and logistical procedures are of paramount importance for retailer efficiency and the design of offers and because they often constitute significant differences between foreign and domestic retailers (e.g., Goldman 2000). Our results support past studies in conceptualizing processes as determinants of offers (e.g., Bourlakis and Bourlakis 2001; Cao and Dupuis 2009; Griffith, Chandra and Ryans 2003; Quintens, Pauwels and Matthyssens 2006). Consequently, both, the efficiency and the determinant argument emphasize the need to consider processes in investigating retailers' format transfers. We propose initial differentiations between process elements, process-offer relationships and marketing and supply chain processes. However, a fine-grained investigation of these factors is required.

This study proposes an important differentiation between more standardized core elements and more adapted peripheral elements within format transfer. The need for this differentiation has been suggested previously in the literature (e.g., Cao and Dupuis 2009; Carman and Langeard 1980; Kaufmann and Eroglu 1999) but this study provides strong empirical evidence that most retailers standardize some elements and adapt others. The observations are stable for both psychically close and distant countries. More importantly, proof of the hierarchical behavior of retailers is provided consistent with the recent literature (Jonsson and Foss 2011). However, the finding that most retailers standardize elements of their offers and processes is novel. Consequently, we cannot conclude that the standardization of processes or high-level features and the adaptation of offers or low-level features (e.g., Chandra, Griffith and Ryans 2002) are consistent among international retailers. Instead, it is advantageous to determine the degree of standardization of visible offers and internal processes for two reasons. First, the conceptualization of core elements may make it easier to address internal consistencies with regard to a format. Discounters, category killers and specialty stores exhibit different but characteristic combinations of location planning, logistic systems and store layouts, as do retailers such as Aldi, Best Buy or The Gap. The latter may have strategic plans or market-based routines to internationalize these core elements. Second, the identified more or less standardized format elements may not be labeled as core or peripheral elements. However, the empirical results yield an approximation of these categories that will be useful for further research. The differentiation emphasizes the varying importance of these elements, which may be used, for instance, to compose indices for categorizing of format strategies (Goldman 2001).

To enhance the empirical findings regarding the performance of international retailers, which have only been addressed in seven studies, and to shed light on successful format strategies, we explore the mediating role of core and peripheral marketing program elements in the relationship between marketing and supply-chain processes and success in a host country. In response to our second research question, i.e., whether and how standardized or adapted processes and marketing programs drive performance, we discuss two major conclusions. Because of the dearth of previous findings, this question is approached in a descriptive manner.

Although retail firms might be successful in a country due to standardization or adaptation (e.g., Cavusgil and Zou 1994, 2002), our study emphasizes that the success of most retailers depends on the standardization and adaptation of certain marketing program elements. These findings are stable in psychically close and distant countries. We are aware that boundary conditions that may affect the analyzed relationships are not controlled for in this study, e.g., internal or environmental contingencies. However, successful retailers employ unchanged core marketing elements (e.g., store types, layouts and locations) and adapt peripheral elements (e.g., assortments, promotions and prices) in a country because this approach encourages reproducible routines and market-based learning while also allowing the retailer to consider local circumstances. This finding contributes to two streams of research. *First*, it contributes to the broad retail literature on peripheral elements. The studies in this domain refer often to PMT reasoning recommending the adaptation of peripheral marketing elements in response to local customer needs. Although these previous findings are supported by this study, we also show that standardized core marketing elements are associated with performance. The latter explains even stronger performance which is noteworthy because standardization is known to determine global performance rather than country-level performance. Various causes can be attributed to this as, e.g., retailers have a preference for a particular store type or routine because all possible types of locations are already being utilized in the host country which also constitutes an important contact point for further research. *Second*, the literature concerning FFR notes that core and peripheral market offers are associated with performance in a country and that retailers' systematic evaluations and market-based learning are important explanations for firm behavior in a given country. Our study supports this finding with a representative retail sample of (non-global) retailers. Although global retailers may adapt format elements after a mostly standardized entry, many retailers may also search for more standardizable format elements. In general, retailers likely transfer modules of a format, e.g., preferred types of store layout, core assortments or categories. Such modular construction systems would be an interesting topic for further research.

Consistent with previous research (Einarsson 2008; Ganesan et al. 2009; Mentzer, Min and Zacharia 2000; Walters 1986), this study emphasizes that marketing and supply chain processes are important in the retail sector. Standardized processes have a direct relationship with performance when offers are not considered, but they are generally indirectly related to performance. This finding is notable because the standardization of processes leads to advantages across countries but does not determine performance in a specific country. Hence, there are two conclusions of interest that are related to successful process-program relationships.

- An equal degree of standardization of core and peripheral processes as well as core and peripheral marketing program elements positively affects performance. This relationship was already mentioned above and seems to emphasize a consistent behavior.
- In contrast, the degree of standardization of core processes positively influences the degree of standardization of peripheral marketing instruments, but the latter negatively affects performance. This finding indicates a possible trade-off, e.g., core processes generate boundary conditions for the design of peripheral elements or advantages across countries and must be balanced against the advantages in a specific country. One could argue that standardized core processes may not diminish a firm's ability to adapt peripheral marketing elements, e.g., when a retailer designs appropriate modules for foreign expansion or when processes do not influence offers in certain environments. The latter case was shown for core marketing processes

in Western countries. Both explanations may be representing interesting avenues for future research.

5.3. *Managerial Implications*

This study provides managerial implications in that it highlights which elements of format transfer must be more standardized or adapted, which are interrelated and whether and how their degree of standardization is associated with performance in foreign countries. We will now discuss two performance-related managerial implications.

Executives who are responsible for foreign activities or a specific country market may learn which the determining factors for performance in a country are with regard to unchanged or adapted format transfer. More specifically, managers may learn that performance depends primarily on visible offers and therefore on the design of marketing program elements. The core elements should be well known and appropriately defined within the organization. These elements should be managed deliberately in the home country, which remains for most retailers the basis for successful retail internationalization. However, such core elements change due to market-based learning and must thus be adjusted with care, especially during an aggressive internationalization process. In turn, it is valuable to adapt peripheral elements. Although such observations might be evident to managers, market exits (e.g., Wal-Mart from South Korea, Carrefour from Switzerland or Best Buy from China) indicate that this approach is not always successfully executed. Consequently, it seems that this study contributes a perspective that might be overlooked by some retailers.

More importantly, this study emphasizes that processes are important for success in a country, but only indirectly and in combination with visible offers. Thus, advantages such as an excellent market and trend analysis or CRM systems, as well as purchasing procedures or store logistics, are helpful only in a country when these elements are consistently designed with core and peripheral marketing program elements. Trade-offs must be observed because negative relationships exist between process standardization, offer adaptation and country-level performance. Furthermore, trade-offs exist between firm performance in a country and across countries. Thus, retail managers should exactly define the relationships between transferred processes and offers as indicated in this study because such relationships vary.

5.4. Limitations and Further Research

To better understand the effects of format transfer strategies on performance, further research is necessary because this study also suffers some limitations.

Although we paid special attention to the data collection process, we cannot guarantee the generalizability of the results to all international retailers. Because we collected data at retail chain headquarters in three countries based on the openness of executives to providing information in face-to-face interviews and concerning two groups of psychically different countries, this study is limited in scope. By broadening the database, a researcher could mitigate this limitation and allow for further conclusions. For example, although German retailers represent the greatest number of retailers in Europe and their international activities may be viewed as representative of those of European retailers, further studies might target one country as the unit of analysis and consider retailers from several countries. However, it can be difficult to obtain large samples of international retail firms because retailers rarely provide information and the largest survey contains 102 retail firms (Evans and Mavondo 2002) but the observation of retailers' foreign entities might be an interesting alternative (Harzing 2000).

Second, we conceptualized and measured the elements of format transfer strategy as precisely as possible. We use the home market as a reference but allow the respondents to choose the foreign countries and entry strategies, e.g., not focusing on the dominant WOS and franchising. Thus, we did not control for seldom observable, fully diversified entries. We measured the degree of standardization on semantic differential scales based on previous research and our experience in the pre-tests, but alternative approaches exist (e.g., Cavusgil and Zou 1994; Schilke, Reimann and Thomas 2009; Vrontis, Thrassou and Lamprianou 2009). Furthermore, processes and marketing elements are inherently complex, and our attempt to adapt the scales to the retail context was exploratory. More fine-grained measures may enhance the precision of the results and enlarge the scope of their implications. One particular concern is the relationships between single processes and elements (e.g., Griffith, Chandra and Ryans 2003).

Third, we focus on marketing elements and two types of processes. However, we have not discussed their different effects in detail or alternative relationships and models as mentioned above. Other elements of format transfer should be examined in future research. Examples can be found in the literature such as retail culture (e.g., Goldman 2001; Jonsson and Foss 2011; Kacker 1988), international retail strategy or retail sectors (Swoboda, Elsner and Morschett 2012). These issues can be viewed as boundary conditions or contingencies that influence the proposed relationships as environmental factors do (e.g., institutional boundaries Huang and Sternquist 2007).

D. Study 3 – Successful Organization and Coordination of International Retail Activities

1. Introduction

When going abroad, retailers are forced to manage their external marketing program and internal organizational structure, which generally involves the most important and challenging decisions a firm has to face in the international marketing arena (e.g., Cavusgil and Zou 1994; Özsomer and Prussia 2000). Regarding the long-lasting debate about marketing program standardization (Schmid and Kotulla 2011), which is defined as employing the same marketing-mix characteristics across several countries (Schilke, Reimann and Thomas 2009), retailers have to find the right balance between standardization and adaptation of their retail marketing program across countries in order to be successful. In order to coordinate the implementation of their retail marketing program, firms have to decide according to Sine, Mitsuhashi and Kirsch (2006) whether to implement mechanistic or organic organizational structures, including the degree of centralized decision-making, i.e., the extent of decision-making authority that is delegated to the local entity (Aiken and Hage 1968), and the degree of formalization of rules and procedures, i.e., the extent to which appropriate behavior is noted in formal rules and procedures (Dalton et al. 1980). However, the overwhelming majority of investigations on these decisions have dealt with manufacturing firms only and their results cannot be transferred to retailers (Burt and Carralero-Encinas 2000) because, through the distribution of manufactured products to the end customer, the retailers' production location is rather location-bound from a marketing perspective, with the result that production and consumption cannot be separated (Bouquet, Hébert and Delios 2004). Thus, as the location of production shifts in the retail context more to the host country, important implications emerge for the management and coordination of the external retail marketing program and the internal organizational structure.

According to Bartlett and Ghoshal's (1987) proposed integration-responsiveness framework, a superior internationalization strategy can be realized using a transnational strategy, meaning a high degree of global integration and a high degree of local responsiveness. Within the scope of their case study-based investigations of nine manufacturers, the authors examine whether these respond to the local environment by employing an adapted marketing program implemented by an integrated organizational structure to achieve economies of scale. However, little is known about the realization of such a transnational strategy by retailers operating internationally (Helfferich, Hinfelaar and Kasper 1997). Most recently, Jonsson and Foss (2011) use the concept of flexible replication in their case study-based investigation of IKEA to indicate that the Swedish retailer replicates its retail format abroad at first, but then makes adjustments after a learning phase by the local entities. Thus, in accordance with previous research, it can be assumed that retailers behave in the same way as manufacturers. On the other hand, it can also be argued that, due to the non-separability of location and production, the providing of goods and services has to take place abroad, resulting in a need for greater autonomy of the local subsidiary and, therefore, a less integrated organizational structure to achieve local responsiveness, but with a more standardized marketing program to realize economies of scale. Accordingly, it can be questioned whether it is more promising to apply a standardized marketing program to realize economies of scale implemented by an organic organizational structure to achieve local responsiveness or an adapted marketing program implemented by a mechanistic organizational structure? Moreover, many studies propose that management of the marketing program and organizational structure is dependent upon the external environment (e.g., Evans, Mavondo and Bridson 2008). Thus, a further question is how the marketing program and the organizational structure are influenced in countries that are psychically close and psychically distant?

These research questions are analyzed on the basis of in-depth, face-to-face interviews with 126 executives at the headquarters of 102 German-speaking retailers for each psychically close and psychically distant country in which the retailers operate in a local store network. With regard to profit maximization theory, it is assumed that it is more beneficial for retailers to employ a standardized marketing program to realize economies of scale implemented by an organic organizational structure to delegate responsibility and to accumulate local knowledge. However, due to the change in the external environment, it is assumed that retailers shift to a more adapted marketing program in psychically distant countries to respond to increasing differences abroad and to a mechanistic organizational structure to respond to increasing risks. Thus, a superior transnational strategy, including benefits of local responsiveness and global integration, can be pursued in both psychically close and psychically distant countries.

According to the call of Quester and Conduit (1996), who claim to investigate the efficiency of marketing program and organizational structure, the results of the conceptual framework provide new insights for scholars and managers. From a theoretical point of view, it can be concluded that the benefits of a standardized marketing program exceed the benefits of an adapted marketing strategy in psychically close and even psychically distant countries, whereas decision-making authority shifts from a more organic to a mechanistic structure in psychically distant countries. Thus, it is suggested that retail managers employ a standardized marketing program across psychically close and psychically distant countries, accompanied by an adjusted organizational structure depending on whether it is serving a psychically close or psychically distant country.

The remainder of this study is as follows. First, the literature review provides an overview of the current knowledge on how the degree of marketing program standardization and the organizational structures employed impact foreign performance. Subsequently, the conceptual framework deduces the hypotheses on the basis of profit maximization theory that are tested in the empirical section. After presenting the results, implications for theory and practice are drawn as well as hints for further research.

2. Literature Review

Due to the long-lasting research tradition dealing with the degree of marketing program standardization and arrangement of the organizational structure, the literature review focuses on the impact of both factors on foreign performance. Thus, the literature review is divided into three parts: 1) studies that investigate how the degree of marketing program standardization impacts foreign performance, 2) studies that investigate how the organizational structure employed impacts foreign performance and 3) studies that investigate simultaneously how both factors impact foreign performance. Furthermore, each part distinguishes between the findings for the manufacturing sector and for the retail sector.

2.1. Impact of the Degree of Marketing Program Standardization on Foreign Performance

In the manufacturing sector, one of the first profound contributions was provided by Samiee and Roth (1992), who show from analyses of 147 globally operating US business units that standardization does not lead to higher profits. By elaborating the interviews of 202 export marketing managers from US firms, Cavusgil and Zou (1994) provide mixed results. The authors estimate that performance of export ventures is influenced by product adaptation, but is negatively influenced by promotion adaptation. Also Baalbaki and Malhotra (1995) come to a divergent solution following an analysis of 74 US firms that a fully standardized marketing program is not beneficial, but should differentiate between the marketing program elements. By considering short- and long-term export performance effects experienced by 98 manufacturers from Israel, Shoham (1999) confirms that product adaptation only enhances performance in the short-run, whereas promotion adaptation enhances both short- and long-term performance. In contrast, standardization of the other elements of the marketing program, such as distribution and prices, always enhances performance. Albaum and Tse (2001) do not find a direct impact of marketing program adaptation on performance, but a mediating effect of this relationship through competitive advantage. Thus, the congruence between competitive advantage and marketing program adaptation leads to higher performance.

In contrast, several studies confirm the beneficial effect of marketing program standardization. In this respect, Zou and Cavusgil (2002) introduce the concept of global marketing strategy (GMS) and confirm a positive impact on global strategic and financial performance, whereas product and promotion standardization in particular show a high impact. By employing the concept of strategic fit, Katsikeas, Samiee and Theodosiou (2006) confirm that higher performance depends on a strategic fit between the degree of marketing strategy standardization and the environment when investigating US, Japanese and German MNCs in the UK. Hence, the more similar home and host countries are, the more beneficial is the use of a standardized marketing strategy. Chung (2009) analyzes the impact of product and promotion standardization on performance and confirm by investigating MNCs from New Zealand in Europe that both lead to a higher market share, but not to higher profits and sales growth. Overall, Schilke, Reimann and Thomas (2009) demonstrate that standardization of the marketing program is generally beneficial. However, the authors find evidence that this impact is even greater if firms are large, sell homogeneous products, pursue a cost leadership strategy and obtain a high degree of global market participation. Moreover, product standardization leads to a higher degree of success followed by promotion standardization and channel structure standardization. Vrontis, Thrassou and Lamprianou (2009) conclude from their investigation of 372 UK-based MNCs that complete standardization cannot be beneficial due to market heterogeneity. However, the authors summarize that the marketing program should be standardized where possible and adapted where needed. In conclusion, most studies find evidence that the higher the degree of standardization of the marketing program, the better the performance abroad. However, it seems also evident that not only complete standardization is beneficial, but that adaptations are also necessary.

Regarding the retail sector, Mårtenson (1987) shows that standardization is even feasible in highly culturally bound industries and leads to success, as the case of the Swedish furniture retailer IKEA shows. Dupuis and Prime (1996) analyze the market operations of Carrefour in the USA and Taiwan and conclude that the retail format should be maintained in general, but adjusted to the local conditions where necessary. The authors note that Carrefour failed in the USA due to missing adaptations, but succeeded in Taiwan due to adaptation to the local environment. Similarly, McGoldrick (1998) investigates the competitive positions of Marks & Spencer and C&A, concluding that even successful retail formats in the domestic markets have to be adapted abroad. Also in the retail context, McGauran (2001) suggests through a comparison of 27 fashion retailers in Paris and Dublin that marketing program adaptations are necessary due to different local tastes and competitive market conditions despite the relatively short distance between the two cities. Burt et al. (2005) show that a retail format can fail abroad in the case of the British retailer Boots, although the retail format is very well accepted in the domestic market. Thus, the authors highlight the importance of adaptations in the retail context because the lack of even minor adaptations can lead to failure abroad. By comparing store decision criteria between consumers of the EU founder countries with those from Central and Eastern Europe, White and Absher (2007) find significant differences in both groups and conclude that cultural differences make it necessary to adapt the marketing program to meet store decision criteria abroad. Among other things, Evans, Mavondo and Bridson (2008) analyze the impact of marketing program adaptation on financial performance by 102 retailers operating internationally, but, contrary to the authors' expectations, find a strong negative impact indicating that the higher the degree of standardization of the marketing program, the better the financial performance. Wigley and Chiang (2009) suggest from the case-study based analysis of the fashion retailer per una in the UK and Taiwan that success can be achieved by standardizing product design, brand image, store layout, logistics and customer relationship management, whereas prices, product assortment and advertising are suggested for adaptation in order to maximize profitability. Similarly, Burt, Johansson and Thelander (2011) and Jonsson and Foss (2011) show from the case of IKEA that the marketing program is mostly standardized, but adaptations are applied where needed. In conclusion and in contrast to the international business literature, studies in the retail context emphasize in particular the importance of marketing program adaptation and of a combination of standardization and adaptation, respectively, as Jonsson and Foss (2011) introduce most recently with their concept of 'flexible replication'. However, with the sole exception of Evans, Mavondo and Bridson (2008), all other studies are only case study-based investigations highlighting the importance of more generalizable results in the retail context.

2.2. *Impact of the Organizational Structure employed on Foreign Performance*

In contrast to the previous section, research on the impact of the organizational structure employed on foreign performance in the manufacturing sector is partly conceptual and partly empirical, so the following studies are categorized accordingly.

Conceptually, the first contribution on the impact of organizational structure on performance has been provided by Dalton et al. (1980). By reviewing the existing literature, the authors do not find a consensus on the impact of formalization and specialization on performance, but they suggest that centralization has a negative effect on performance. More specifically, Govindarajan (1986) examines the impact of the degree of decentralization on the effectiveness of strategic business units. By reviewing previous research studies, the author concludes that centralization leads to higher performance in terms of a high need of interdependence between headquarter and subsidiary to make coordination between the two more effective. Furthermore, centralization is effective for low-cost business units, whereas decentralization is more effective for differentiator business units. Finally, Chang and Harrington (2000) assume by referring to their computational simulation that decentralization is beneficial in terms of heterogeneous markets, consumers that are non-sensitive to store practices sensitive to store practices, a long-term horizon and a stable market environment. In contrast, centralization is more advantageous in terms of homogenous markets, consumers that are sensitive to store practices to store practices, a short horizon and a turbulent market environment.

Empirically, only a few studies have so far analyzed how the organizational structure employed impacts foreign performance. Miller (1987) shows in an analysis of 97 manufacturing firms that the degree of centralization of decision-making must correspond to the strategy-making process in order to achieve higher performance. Nohria and Ghoshal (1994) find evidence through an investigation of subsidiaries of 54 MNCs that a decentralized and informal organizational structure becomes more efficient as the external environment becomes more complex. Moreover and similar to Miller (1987), the authors demonstrate that a fit between the organizational structure and the internal circumstances of the subsidiaries leads to higher performance. Lin and Germain (2003) show from an investigation of 274 Chinese state-owned enterprises that centralization of decision-making and formal control have a positive impact on performance, whereas market orientation is positively influenced by a high degree of decentralization and in combination with formal control. Auh and Menguc (2007) examine 260 large Australian companies and find evidence that centralization has a negative impact on customer orientation, whereas formalization reinforces the impact of customer orientation on firm performance because transparent rules minimize redundancy and confusion on how to be customer-oriented. Finally, Chung (2008) shows in an analysis of 78 companies from New Zealand operating in Europe that decentralized decision-making leads to a greater profitability, whereas centralized decision-making leads to higher sales growth and profit in interaction with a very different environment and a low level of local knowledge. In conclusion, most studies in the manufacturing context suggest that a high degree of centralization, mostly in combination with a high degree of formalization, leads to higher performance.

In the retail context, only two studies have yet been provided. Harris (2000) interviews 107 store managers of large UK retailers and concludes that centralization and formalization leads to efficient decision-making, but the innovativeness and market orientation of the retailers are hampered. By referring to case study-based analyses of 10 international retailers with operations in the UK, Moore, Birtwistle and Burt (2004) suggest that retailers with decentralized decision-making and a low degree of formalization face fewer problems with the local management and are therefore more likely to be successful. In conclusion, it appears that a high degree of market orientation might be achieved through a high degree of decentralization. However, the impact of the organizational structure employed on foreign performance has not yet been investigated in the retail context.

2.3. *Impact of Both on Foreign Performance*

By investigating 45 MNCs that operate in Turkey, Özsomer and Prussia (2000) show that a standardized marketing strategy only influences subsidiary performance indirectly through a centralized marketing structure, whereas centralization of the marketing structure has a negative effect on subsidiary performance. The authors conclude that an adapted marketing strategy in combination with a decentralized marketing structure leads to superior performance. Özsomer and Simonin (2004) conclude in an investigation of Japanese and Turkish subsidiaries of MNCs that standardization of the marketing program leads to higher performance at subsidiary level, but cultural differences impede standardization and firms are forced to adapt to local conditions to a certain extent. Regarding the degree of centralization of decision-making, centralization of product decisions does not show a significant effect on performance compared to centralization of non-product decisions, which has a significantly negative effect on performance. The authors argue that centralization of non-product decisions limits flexibility and thus leads to a lower performance. Finally, Chung (2009) shows from the analysis of 78 MNCs from New Zealand operating in Europe that the structure of decision-making, i.e., the degree of authorization given to a firm's local representation, does not influence financial performance directly, but only indirectly in congruence with the degree of marketing program standardization. In conclusion, it is evidenced by these studies that marketing program and organizational structure have to fit one another in order to enhance performance.

In the retail context, Arnold and Fernie (2000) analyze the market entry of Wal-Mart into the UK. In order to be successful, Wal-Mart employed a mixture of standardization and adaptation of their marketing program, implemented with a decentralized and informal organizational structure. This study is, therefore, the only one that investigates simultaneously how the degree of standardization of the marketing program and how the organizational structure employed impact foreign performance in the retail context, but only in a case-study based research design, which means that the results provided have to be viewed with care. Furthermore, as already indicated in the literature review, Swoboda and Anderer (2008), identify several coordination dimensions in retailing and emphasize in their empirical analysis that organizational structure has itself no direct effect on success but instead the instruments of coordination. All in all, due to the narrow research status the question is how the degree of marketing program standardization, the centralization of decision-making and the formalization of rules and procedures influence performance by international operating retailers in psychically different countries?

3. Theoretical Foundation

Scholars have examined the standardization and adaptation decision from different angles, such as contingency theory, profit maximization theory, resource-based view, internationalization and institutional theory (Schmid and Kotulla 2011), as well as the decision about the arrangement of the organizational structure by contingency theory (e.g., Chang and Harrington 2000), agency theory (e.g., Moore, Birtwistle and Burt 2004) and control theory (e.g., Auh and Menguc 2007). To address the above mentioned research questions, the profit maximization theory (PMT) has been employed to explain the successful usefulness of marketing program standardization and the arrangement of organizational structure from an economic perspective. Using this approach broadens the existing arguments by determining the successful balance between benefits and costs of marketing program standardization and the arrangement of organizational structure.

The PMT focuses on explaining foreign performance through the successful implementation of strategies (Schmid and Kotulla 2011). The theory postulates that a firm's main goal is to maximize profits, achieved through the realization of economies of scale or the benefits of market segmentation (Samiee and Roth 1992). Economies of scale can be realized by employing a standardized marketing program across countries, with centralized decision-making supported by formalized rules and procedures so that costs are reduced and profits are enhanced under the assumption that sales are maintained constant. On the other hand, through the adaptation of the marketing program, the decentralization of decision-making and informal rules and procedures, adjustments to the local host country conditions are allowed by segmenting the host countries into homogeneous markets, resulting in higher sales so that profits are enhanced under the assumption that the increase in costs, for example through adaptation, are exceeded by the increase of sales. In conclusion, integration of activities is favored as long as economies of scale exceed benefits through increasing sales, whereas local responsiveness of activities is favored as long as benefits through increasing sales exceed economies of scale.

4. Conceptual Framework and Hypotheses Development

In this section, the proposed hypotheses are deduced. The conceptual model summarizes the set of relationships examined in this study (Figure D-1).

It is assumed at first that retailers differ considerably from manufacturers due to the local nature of the retail business (e.g., Bouquet, Hébert and Delios

2004). Hence, specific effects can be assumed by the degree of standardization of the marketing program, the degree of centralization of decision-making and the degree of formalization of rules and procedures on foreign performance. Although numerous potential structural characteristics exist (Hempel, Zhang and Han 2012), the degree of specialization, i.e., the extent of the division of labor within a firm, represents another dimension of organizational structure according to Pugh et al. (1968). However, similar to many previous studies that investigate the success of organizational structure (e.g., Auh and Menguc 2007; Caruana, Morris and Vella 1998; Deshpandé 1982; Ghoshal and Nohria 1993) this dimension is not considered in this study because the extent of the division of labor within a firm do not influence the market orientation of a firm (Jaworski and Kohli 1993) and therefore performance in a foreign country, particularly in retailing (Harris 2000).

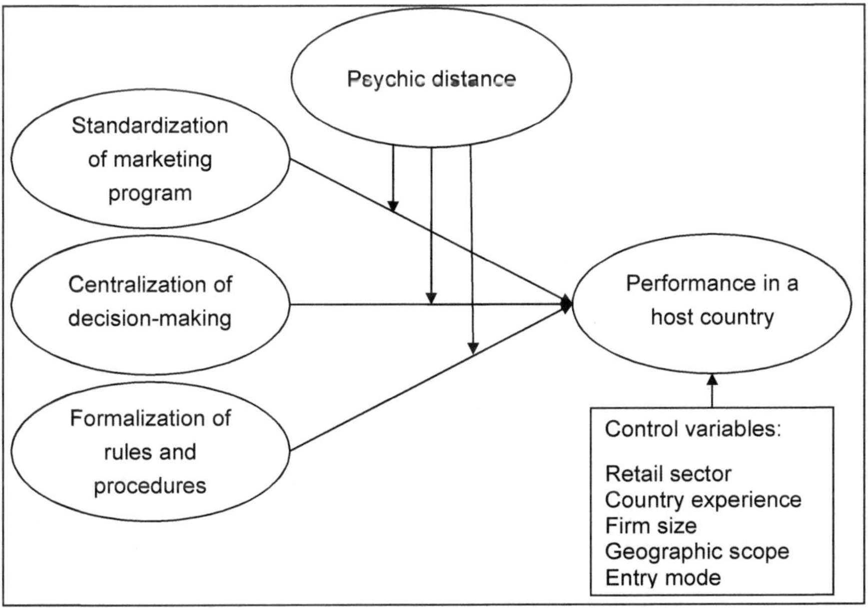

Figure D-1: Conceptual Framework
Source: Own creation.

In this study, it is proposed that retailers strive for efficiency by rolling out a highly standardized retail format in foreign countries to realize economies of scale implemented by a high degree of formalization of rules and procedures and a low degree of centralization of decision-making to respond to the local host country conditions. Furthermore, it is proposed that retailers depart from this default strategy when entering psychically distant countries. Due to the considerable dissimilarities between home and host countries, it is proposed that retailers are forced to employ a low degree of standardization to respond to the local host country conditions implemented by a low degree of formalization of rules and procdures and a high degree of centralization of decision-making to strive for efficiency. Hence, it is proposed that psychic distance moderates the effects that marketing program standardization and the organizational structure employed have on foreign performance.

In the following, the effects of the degree of markeitng program standardization, the degree of centralization of decision-making and the degree of formalization of rules and procedures for psychically close and psychically distant countries are discussed from a theoretical perspective and empirical evidence is provided for each proposition.

4.1. The Degree of Marketing Program Standardization and Foreign Performance

Marketing program standardization means the use of the same marketing-mix characteristics across several countries (Schilke, Reimann and Thomas 2009). With regard to psychically close countries, it can be assumed that these countries are very similar to the retailers' home countries so that a high potential is offered for realizing of economies of scale. In contrast, due to the high similarity, fewer adaptations are necessary, resulting in fewer expected benefits through increased sales. Hence, as the amount of economies of scale might exceed the benefits through increased sales, it can be assumed that the more standardized the retail marketing program in psychically close countries, the higher the foreign performance.

Empirically, scholars provide indecisive results about the effect of marketing program standardization on foreign performance. Some researchers observed no effect of standardization towards performance (e.g., Samiee and Roth 1992), whereas others estimate a positive impact of product adaptation on foreign performance (e.g., Shoham 1999) or demonstrate a positive influence of a standardized global marketing strategy on foreign performance (Zou and Cavusgil 2002). Because of these inconsistent results, some researchers recommend considering standardization of the marketing program depending on the external environment. Accordingly, Chung (2003) reports the efficiency of promotion and product standardization if operating in similar markets. Özsomer, Bodur and Cavusgil (1991) illustrate the appropriateness of a standardized approach with regard to similarities in the nature of competition, retail structure, target customer segments, marketing legislation and product life cycle stages between home and host countries. By considering the retail sector, Evans, Treadgold and Mavondo (2000) find evidence that marketing program standardization seems to be most beneficial in homogenous countries. Also, the results of Evans and Bridson (2005) indicate that the smaller the perceived psychic distance, the smaller the need for marketing strategy adaptation. Therefore, it is assumed:

Hypothesis 1a: The more standardized the retail marketing program, the higher the performance in psychically close countries.

With regard to psychically distant countries, it can be assumed that these countries have little similarity to the retailers' home country. Thus, it can be expected that marketing program adaptation will result in greater benefits through increased sales. Furthermore, marketing program standardization is less feasible in psychically distant countries and therefore offers a low potential for realizing economies of scale. Hence, as benefits through increased sales might exceed the amount of economies of scale, it can be assumed that the more adapted the retail marketing program in psychically distant countries, the higher the foreign performance.

While assuming the prevalence of a standardized marketing program for operations in psychically close countries, the profitability of an adapted marketing program in psychically distant countries is inherent (White and Absher 2007). Accordingly, Sousa and Bradley (2005) show that a greater psychic distance leads to a higher proportion of marketing program adaptation, particularly with regard to price and promotion activities. In the retail context, Beninati, Evans and McKinney (1997) state that assortment management at local level will result in increasing profits and greater customer loyalty in foreign countries. By explicitly referring to the concept of psychic distance, Evans and Bridson (2005) demonstrate a positive effect of retail offer adaptation on foreign performance in psychically distant countries. Thus, due to substantial environmental differences, a greater need is assumed for adaptation in psychically distant countries in order to be successful.

Hypothesis 1b: The more adapted the retail marketing program, the higher the performance in psychically distant countries.

4.2. The Degree of Centralization of Decision-making and Foreign Performance

The centralization of decision-making is the amount of decision-making authority that is held by the headquarter (Aiken and Hage 1968). With regard to psychically close countries, it can be assumed that retailers are familiar with the local host country conditions and retailers are able to leave autonomy to the local entity, which is necessary in retailing as the production location is the store abroad that delivers manufactured products to the end-customer. Thus, the decentralization of decision-making makes it possible to respond to the local host country conditions, resulting in greater benefits through increased sales. In contrast, the centralization of decision-making is less feasible as the production location is abroad and therefore offers low potential for realizing of economies of scale. Hence, as benefits through increased sales might exceed the amount of economies of scale, it can be assumed that the more decentralized the structure of organizational decision-making in psychically close countries, the higher the foreign performance.

Empirically, the literature in the review also provides indecisive results on how centralization of decision-making impacts foreign performance, as Dalton et al. (1980) has already shown. Some scholars come to the conclusion that centralization of decision-making has a positive impact on foreign performance (e.g., Lin and Germain 2003), whereas other researchers find that decentralization of decision-making influences foreign performance positively (e.g., Auh and Menguc 2007). Thus, further scholars postulate that the degree of centralization must correspond to the external environment in order to be successful (e.g., Chung 2008; Ruekert, Walker and Roering 1985). Hence, the external environment plays an important role in choosing the extent of decision-making authority that is held by the headquarters and also Nohria and Ghoshal (1994) demonstrate that the degree of centralization of decision-making depends upon the complexity of the external environment. Due to the local nature of the retail business (Bouquet, Hébert and Delios 2004), decentralization of decision-making can generally be assumed to be a successful default organizational structure for several reasons and as the fast growing franchise retail format shows. First, in decentralized decision-making, trust is given to local managers, who commonly reward this with greater degrees of involvement and efficiency (Aghion and Tirole 1997; Singh 1986). Second, local managers have access to specific local information that might be difficult to communicate to central managers, as the managers at headquarters might not see the necessity to consider certain aspects (Malone 1999). Third, due to the self-reliance of local managers, the complexity of global operations and the possibility that conflicts might emerge are reduced (Aghion and Tirole 1997). Hence, by the decentralization of decision-making, local responsiveness is assured. As the literature in the review indicates, the degree of centralization of decision-making for retailers operating internationally is mainly only investigated in case-study based analyses. In this regard, Arnold and Fernie (2000) illustrate the successful market entry of Wal-Mart in the UK by decentralized decision-making. By investigating the success factors of the world's best retailers, Arnold (2002) concludes among others that decentralized decision-making leads to a more motivational organizational structure and Moore, Birtwistle and Burt (2004) find that retailers with decentralized decision making are likely to have fewer problems with subsidiary management. Furthermore, Harris (2000) concludes from the investigation of several store managers that decentralized decision-making leads to a better market orientation. In the light of the above mentioned theoretical rationale and according to previous research, it can be assumed that the decentralization of decision-making enables retailers to respond to local conditions, which in turn enhances foreign performance.

Hypothesis 2a: The more decentralized the decision-making, the higher the performance in psychically close countries.

With regard to psychically distant countries, it can be assumed that retailers are less familiar with the local host country conditions so that retailers perceive greater risks in leaving autonomy to the local entity. Thus, the centralization of decision-making makes it possible to reduce risk and to realize economies of scale. In contrast, the decentralization of decision-making is less feasible due to greater perceived risks, resulting in fewer benefits. Hence, as the amount of economies of scale might exceed the benefits through increased sales, it can be assumed that the more centralized the decision-making in psychically distant countries, the higher the foreign performance.

As the literature in the review shows, centralized decision-making is suggested by Chang and Harrington (2000) when operating in unstable markets because uncertainties exist about whether a firm's enunciated policies are followed or whether there is idiosyncratic behavior by the local management. Therefore, control is a viable option to counteract such adverse behavior (Cray 1984). In this regard, Boyacigiller (1990) finds evidence that firms respond to greater risks by employing associates from their home market and Garnier (1982) demonstrates a general tendency to increase centralization if the perceived risk of foreign operations increases. Regarding the retail sector, Evans, Mavondo and Bridson (2008) state that decentralized decision-making is more likely to be applied in psychically distant countries, but the authors cannot detect a significant influence. Hence, due to uncertainties associated with operations in psychically distant countries, including both market risks and the danger of misleading individual behavior, it is assumed that the more centralized the decision-making, the better the performance in psychically distant countries.

Hypothesis 2b: The more centralized the decision-making, the higher the performance in psychically distant countries.

4.3. The Degree of Formalization of Rules and Procedures and Foreign Performance

The formalization of rules and procedures is understood as the extent to which appropriate behavior is noted (Dalton et al. 1980). With regard to psychically close countries, it can be assumed that these countries are very similar to the retailers' home country so a high degree of formalization is necessary to implement a standardized marketing program resulting in high potential for realizing economies of scale as this also allows faster decision-making. In contrast, due to the high similarity, a lower degree of formalization is not appropriate as not many benefits can be achieved through increased sales. Hence, as the amount of economies of scale might exceed the benefits through increased sales in psychically close countries, it can be assumed that the more formalized rules and procedures in psychically close countries, the higher the foreign performance.

As the literature in the review shows, Lin and Germain (2003) demonstrate that formalized rules and procedures result into higher performance in Chinese state-owned enterprises and Morrison and Roth (1993) support the proposal that firms with a purely global strategy employ a high degree of formalization, whereas firms that pursue a country-specific strategy employ a low degree of formalization. In the retail context, Arnold (2002) points out that successful retailers, such as Wal-Mart and Home Depot, rely on formal rules and Verity (2005) highlights the importance of written plans and formal rules for the gas-station giant Shell in order to be successful abroad. In conclusion, it is assumed in this study that the greater the formalization of rules and procedures in psychically close countries, the higher the foreign performance.

Hypothesis 3a: The more formalized rules and procedures are, the higher the performance in psychically close countries.

With regard to psychically distant countries, it can be assumed that these countries are very dissimilar to the retailers' home country so a low degree of formalization is necessary to implement an adapted marketing program, resulting in greater benefits through increased sales. In contrast, a high degree of formalization is not appropriate in psychically distant countries due to the huge dissimilarities between home and host countries. Hence, as benefits through increased sales might exceed the amount of economies of scale in psychically distant countries, it can be assumed that the less formalized the rules and procedures in psychically distant countries, the higher the foreign performance.

As the literature in the review shows, only Nohria and Ghoshal (1994) suggest that when complexity of the external environment increases, a low degree of formalization is more efficient. However, no study known to the author has yet considered the degree of formalization for retailers operating internationally in dependence upon the external environment. With respect to the above mentioned rationale, however, it is assumed that less formalized rules and procedures lead to higher performance in psychically distant countries.

Hypothesis 3b: The less formalized rules and procedures are, the higher the performance in psychically distant countries.

In conclusion, it is assumed for psychically close countries that it is most beneficial when retailers employ a standardized marketing program with a high degree of formalization of rules and procedures to realize economies of scale, implemented by decentralized decision-making to ensure local responsiveness. In contrast, it is assumed for psychically distant countries that retailers employ an adapted marketing program with a low degree of formalization of rules and procedures to ensure local responsiveness, implemented by centralized decision-making to realize economies of scale and to reduce risk.

5. Empirical Study

5.1. Data Collection and Sample Characteristics

To test the proposed conceptual framework empirically, primary-data have been collected by conducting in-depth, face-to-face interviews with German-speaking retailers with headquarters located in Austria, Germany and Switzerland, who conduct their sales activities abroad in at least two countries. The focus on German-speaking retailers is inevitable in order to avoid any measurement variances across countries (Hult et al. 2008) and to ensure that the countries considered were always interpreted in the same way with regard to psychic distance. In order to identify appropriate retailers, the Hoppenstedt database was searched, which is one of the largest business data providers in Europe (e.g., Schilke and Goerzen 2010). First, the database was searched according to the criteria of the German Classification of Economic Activities of the Federal Statistical Office (2003). Consistent with this classification, traditional retailers belong to section G 52 "Retail trade, except of motor vehicles and motorcycles" resulting in 758 retailers. After duplications were erased, each retailer was checked via internet research to ensure that the retailer's headquarter is located in one of the above mentioned German-speaking countries and operates in at least two foreign companies. Additionally, retail associations were contacted, requesting identification of further retailers operating internationally, which resulted in a potential sample size of 193 firms.

Using this database, an interview was requested from the CEOs or expansion managers at the firms' headquarters first by standard mail and then by electronic mail followed by telephone calls two weeks later. Sixty-five retailers declined as they generally do not provide any information. Other retailers did not react to mails and telephone calls. However, 126 managers (53% CEOs/ heads of chains, 47% expansion managers) from 102 retail chains agreed to interviews, which resulted in a comparatively high response rate of 53% (e.g., Baalbaki and Malhotra 1995; Schilke, Reimann and Thomas 2009). As Table D-1 indicates, the average retailer in the data sample generates total sales of about 5.7 billion € and employs 25,500 employees, whereas 40% of total sales and employees came from abroad in each case. Furthermore, the average retailer has almost 19.5 years of experience in psychically close and 10.9 years of experience in psychically distant countries and operates in 19 countries.

	Mean value	Std	Close countries[1]		Distant countries	
Number of total sales in m €	5,772	10,371	Western Europe	85.3%	Eastern Europe	46.1%
Sales abroad in %	41.6	25.9	Eastern Europe	11.8%	Asia	31.4%
Number of employees	25,508	56,268	Other	2.9%	Americas	17.6%
Employees abroad in %	40.4	25.9			Other	4.9%
Number of operating countries	19.1	23.5	**Entry modes**			
International experience in years	23.7	17.1	WOS	62.8%	WOS	54.9%
Country experience in close countries (years)	19.5	14.1	Franchising	16.7%	Franchising	22.5%
Country experience in distant countries (years)	10.9	5.2	M&A	13.7%	M&A	11.8%
Retail sector	39.2% food		Joint Venture	3.9%	Joint Venture	5.9%
	60.8% non-food		Other	2.9%	Other	4.9%

N=102; Country of origin: German = 80.4%, Austria = 11.8%, Switzerland = 7.8%.
[1] Please choose two different countries to evaluate in which your company operates for at least five or more years: one psychically close country (with similar legal, political, economic, business and cultural environment compared to your home country) and a psychically distant country. The country selection has been controlled according to Evans and Mavondo (2002) by using ten business and cultural dimensions; all mean value differences are significant at a p<.001 level (two-sided).

Table D-1: Sample Characteristics
Source: Own creation.

In investigating the differences between psychically close and psychically distant countries, this study follows the procedure of Evans and Mavondo (2002) as each construct has been evaluated by the respondents for a respective close and distant country. Therefore, the respondents had to choose one psychically close and one psychically distant country in which the retailer operates before the survey. In order to check for validity, each respondent evaluated for both countries the cultural and business distance between the home and the respective host country based on Likert-type scales, from 1=exactly the same to 5=entirely different. The mean value comparisons between psychically close and psychically distant countries show that the first are perceived significantly more similar to the home country in terms of cultural and business distance so it can be concluded that the categorization into psychically close and psychically distant countries is appropriate. The countries chosen are linked to Western and Eastern Europe for psychically close countries and to Eastern Europe, Asia and the Americas for psychically distant countries.

Several tests have been conducted to assure that the data sample is not biased. Single response bias is assumed to be reduced due to the focus on senior executives (Venkatraman and Grant 1986). Furthermore, as no significant differences could be found between single and second informants in 22 cases, it can be assumed that single informant biases are not likely to occur (Kumar, Stern and Anderson 1993). The probability of non-response bias is also assumed to be reduced as no significant differences were found between early and late respondents, nor between respondents and non-respondents in terms of sales and number of employees (Armstrong and Overton 1977). In order to reduce common method bias a-priori, the structure of the questionnaire has been designed by a mixed order of questions (Kline, Sulsky and Rever-Moriyama 2000). Moreover, the Harman's single-factor test has been carried out ex-post, but no general factor accounted for the majority of the covariance between the measures and no single factor emerged (Chang, van Witteloostuijn and Eden 2010; Podsakoff et al. 2003). Therefore, it can also be assumed that common method bias also does not constitute a problem in this study.

5.2. Measurement of Variables

With regard to the survey design, general aspects have been considered, e.g., the hierarchy of effects and the visual design. All questions used in the survey are adapted from previous studies. In measuring performance, this study follows Evans and Mavondo (2002), who refer to Cavusgil and Zou (1994) and Shoham (1996) by measuring three financial performance indicators (sales development, return on investment and market share) on average over the past three years on a five-point Likert-type scale ([1] declining/ constant, [2] increase of up to 10%, [3] increase of 11-20%, [4] increase of 21-30%, [5] increase of more than 30%) and one strategic effectiveness indicator (degree of satisfaction with the past development) also on average over the past three years on a five-point Likert-type scale ([1] very unsatisfied to [5] very satisfied). However, as illustrated in Table D-4, the latter indicator which targets the subjective satisfaction level of managers has been dropped because it can be assumed due to the high mean value that the responses are assumed to be biased by social desirability (Podsakoff and Organ 1986) and because the value of the indicator reliability falls significantly below the recommended threshold in both psychically close and psychically distant countries (Table D-2).

In order to conceptualize the standardization of the retail marketing program, most studies refer to McCarthy's (1964) "4P" classification (e.g., Schilke, Reimann and Thomas 2009; Sousa and Lengler 2009). However, this classification has to be modified for the retail sector because other marketing elements, such as store layout, have to be considered due to the direct contact between the retailer and the end-customers (Mulhern 1997). Thus, while adapting the marketing program elements of price and advertising, those of product and distribution have been replaced by assortment and store layout (McGoldrick 1998). All these items have been measured on a five-point Likert-type scale ranging from [1] fully adapted to [5] fully standardized compared to the degree of standardization in the home country (e.g., Baalbaki and Malhotra 1995; Zou and Cavusgil 2002).

In order to conceptualize the organizational structure, this study investigates the degree of centralization of decision-making and the degree of formalization of rules and procedures, as outlined above, as the most important organizational structure dimensions (e.g., Caruana, Morris and Vella 1998), even in the retail context (e.g., Harris 2000). To measure both dimensions, most studies refer to Aiken and Hage (1968) and Pugh et al. (1968) (e.g., Auh and Menguc 2007). However, due to the characteristics of the retail sector, the scale established has to be adapted to the retail context according to Lin and Hsieh (2010) by measuring three important business functions (planning, investments and controlling) according to a five-point Likert-type scale ranging from [1] fully decentralized to [5] fully centralized and from [1] fully unformulated to [5] fully formulated, respectively. Finally, all items were measured reflectively because the indicators measured reflect the underlying construct (Hulland

1999). Thus, changes in the latent variables of marketing program standardization, centralization and formalization cause simultaneous variation in all measures. Furthermore, indicators are interchangeable and the removal of one item does not influence the nature of the underlying construct (Diamantopoulos and Winklhofer 2001).

Table D-2 illustrates the reliability and validity of the measurement models. However, as some changes must have been conducted compared to previous research, extensive pre-tests were conducted at first to ensure content validity (Churchill 1979). Three retail experts were asked in focus interviews to assess all indicators to ensure that each construct is measured fully. Moreover, seven and nine expansion managers, respectively, from two top management seminars on retail internationalization were asked to evaluate their own and competing retail chains according to these indicators in order to pretest the indicators compiled. After eliminating comprehension problems and in accordance with the rationale emphasized above, four items were defined for measuring the degree of standardization of retail marketing programs and three items each for measuring the degree of centralization of decision-making and the degree of formalization of rules and procedures.

Before checking for reliability and validity of the measured variables, one-dimensionality of each construct was checked first by an explorative factor analysis (Gerbing and Anderson 1988). As each item per construct loads only on one factor, the assumption of one-dimensionality for all constructs is fulfilled. To check for indicator reliability, almost all indicators in Table D-2 exceed the recommended threshold of 0.3 (Bagozzi 1994), except for assortment and advertising. However, the indicators have not been discarded as reliability of the construct is not improved significantly by elimination and both are important for the whole marketing program, as the 4P classification indicates (Henseler, Ringle and Sinkovics 2009). In assessing construct reliability, Cronbach's alpha, the composite reliability and the average variance extracted (AVE) are considered. The Cronbach's alpha values and those of the composite reliability almost exceed the recommended threshold of 0.7 and 0.6 (Nunally and Bernstein 1978; Peterson 1994) and 0.6 (Bagozzi and Yi 1988), respectively, for psychically close and psychically distant countries. Furthermore, almost all values of the average variance extracted (AVE) exceed the recommended threshold of 0.5

except for the marketing program in the case of psychically close countries. However, construct reliability can be assumed as the more strict Fornell-Larcker criterion below is fulfilled, as indicated in Table D-3 (Fornell and Larcker 1981).

Construct	Item	Factor loadings EFA (> .50)	KMO (X²) (>.50)	Factor-loading PLS	Indicator reliability (>.30)	AVE (>.50)	Composite reliability (>.60)	Cronbach's alpha (> .60/.70)	Factor loadings EFA (> .50)	KMO (X²) (>.50)	Factor-loading PLS	Indicator reliability (>.30)	AVE (> .50)	Composite reliability (>.60)	Cronbach's alpha (> .60/.70)	Sources
		Close countries							Distant countries							
Standardization of marketing program[1]	Store layout	.709		.626	.392				.666		.879	.773				Acc. to McCarthy (1964); McGoldrick (1998); Mulhern (1997)
	Assortment	.778	.697 (76.563)	.115	.013	.307	.591	.696	.757	.734 (61.219)	.585	.343	.473	.775	.697	
	Price	.665		.752	.565				.736		.534	.286				
	Advertising	.739		.509	.259				.734		.699	.489				
Centralization of decision-making[2]	Planning	.861		.946	.895				.903		.930	.865				Acc. to Aiken and Hage (1968); Lin and Hsieh (2010); Pugh et al. (1968)
	Investment	.487	.612 (144.924)	.609	.370	.718	.881	.803	.689	.619 (102.687)	.582	.338	.684	.862	.772	
	Controlling	.828		.942	.889				.888		.921	.848				
Formalization of rules & procedures[3]	Planning	.888		.815	.665				.914		.895	.800				Acc. to Aiken and Hage (1968); Lin and Hsieh (2010); Pugh et al. (1968)
	Investment	.919	.741 (168.964)	.975	.950	.790	.918	.887	.923	.755 (185.638)	.953	.908	.836	.938	.902	
	Controlling	.903		.870	.756				.915		.894	.799				
Performance in a host country[4]	Sales development	.903		.888	.789				.891		.871	.758				Acc. to Evans and Mavondo (2002)
	Return on investment	.850	.812 (200.235)	.857	.735	.794	.920	.873	.889	833 (254.477)	.907	.823	.822	.933	.893	
	Market share	.865		.926	.858				.900		.941	.886				
	Satisfaction	.764		.389	.151				.865		.452	.204				

[1]How strongly does your company standardize the following marketing elements abroad in comparison to the home country? *[Please estimate as follows [1] totally adapted to [5] totally standardized.*
[2]How strongly does your company centralize the following management decisions? *[Please estimate as follows [1] totally decentralized to [5] totally centralized].*
[3]How strongly does your company formalize the following management decisions? *[Please estimate as follows [1] totally unformulated to [5] totally formulated].*
[4]How successful was your company internationally on average over the past three years? *[Please estimate as follows [1] Declining/ constant, [2] Increase of up to 10%, [3] Increase of 11-20%, [4] Increase of 21-30%, [5] Increase of more than 30%.].* How satisfied are you with the overall development? *[1 = very unsatisfied to 5 = very satisfied].*

Table D-2: Reliability and Validity of the Measurement Model

Source: Own source.

In order to estimate indicator validity, content validity is already assured by conducting intensive pre-tests (Nunally and Bernstein 1967). In assessing construct validity, convergent, discriminant and nomological validity were estimated. Convergent validity can be estimated through the strength of association between the indicator variables that are assigned to one construct (Bagozzi and Yi 1988). In this respect, all AVE values are close to 0.5, indicating a high degree of convergent validity (Fornell and Larcker 1981). Discriminant validity refers to the extent that a concept differs from other concepts, which can be estimated by the Fornell-Larcker-Criterion (Fornell and Larcker 1981). Accordingly, the AVE values estimated should be higher than the squared correlations between two variables. As Table D-3 illustrates, this is achieved for all constructs. Thus, discriminant validity can be confirmed. Finally, nomological validity is given as well, as the structural equation model is sufficiently specified, as will be estimated in the next section (Peter 1981). In conclusion, reliability and validity can be assumed for all indicators and constructs.

			Squared latent variable correlation								
		AVE	1	2	3	4	5	6	7	8	9
	VIF		1.322	1.406	1.427	1.028	1.491	1.102	1.143	1.207	1.160
	AVE		.307	.718	.790	.794	1.000	1.000	1.000	1.000	1.000
1	Standardization of marketing program	.473	-	.183	.010	.064	.091	.001	.032	.004	.029
2	Centralization of decision-making	.684	.113	-	.217	.004	.099	.007	.013	.012	.007
3	Formalization of rules & procedures	.836	.087	.142	-	.012	.022	.012	.003	.041	.065
4	Performance in a host country	.822	.077	.111	.032	-	.005	.012	.003	.049	.041
5	Retail sector	1.000	.037	.018	.000	.001	-	.000	.114	.134	.014
6	Country experience	1.000	.000	.009	.025	.000	.000	-	.059	.113	.000
7	Firm size	1.000	.041	.002	.001	.001	.114	.000	-	.008	.016
8	Geographical scope	1.000	.002	.000	.004	.003	.134	.000	.008	-	.000
9	Entry mode	1.000	.000	.035	.137	.019	.002	.000	.049	.000	-

Close countries above (distant countries below) the diagonal; Discriminant validity: Squared correlation<AVE.

Table D-3: Bivariate Correlations

Source: Own creation.

Five control variables are included, which were most commonly used in previous studies. First, as the retail sector consists particularly of several subsectors and prior research confirmed distinctive sectoral differences, this study controls for subsector effects by including a binary variable, distinguishing between food and non-food retailers (e.g., Swoboda, Elsner and Morschett 2012).

Second, country experience measured by the number of years that a firm operates in the respective psychically close and psychically distant country is included as a control variable because previous research has evidenced a positive impact on performance (e.g., Carlsson, Nordegren and Sjöholm 2005). Third, previous results indicate that differences in performance between diversified firms can be attributed to differences in firm size (Chang and Thomas 1989). Thus, firm size is included as a control variable and is measured by the number of employees (e.g., Xu, Cavusgil and White 2006). Fourth, several researchers conclude that geographic scope measured by the number of countries in which the retailer operates also has a positive impact on performance so the impact of this control variable is incorporated as well (e.g., Cavusgil and Zou 1994). Finally, entry mode choice has been controlled by a dummy variable (full- vs. shared-controlled mode) because the mode of operation might significantly determine performance (Brouthers 2002).

5.3. Methodical Approach

In order to test the hypothesized relationships, the variance-based partial least squares (PLS) approach was applied. Although the shortcomings of this method are acknowledged (Hulland 1999), the PLS approach is particularly suitable in this research context because small sample sizes and research at a rather early stage of theoretical development are particularly supported due to fewer restrictions regarding distributional assumptions (Chin, Marcolin and Newsted 2003; Reinartz, Haenlein and Henseler 2009).

Although the correlations between the constructs as illustrated in Table D-3 are comparatively low, the variance inflation factors (VIF) were calculated in addition in order to exclude biases from multicollinearity. As all values are lower than the recommended threshold of 10 (Diamantopoulos and Winklhofer 2001), it can be concluded that multicollinearity is not a serious problem in this study.

5.4. Results

The descriptive results illustrated in Table D-4 indicate that standardization of the retail marketing program is more exigent in psychically close countries. Except for the standardization of store layout, the standardization of other marketing program elements shows a significantly higher degree of adaptation in psychically distant countries. However, the mean values of the degree of centralization of decision-making and the degree of formalization do not differ significantly between psychically close and psychically distant countries. Interestingly, the mean values of the financial performance tend to be higher for psychically distant countries and are even significantly different in terms of market share. Thus, the descriptive results suggest evidence for the psychic distance paradox according to O'Grady and Lane (1996), meaning that firms are more successful in psychically distant countries.

	Construct	Mean value		Standard deviation		Mean value differences[1]
		Close countries	Distant countries	Close countries	Distant countries	
1	**Standardization of marketing program**					
	Store layout	3.81	3.59	1.266	1.259	.220 ns
	Assortment	3.49	3.16	1.066	1.048	.330 *
	Price	3.07	2.75	1.219	1.238	.320 †
	Advertising	3.01	2.71	1.206	1.131	.296 †
2	**Centralization of decision-making**					
	Planning	3.09	3.02	1.306	1.316	.068 ns
	Investment	3.87	3.60	1.272	1.383	.271 ns
	Controlling	3.20	3.18	1.343	1.287	.012 ns
3	**Formalization of rules & procedures**					
	Planning	3.80	3.63	1.235	1.350	.171 ns
	Investment	3.88	3.71	1.180	1.260	.168 ns
	Controlling	3.74	3.48	1.234	1.310	.256 ns
5	**Performance in a host country**					
	Sales development	2.66	2.87	1.010	1.118	-.211 ns
	Return on investment	2.58	2.72	1.084	1.170	-.140 ns
	Market share	2.38	2.69	0.944	1.134	-.310 *
	Satisfaction	3.50	3.37	1.032	1.247	.130 ns
6	Retail sector (food/ non-food)			39.2%/ 60.8%		
7	Country experience (in years)	19.47	10.88	14.145	5.228	8.60 ***
8	Firm size (number of employees)	25,508		56,268		
9	Geographical scope (number of countries)	19.1		23.5		
10	Entry mode (full/ shared-controlled)	76.5%/ 23.5%		66.7%/ 33.3%		

[1] Two-sided test of significance: ***p<.001, **p<.01, *p<.05, †p<.10, ns=not significant

Table D-4: Descriptive Results

Source: Own creation.

The results of the proposed hypotheses are illustrated in Table D-5, where model 2a for psychically close countries and model 2b for psychically distant countries serve as the final models for testing the proposed relationships.

As stated by *hypothesis 1a*, a standardized marketing program results in superior performance in psychically close countries due to greater similarities between home and host countries. In this respect, the positive beta coefficient of .391 with a t-value of 8.080 confirms hypothesis 1a at a $p < .001$ level. In contrast, *hypothesis 1b* assumes due to greater dissimilarities between the home and psychically distant countries that the lower the degree of standardization of the marketing program, the higher the financial performance. However, the beta coefficient in model 2a shows a positive value of .200 with a t-value of 5.598 so a positive impact of the degree of standardization of marketing program on foreign performance is supported at a $p < .001$ level. Thus, hypothesis 1b has to be rejected and contradicts previous research suggesting that particularly psychically distant countries force firms to adapt their marketing program. Instead, it can be concluded that retailers rather strive to employ the same marketing program independently of the position of the host country compared to the home country.

With regard to the organizational structure, *hypothesis 2a* assumes that the centralization of decision-making has a negative influence on financial performance because the decentralization of decision-making is more beneficial due to the local idiosyncrasies of the retail business, as benefits are assured through the accumulation of local knowledge as well as reduced costs of control. The negative path coefficient of -.348 indicates the appropriateness of decentralized decision-making in psychically close countries and the t-value of 3.839 supports the hypothesis at a $p < .001$ level. Thus, hypothesis 2a is supported. In contrast, *hypothesis 2b* predicts that the centralization of decision-making has a positive impact on financial performance in psychically distant countries. It has been argued that psychically distant countries are associated with higher risks and that corporate policies might be replaced by idiosyncratic behavior. In order to respond to those risks and uncertainties, it is beneficial to employ centralized decision-making as benefits are secured through the implementation of knowledge from the headquarters and costs are reduced due to fewer risks and uncertainties. The respective path coefficient is positive and amounts to .249 with a t-value of 5.083 so that hypothesis 2b is also supported at a $p < .001$ level.

Hypothesis 3a assumes that the higher the degree of formalization, the higher the financial performance in psychically close countries because a high degree of formalization is most beneficial because benefits are assured through the transfer of established knowledge and costs are reduced due to fewer mistakes and redundancies. The path coefficient of .197 indicates a positive impact of the degree of formalization of rules and procedures on foreign performance in psychically close countries with a t-value of 3.386 so hypothesis 3a is supported at a $p < .001$ level. Regarding psychically distant countries, it is assumed by *hypothesis 3b* that a low degree of formalization is more beneficial because benefits can be enhanced by leaving enough space for adjustments to the idiosyncrasies of psychically distant countries and costs are reduced because there are no predetermined rules and procedures implemented that might not fit the environment. The path coefficient amounts to -.017 with a t-value of 0.624 and is therefore not significant. Thus, hypothesis 3b is rejected.

Finally, the impacts of control variables were proven to be almost insignificant for both types of countries. Only the mode of entry shows a significant positive impact on foreign performance so it can be concluded that full control modes lead to a higher financial performance in psychically close and psychically distant countries.

	Model 1a	***Model 1b***	***Model 2a***	***Model 2b***
	Close countries	Distant countries	Close countries	Distant countries
Direct performance effects				
H1: Standardization of marketing program → Performance			.391 ***	.200 ***
H2: Centralization of decision-making→ Performance			-.348 **	.249 *
H3: Formalization of rules & procedures → Performance			.197 **	-.017 ns
Control variables				
Retail sector	.038 ns	.075 ns	.047 ns	-.011 ns
Country experience (log)	.095 †	.009 ns	-.026 ns	-.010 ns
Firm size (log)	.007 ns	-.053 *	.048 †	-.023 ns
Geographical scope (log)	.136 *	-.064 ns	.031 ns	-.045 ns
Entry mode	.144 **	.186 ***	.105 *	.132 **
R^2 of performance	6.4%	4.2%	15.4%	16.3%

***p<.001, **p<.01, *p<.05, †p<.10, ns=not significant; standardized coefficient and p-value are illustrated.

Table D-5: Results

Source: Own creation.

Regarding the overall quality of the structural model, the Stone-Geisser criterion Q^2 for assessing the prediction relevance of the structural model amounts to .079 for psychically close and .107 for psychically distant countries. As both values are positive, prediction relevance can be assumed (Fornell and Bookstein 1982). Additionally, the effect-sizes f^2 that estimate the direct effect of a latent variable on the structural model (Cohen 1988) have to be considered for each path. While the standardization of marketing program reaches a value of .106 in psychically close and a value of .036 in psychically distant countries, the centralization of decision-making shows a value of .085 and .059, respectively. The f^2 values of the formalization accounts for .033 in psychically close and .001 in psychically distant countries. In this regard, the R^2 values achieve relatively low values of 15.4% for psychically close and 16.3% for psychically distant countries. However, as only the standardization of the marketing program, the centralization of decision-making and the formalization of rules and procedures are considered and since performance is dependent upon several other factors, the estimated R^2 values are suitable and in line with previous studies in strategic management that investigate performance effects (e.g., Birkinshaw and Morrison 1995; Peña-Vinces, Cepeda-Carrión and Chin 2012).

6. Discussion

According to the above mentioned literature review, the present study contributes to previous research by examining the impact of marketing program standardization, the centralization of decision-making and the degree of formalization on foreign performance in dependency on psychically close and psychically distant countries based on a large company survey of retailers operating internationally. The study contributes to the international marketing research, in particular to the relatively young research field of retail internationalization. The results allow two major theoretical implications and conclusions to be deduced for managers.

6.1. Main Conclusions

With respect to the above mentioned research questions, the results of the conceptual framework indicate according to previous research that the more standardized the retail marketing program the higher the foreign performance in psychically close countries (e.g., Jain 1989; Walters 1986). Moreover, evidence was also found to support the proposal that a standardized marketing program enhances foreign performance in psychically distant countries. This result contradicts current research, which concluded that the marketing program has to be adapted in psychically distant countries (e.g., Evans and Bridson 2005; Sousa and Bradley 2005). Thus, it can be assumed that the benefits of a standardized approach, such as economies of scale, outweigh the benefits of marketing program adaptation, even with regard to psychically distant countries. However, this result does not contradict the need for more adaptation in psychically distant countries, as the moderating effect of psychic distance can change the strength (beta-coefficient) and the amount (degree of mean value) of the respective predictor variables (MacKenzie and Spreng 1992). As illustrated by the descriptive statistics, the retail marketing program is partly significantly more adapted in psychic distant countries. Thus, it can be summarized that retail marketing programs should be standardized as much as possible across psychically close and psychically distant countries to realize economies of scale and should be adapted as is necessary to increase benefits through responding to local tastes and needs, particularly in psychically distant countries.

Regarding the impact of the centralization of decision-making, the results provide evidence that the higher the degree of decentralization of decision-making, the higher the foreign performance in psychically close countries. Contrasting this, Ruekert, Walker and Roering (1985) suggest in their conceptual work that centralized decisions are assumed to be most efficient in stable environments and a decentralized structure of organizational decision-making is superior in more dynamic environments. Likewise, Chang and Harrington (2000) assume on the basis of their computational model that decentralization of decision-making outperforms centralization when operating in heterogeneous countries. However, both studies do not test their assumptions empirically. Furthermore, Chang and Harrington (2000) predict also that decentralization outperforms centralization in stable markets. As it can be assumed that psychically close countries to Western retailers are more stable and due to the inherent local nature of the retail sector, decentralized decision-making is most promising for in psychically close countries as retail managers of local entities tend to reward trust with higher degrees of involvement. This result has already been suggested by the case study-based analysis of Arnold (2002) by showing that retailers such as Ahold, Home Depot and IKEA benefit from decentralized decision-making. In contrast, due to the risk associated with operations in psychically distant countries, the advantages of decentralized decision-making must be questioned. This result is in accordance with Garnier (1982), who states that decision making should be centralized when the perceived risk arises, e.g., a higher psychic distance. Evans, Mavondo and Bridson (2008) support this notion for the retail sector by stating that decentralized decision-making is less effective in distant countries.

Regarding the effect of the degree of formalization of rules and procedures, the results indicate that a higher degree of formalization results in higher foreign performance in psychically close countries. This finding is according to Baum and Wally (2003), who find formalization to be positively related to fast decision-making, which in turn has a positive impact on performance. In psychically distant countries, the beta coefficient for formalization shows no significant effect on foreign performance. This result contradicts the hypothesis and therefore also the finding of Nohria and Ghoshal (1994) that a lower degree of formalization is more beneficial in complex environments. Similarly, Harris (2000) confirms for the retail sector that a high degree of formalization is negatively related to market orientation meaning that less formalization strengthens local responsiveness.

Overall, the results show for psychically close countries that a standardized marketing program is best implemented by decentralized decision-making to transfer responsiveness to the local entity and by a high degree of formalization to realize a standardized marketing program. In contrast, it has been assumed that an adapted marketing program is implemented by centralized decision-making and a low degree of formalization in psychically distant countries. However, the results indicate that a standardized marketing program is implemented by centralized decision-making. According to these results, important implications could be drawn for research and practice.

6.2. Implications for Research and Practice

With respect to the results, two major implications can be deduced for research. First, the proposed conceptual framework focuses on important strategic decisions with consideration to psychically distant operations. While research concerning the standardization-adaptation debate, with consideration to psychic distance, is processed, investigations of psychic distance with regard to the organizational structure of retailing firms are rare (Evans and Bridson 2005; Evans, Treadgold and Mavondo 2000). Thus, the organizational structure of retail firms operating internationally is considered using the degree of centralization of decision-making and the degree of formalization. Second, the results indicate the importance of considering sector-specific influences. Particularly due to the local nature of the retail business, the production location of retail firms is abroad so transferring responsibilities to the local entity is beneficial at least in psychically close countries.

From a managerial point of view, managers should recognize standardization as a desirable objective in order to improve performance by realizing economies of scale regardless of whether psychically close or psychically distant countries are served. However, the need for adaptation, particularly through product-related marketing programs including assortment, price and advertising, should not be neglected. Second, managers should exploit the benefits of decentralized decision-making in psychically close countries. The concept of a standardized marketing program implemented by a high degree of formalization of rules and procedures and decentralized decision-making is promising because benefits can be realized through economies of scale and local responsiveness, as already employed by specific retailers. For instance, franchise concepts offer a standardized marketing program that is implemented in a decentralized structure by the franchisee. Such concepts are related to the approach of structural empowerment, i.e., formalized decentralization, as already introduced by (Mintzberg 1979). Therefore, all advantages of global integration and local responsiveness can be achieved. Moreover, the complexity of global operations is reduced as decision autonomy can be delegated successfully to the local entity. For psychically distant countries, a standardized marketing program should be implemented by a centralized structure of organizational decision-making to reduce risk as perceived in more distant countries. However, due to the lack of adaptation to local conditions, it can be assumed that the implementation of a standardized strategy by a centralized structure is only a somewhat second-best solution.

6.3. *Limitations and Further Research*

As with all studies, this study also suffers some limitations. First, the investigation is restricted to German retailers, so generalizations might be difficult. Second, one could argue that a sample of 102 retailers is not sufficient to provide a high degree of generalizability. Reinartz, Haenlein and Henseler (2009), however, argue that a sample size of 100 is adequate for delivering statistically satisfying results within PLS. A third limitation is related to the concept of psychic distance. While the difference between psychically close and psychically distant countries is estimated by the perceptions of the interviewee, the assessment is rather subjective to the respondent. Fourth, although the reliability and validity of the measurement of the standardization of the retail marketing program is sufficient in this study, it can be improved by distinguishing between core and peripheral elements of the retail marketing program according to previous research (Kaufmann and Eroglu 1999). However, the retail marketing program has been considered comprehensively in this study to ensure comparability with previous studies (e.g., Quester and Conduit 1996). The last limitation addresses implementation of the results. While a standardized marketing program is useable for implementation in psychically close and psychically distant countries, the difference in the structure of organizational decision-making is more challenging to implement in retail practice.

However, this study also shows the need for future research. First, as this study addresses marketing program and organizational structure, several other impacts could be conceptualized, such as the degree of standardization of internal processes. Second, the results could also be tested for other service sectors, confirming that whenever the production location is local, a decentralized structure of organizational decision-making might be successful. Third, this study does not investigate the fit between retail marketing program standardization and organizational structure because previous research, as indicated in the literature review, has already shown that a fit between both leads to success in foreign countries and because the detection of a fit suffers the limitation that nothing is said about which strategy is actually successful. However, the investigation of a fit between both might be interesting to investigate in the retail context. Finally, an interesting point of contact for further research is whether a standardized marketing program could be implemented by decentralized decision-making in psychically distant countries when risk and uncertainty are decreased, which requires consideration of the internationalization process over the course of time.

E. Final Remarks

1. Discussion and Conclusions

1.1. Core Results

As initially stated, retailers have been expanding increasingly since the nineties, and the internationalization of retailing firms is characterized by specific challenges due to the inherent local nature of the retail business, unlike the internationalization of manufacturing firms. For instance, El-Amir and Burt (2008) provide the example of Sainsbury's market engagement in Egypt, where a cutting-edge retail format with low prices, high-quality products and services, and even salaries above average was offered. However, Sainsbury failed to recognize the socio-economic norms of the Egyptian customers, who were not used to such a retail format, which finally resulted in theft and fraud as the customers opened the food packages and tested the products before buying. In conclusion, the exploration of retail firms with international operations is highly relevant from a managerial perspective due to the increasing degree of internationalization and the specific characteristics of the retail sector. Furthermore, most studies in international business literature have been conducted in the context of manufacturing firms, so the research status in the context of retail firms is still fairly narrow as the literature review in this thesis also indicates. Additionally, as results cannot be transferred from the manufacturing sector to the retail sector due to the above mentioned differences, investigations in the retail context are also highly relevant from a research perspective.

With respect to the high relevance of exploring retail internationalization from a research and managerial perspective, important issues of the internationalization of retailing have been illustrated. Hence, the following general research questions regarding 1) retail entry mode choice, 2) retail format transfer and 3) organization and coordination of international retail activities are of paramount importance in the domains of going and of being international:

(1) How do retailers choose their entry mode when going international in the area of conflict between full- and shared-controlled entry modes and how is their choice influenced by the internal and external environment?

(2) How can international retailers during the being international transfer their retail format successfully to foreign countries by standardizing or adapting the internal and external elements of their retail format?

(3) How can international retailers during the being international successfully coordinate the implementation of their retail marketing program to culturally different countries?

The core results of these general research questions provide new insights for each domain and can be summarized as follows.

By answering the first general research question, study one examines on a sound theoretical basis of institutional theory and the RBV how retail entry modes are chosen in the area of conflict between full- and shared-controlled entry modes. On the basis of institutional theory, a strong effect was determined by an institutionalized entry mode, i.e., the entry mode that was used predominantly in the past, on the choice of subsequent entry modes. However, this influence is attenuated, as institutional theory also suggests. Hence, as soon as differences between the home and host country with regard to the regulative environment, i.e., political distance, increase, retailers are forced to depart from their institutionalized entry mode. The same impact has been suggested by institutional theory for the normative environment, i.e., cultural distance, but no significant effect could be confirmed in this study so the moderating effect initially hypothesized has to be rejected. This result could be explained because the choice of retail entry mode is usually made before market entry, with the result that the cultural distance between the home and the host country may not influence the effect of using an institutionalized entry mode for subsequent initial market entries. In contrast to the external institutional environment, it was assumed that the internal environment reinforces the use of an institutionalized entry mode. It has, therefore, been hypothesized on the basis of the RBV that as soon as internal capabilities arise with regard to entry mode choice, the use of an institutionalized entry mode is reinforced. The results confirm this reasoning by illustrating a significant positive moderating effect of international experience and the speed of internationalization. Hence, the actual choice of retail market entry mode depends mainly on habitual behavior in correspondence with the increase in internal capabilities, but is forced to change by the boundary conditions of the external institutional environment.

By answering the second general research question, study two explores on the basis of the FFR approach and the PMT how the retail format can be transferred abroad successfully in the area of conflict between the standardization and adaptation of the retail format elements. Thus, the retail format has been divided according to Goldman (2001) into internal processes and external marketing programs. It is assumed that internal processes, i.e., marketing and supply chain processes, form the basis of success as they are able to drive efficiency, whereas the external marketing program is able to attract local customers. More specifically, it is assumed on the basis of the FFR approach that each of the internal processes and the external marketing program have to be subdivided into core and peripheral elements that are interrelated positively between both sides of the retail format, which is also supported by almost all hypotheses. To investigate their impact on performance in a host country, it has been argued on the basis of the PMT that the standardization of internal processes and of core retail marketing program elements is beneficial due to the greater potential for realizing economies of scale. In contrast, it is argued that the adaptation of peripheral retail marketing program elements is beneficial because it offers a higher potential to increase local sales. Hence, these elements are an important part of the retail format transfer to respond to the idiosyncrasies of the local host country. The results partly support these assumptions. Although the internal processes do not directly influence performance in a host country, performance is influenced by the mediating role of core and peripheral retail marketing program elements. The latter in turn influence performance, as previously proposed by a higher degree of standardization of core elements and a higher degree of adaptation of peripheral elements. Finally, the results are similar in psychically close and psychically distant countries, so that the successful transfer of the retail format to both kinds of host countries takes place in a similar vein.

By answering the third general research question, study three investigates how the retail marketing program can be implemented successfully by the organizational structure in psychically close and psychically distant countries for the domain of being international and on the basis of the PMT. With regard to the ideal strategy, including the realization of economies of scale due to global integration and the increase of local sales due to local responsiveness, it is argued for psychically close countries that it is most beneficial for retailers to employ a standardized marketing program implemented by a high degree of formalization of rules and procedures and a low degree of centralization in decision-making. In contrast, it is assumed for psychically distant countries that it is most beneficial to apply an adapted marketing program implemented with a low degree of formalization of rules and procedures and a high degree of centralization of decision-making. Hence, the advantages of global integration and local responsiveness can be exploited in both situations. The results demonstrate that the hypothesized relationships can be confirmed fully for psychically close countries. However, for the case of psychically distant countries, it could also be confirmed that a higher degree of standardization in the marketing program leads to better performance in a host country and no significant impact could be estimated by the degree of formalization of rules and procedures on foreign performance. This result shows that retailers use the same standardized retail marketing program from the home market, not only in psychically close but also in psychically distant countries. Hence, benefits from the realization of economies of scale may also outweigh the benefits of increased local sales in psychically distant countries. Regarding the degree of formalization, the prefix of the estimated beta coefficient points in the right direction, but is statistically not significant, which might be due to the relatively small sample size.

In conclusion, the core results summarized provide new insights for research and practice. Thus, the theoretical and managerial implications provided are illustrated in the following section, and subsequently the avenues for further research are highlighted.

1.2. Research Implications

All three studies provide research implications from different angles. Each is addressed in the following within the domain of each study.

According to study one, including the investigation of entry mode choice on the basis of institutional theory and the RBV, three important implications could be drawn. First, from a methodological perspective, this study takes a different perspective in exploring the choice of foreign entry mode in the course of time by using a longitudinal data set. As a result, this study is able to modulate particularly those factors that imprint specific decisions, such as the institutionalized entry mode that is also suggested by institutional theory instead of evaluating the cognitive dimension retrospectively, as employed by previous research (e.g., Davis, Desai and Francis 2000). With this approach the study therefore responds to several calls for investigating the choice of entry mode over the course of time (e.g., Brouthers and Hennart 2007). Second, from a theoretical perspective, all dimensions of institutional theory are considered and also hypothesized as being interrelated due to the moderating effect instead of considering them as independent effects, as was mostly the case in previous research (e.g., Yiu and Makino 2002). Hence, this study contributes to the notion of institutional duality, i.e., different pressures from the internal and external environment that counteract each other. Furthermore, this study combines institutional theory and the RBV, as requested by previous research (Brouthers and Hennart 2007), and demonstrates this in a new way by incorporating the arguments of both theories, i.e., increasing capabilities combined with habitual behavior over the course of time, bounded by the external institutional environment. Thus, the compatibility of both theories is emphasized. Third, from the perspective of previous research, this study addresses the study of Huang and Sternquist (2007), which provides new insights on a conceptual basis as to how institutional theory helps to explain entry mode choice in the retail context. This has been enhanced and validated in this study by employing a substantial dataset of more than 300 market entries by grocery retailers with international operations.

By investigating successful transfer of the retail format in study two on the basis of the FFR approach and the PMT, several important research implications could be drawn. At first and with regard to the identification and measurement of constructs, important retail marketing program elements and, particularly, retail marketing and supply chain processes have been identified. Therefore, this study addresses both sides of the retail format, i.e., the internal background conditions and the external retail marketing program visible to the end-customer, as requested by previous research (Goldman 2001; Jain 1989; Walters 1986). Furthermore, as argued by the FFR approach and as the results confirm, internal processes and the external marketing program have to be divided into core and peripheral elements, as suggested by previous conceptual studies (Carman and Langeard 1980; Kaufmann and Eroglu 1999). Second and with regard to the conceptualization of retail format transfer and to the research question as to whether and how internal processes and the external marketing program correspond to one another, the results show that both sides of the format interact in a similar way instead of in opposite directions. Furthermore, the degree of standardization of internal processes does not significantly influence performance in a host country, but is important due to interaction with the degree of standardization of the marketing program. So, in order to explain the successful transfer of the retail format, it is important to consider both sides of the retail format, but also with more differentiation by distinguishing between core and peripheral elements. Third, from a theoretical perspective, the research domain of standardization and adaptation is traditionally characterized as a research stream with less theoretical foundation (Schmid and Kotulla 2011). However, the FFR approach and the PMT serve as suitable theories to explain successful transfer of the retail format. Finally, the results of the retail format transfer have been validated by one of the largest surveys, covering 102 retail firms with international operations.

The investigation of the successful organization and coordination of international retail activities in different countries on the basis of the PMT provides new insights from a conceptual and an empirical perspective. Regarding the former, this study highlights the consideration of the production location. Studies in the manufacturing context show different results, so that the importance of sector-specific studies is emphasized. Furthermore, the degree of perceived distance at which the retailers operate plays an important role for the organization of international retail activities. Hence, psychic distance has to be considered, as also emphasized by previous research (e.g., Evans and Mavondo 2002). From an empirical perspective, this study measures the organization and coordination of international retail activities, although on a rather exploratory level, validated through extensive pre-tests and in-depth face-to-face interviews at 102 retail firms with international operations, representing one of the largest samples in the research domain of international retailing.

In summary, all three studies provide important implications for research from different perspectives. Hence, this thesis contributes to the international management literature and particularly to the emerging research field of retail internationalization. However, managerial implications were also derived, as the following section demonstrates.

1.3. Managerial Implications

Although retailers have internationalized increasingly since the nineties, the internationalization process is still of considerable interest to retail managers. The growth of retail sales worldwide can be assumed as a reliable indicator of the future development of retail internationalization. As illustrated in Figure E-1, the total and grocery retail sales have increased steadily in the past, and it can be assumed that retail internationalization will become even more important in the forthcoming years in the course of globalization. Accordingly, Planet Retail (2011b) expects an ongoing increase in total and grocery retail sales.

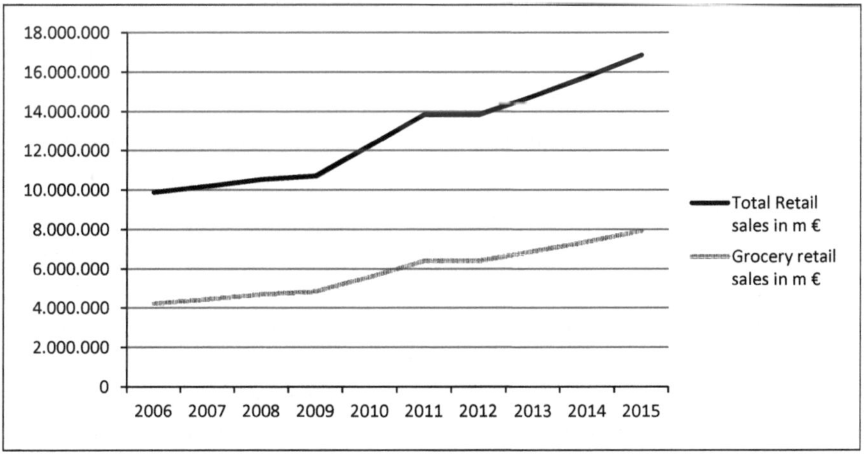

Figure E-1: Growth of Total Retail Sales and Grocery Retail Sales Worldwide
Source: (Planet Retail 2011b).

In view of these opportunities, retail managers face the challenge of managing retail internationalization properly. The following managerial implications regarding the three issues investigated in this thesis are intended to assist managers with their decisions and are explained in the following.

By investigating the choice of retail entry modes, it is confirmed that retailers usually use an institutionalized entry mode instead of searching for alternatives, which is even reinforced over the course of time due to factors from the internal environment and mitigated by the external environment. Based on this finding, retail managers must scrutinize both the institutionalized entry mode and alternative entry modes to establish which are more advantageous. Furthermore, retail managers have to consider entering those countries that are most appropriate to their institutionalized entry mode or entering other even more promising foreign countries, but with a different entry mode to the institutionalized one. As cultural distance does not seem to play an important role, at least for entry modes that are applied when retailers enter a foreign market for the first time, retail managers must consider the regulative environment of the potential host country in particular. In summary, a broad understanding is provided for retail managers as to how market entry mode choices are actually made, which helps to understand the interrelationships between the external and internal environment as well as to distinguish between other important decisions with regard to retail internationalization, such as market selection.

The findings of the investigation of retail format transfer suggest that retail managers must consider the transfer of the retail format more holistically by incorporating internal background processes and external front-end offers. Furthermore, the distinction between core and peripheral elements of the marketing program is of paramount importance because they yield different performance effects. Hence, the notion is emphasized that a certain template is implemented across countries through the standardization of internal processes in association with core marketing program elements, whereas the peripheral marketing program elements serve to adapt to the local host country conditions. Thus, the standardization of core marketing program elements (store type, store layout and store locations) and the adaptation of peripheral marketing program elements (assortment, sales promotion and price) are the main drivers of success in host countries, whereas standardization of internal processes itself only influences performance in association with the retail marketing program.

The investigation of the organization and coordination of international retail activities demonstrates that the retailers' most successful default strategy is to implement their standardized marketing program with a high degree of formalization of rules and procedures to realize economies of scale and decentralized decision-making to respond to the idiosyncrasies of the host country. However, when expanding to countries that are psychically more distant, the risk increases, making it necessary to centralize decision-making. In summary, it is advantageous for retail managers to use the same marketing program in psychically close and psychically distant countries, although the need for adaptations should not be neglected. Only the degree of centralization varies between both types of countries, emphasizing the importance of considering psychically different countries for the organization and coordination of international retail activities.

The implications for managers can be summarized in the following points:

- As retailers mainly use entry modes that have been used predominantly in the past, their effectiveness for success must be reconsidered continuously. Furthermore, retail managers have to pay attention to the regulative environment of the host country in particular because the external environment imposes important boundary conditions for the use of an institutionalized entry mode.
- Retailers who adapt their marketing program abroad are not necessarily successful as previous research indicates. Instead, the use of a standardized marketing program pays off in psychically close countries and also in psychically distant countries.
- Internal process elements, and particularly the marketing program, have to be distinguished into core and peripheral elements due to their different effects on foreign performance.
- Process standardization is not able to increase performance except in combination with the standardization of the marketing program.
- Retail activities must be managed differently in psychically close and psychically distant countries by decentralized decision-making in the former case and centralized decision-making in the latter case.
- The formalization of rules and procedures supports standardization of the retail marketing program and the implementation of decentralized decision-making according to the notion of structural empowerment.

2. Further Research

As avenues for further research have already been addressed at the end of each study, the subsequent issues concern general fields for further research. These are emphasized in the following from the perspective of each study and address conceptual, theoretical or methodological issues.

By analyzing retail entry mode choice, two important issues emerge from a conceptual perspective as well as from a methodological perspective. First, as more than 200 antecedents have already been identified for the most appropriate entry mode (Canabal and White 2008), further research should instead address the difference between the most appropriate and the entry mode actually applied (Brouthers and Hennart 2007). The diagram by Sarkar and Cavusgil (1996) illustrates this issue (Figure E-2).

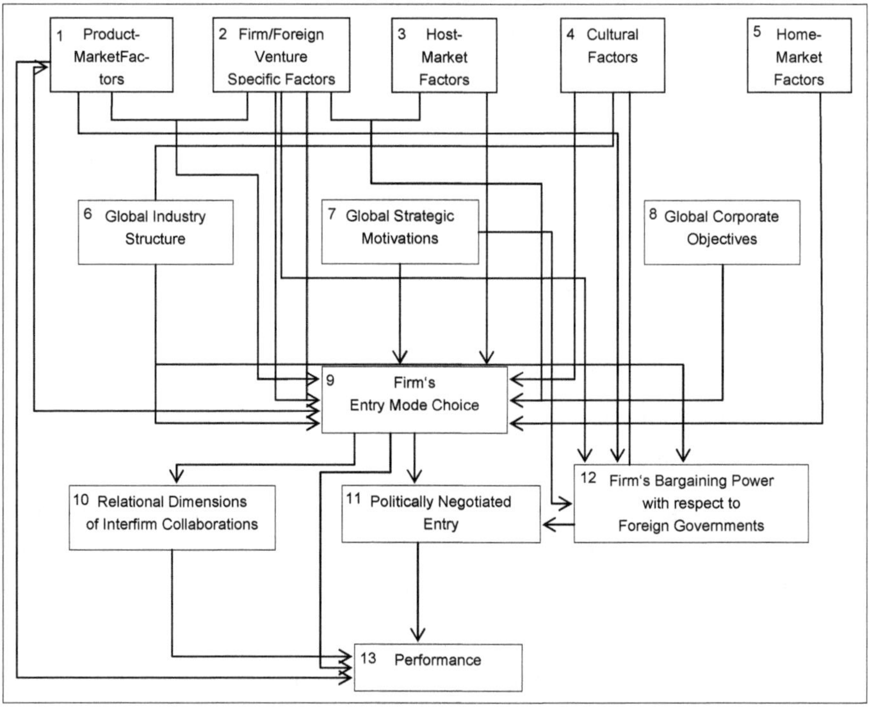

Figure E-2: Classification of Research on Entry Mode Choice

Source: Sarkar and Cavusgil (1996).

Hence, several factors from the internal and external environment (1-8) have been identified as influencing entry mode choice (9). However, there might be a difference between the most appropriate entry mode (9) and the entry mode finally applied (10-12) itself and their impact on success. In conclusion, the question is whether managers use an 'efficiency-satisfying' or an 'efficiency-maximizing' solution. Second, although previous research has advanced by investigating the most efficient entry mode, the circumstances for the most beneficial entry mode of retailers with international operations are still unclear. From a methodological perspective, further research should address multi-level effects in entry mode choice because higher levels, such as corporate or country levels, might be important indicators, particularly in the research domain of entry mode choice. With regard to retail entry mode choice, the entry modes of sectors other than the grocery sector should be considered in large-scale studies to increase generalizability.

By analyzing retail format transfer, it has been shown that elements of the retail format are transferred in a standardized way or adapted to foreign countries. Although studies in this research domain belong to a long research tradition, only a very small number of studies are based on sound theoretical foundations (Schmid and Kotulla 2011). Thus, explanation of the effects of standardization and adaptation with sound theoretical arguments would be desirable in future research. Furthermore, in spite of the comprehensive research status, research in the context of retailers with international operations is still fairly narrow. Most studies only investigate on the basis of small-N research, with the result that the standardization or adaptation of specific marketing program elements is more or less useful, but further research should also consider the antecedents of this decision from the internal and external environment. From a methodological perspective, large primary data investigations on retailers with international operations might help to shed more light on this issue by increasing the generalizability of the results. Furthermore, the analysis of changes over the course of time due to local learning, as provided by the case-study based investigation of IKEA by Jonsson and Foss (2011), on the basis of a longitudinal data set might provide interesting new insights. Finally, as the importance of internal processes has been highlighted by study two in this thesis, further research could contribute by establishing scales for measurement of the internal processes.

Analysis of the organization and coordination of international retail activities has shown how the advantages of global integration and local responsiveness can be incorporated by retailers with international operations. By highlighting the importance of the production location for the organization and coordination of international retail activities, further research could address this issue for other sectors in the service industry, for example for hard and soft service firms (Erramilli 1990), to increase generalizability. From a conceptual perspective, the analysis of the organization and coordination of international retail activities was conducted from the viewpoint of the retailers' headquarters. However, in order to investigate the usefulness of a standardized or an adapted marketing program implemented by a centralized or decentralized organizational structure, further research should investigate this issue from the perspective of subsidiaries as their perceptions might differ from those of the headquarters. From a methodological perspective, the psychic distance construct is particularly subject to the individual perception of each manager so that changes in the perceived distance between two countries might occur in the course of time (Stöttinger and Schlegelmilch 2009), for example due to learning, and might influence the organizational structure, constituting an interesting point of contact for further research. Finally, further studies in the context of retailers with international operations could contribute towards measurement of the organizational structure, as several dimensions other than the traditional centralization and formalization could be considered.

References

Agarwal, Sanjeev and Sridhar N. Ramaswami (1992), "Choice of Foreign Market Entry Mode: Impact of Ownership, Location and Internalization Factors," *Journal of International Business Studies*, 23 (1), 1–27.

Aghion, Philippe and Jean Tirole (1997), "Formal and Real Authority in Organizations," *Journal of Political Economy*, 105 (1), 1–29.

Aiken, Leona S. and Stephen G. West (1991), *Multiple Regression. Testing and Interpreting Interactions.* Newbury Park, CA: Sage.

Aiken, Michael and Jerald Hage (1968), "Organizational Interdependence and Intra-Organizational Structure," *American Sociological Review*, 33 (6), 912–930.

Akaah, Ishmael P. (1991), "Strategy Standardization in International Marketing," *Journal of Global Marketing*, 4 (2), 39-62.

Albaum, Gerard S. and David K. Tse (2001), "Adaptation of International Marketing Strategy Components, Competitive Advantage, and Firm Performance: A Study of Hong Kong Exporters," *Journal of International Marketing*, 9 (4), 59–81.

Alexander, Andrew (2008), "Format development and retail change: supermarket retailing and the London Co-operative Society," *Business History*, 50 (4), 489–508.

Alexander, Nicholas (1990), "Retailing Post-1992," *Service Industries Journal*, 10 (1), 172–187.

Alexander, Nicholas and Andrew Lockwood (1996), "Internationalisation: A Comparison of the Hotel and Retail Sectors," *Service Industries Journal*, 36 (4), 458–473.

Alexander, Nicholas and Anne M. Doherty (2004), "International Market Entry: Management competencies and environmental influences," *European Retail Digest*, 42 (Summer), 14–19.

Alexander, Nicholas and Barry Quinn (2002), "International retail divestment," *International Journal of Retail and Distribution Management*, 30 (2), 112–125.

Alon, Ilan (2006), “Market conditions favoring master international franchising,” *Multinational Business Review*, 14 (2), 67–82.

Alon, Ilan and David McKee (1999), “Towards a Macro Environmental Model of International Franchising,” *Multinational Business Review*, 7 (1), 76–82.

Alpert, Frank H, Michael A. Kamins, Tomoaki Sakano, Naoto Onzo and John L. Graham (1997), “Retail Buyer Decision-making in Japan: what US Sellers Need to Know,” *International Business Review*, 6 (2), 91–112.

Amburgey, Terry L. and Anne S. Miner (1992), “Strategic momentum: The effects of repetitive, positional, and contextual momentum on merger activity,” *Strategic Management Journal*, 13 (5), 335–348.

Amit, Raphael and Paul J. H. Schoemaker (1993), “Strategic Assets and Organizational Rent,” *Strategic Management Journal*, 14 (1), 33–46.

Andersen, Otto (1997), “Internationalization and Market Entry Mode: A review of Theories and Conceptual Frameworks,” *Management International Review*, 37 (2), 27–42.

Anderson, David R, Dennis J. Sweeney and Thomas A. Williams (2010), *Statistics for Business and Economics.* Hampshire: South-Western College Publishing.

Anderson, Erin and Hubert Gatignon (1986), “Modes of Foreign Entry: A Transaction Cost Analysis and Propositions,” *Journal of International Business Studies*, 17 (3), 1–26.

Armstrong, Scott J. and Terry S. Overton (1977), “Estimating Nonresponse Bias in Mail Surveys,” *Journal of Marketing Research*, 14 (3), 396–402.

Arnold, Stephen J. (2002), “Lessons Learned from the world's best retailers,” *International Journal of Retail and Distribution Management*, 30 (11), 562–570.

Arnold, Stephen J. and John Fernie (2000), “Wal-Mart in Europe: prospects for the UK,” *International Marketing Review*, 17 (4/5), 416–432.

Asmussen, Christian G, Gabriel R. G. Benito and Bent Petersen (2009), “Organizing foreign market activities: From entry mode choice to configuration decisions,” *International Business Review*, 18 (2), 145–155.

Assaf, A. G, Alexander Josiassen, Brian T. Ratchford and Carlos P. Barros (2012), "Internationalization and Performance of Retail Firms: A Bayesian Dynamic Model," *Journal of Retailing*, 88 (2), 198–212.

Auh, Seigyoung and Bulent Menguc (2007), "Performance implications of the direct and moderating effects of centralization and formalization on customer orientation," *Industrial Marketing Management*, 36 (8), 1022–1034.

Baalbaki, Imad B. and Naresh K. Malhotra (1995), "Standardization versus Customization in International Marketing: An Investigation Using Bridging Conjoint Analysis," *Journal of the Academy of Marketing Science*, 23 (3), 182–194.

Bagozzi, Richard P. and Youjae Yi (1988), "On the evaluation of structural equation models," *Journal of the Academy of Marketing Science*, 16 (1), 74–94.

Bagozzi, Richard P, ed. (1994), *Principles of Marketing Research. Measurement in Marketing Research*. Cambridge: Blackwell.

Barkema, Harry G. and Freek Vermeulen (1998), "International Expansion through Start-up or Acquisition: A Learning Perspective," *Academy of Management Journal*, 41 (1), 7–26.

Barney, Jay B. (1991), "Firm resources and sustained competitive advantage," *Journal of Management*, 17 (1), 99-121.

Barratt, Mark and Adegoke Oke (2007), "Antecedents of supply chain visibility in retail supply chains: A resource-based theory perspective," *Journal of Operations Management*, 25 (6), 1217–1233.

Bartlett, Christopher A. and Sumantra Ghoshal (1987), "Managing across borders: new strategic requirements," *Sloan management review*, 28 (4), 7–17.

——— (1989), *Managing across borders the transnational solution*, Vol. 1. Boston, Mass: Harvard Business School Press.

Baum, Robert J. and Stefan Wally (2003), "Startegic Decision Speed and Firm Performance," *Strategic Management Journal*, 24 (11), 1107–1129.

Beck, Nikolaus, Josef Brüderl and Michael Woywode (2008), "Momentum or deceleration? Theoretical and methodological reflections on the analysis of organizational change," *Academy of Management Journal*, 51 (3), 413–435.

Bengtsson, Anders, Ulf Elg and Ulf Johansson (2001), "The process of internationalization: how Swedish food retailers perceive their domestic supplier relationships," *International Review of Retail, Distribution and Consumer Research*, 10 (4), 321–334.

Beninati, Marie, Paul Evans and Joseph McKinney (1997), "A Blueprint for Local Assortment Management," *Chain Store Age*, 73 (2), 27–34.

Benito, Gabriel R. G, Bent Petersen and Lawrence S. Welch (2009), "Towards more realistic conceptualisations of foreign operation modes," *Journal of International Business Studies*, 40 (9), 1455–1470.

Berry, Heather, Mauro F. Guillén and Nan Zhou (2010), "An institutional approach to cross-national distance," *Journal of International Business Studies*, 41 (9), 1460–1480.

Bianchi, Constanza C. (2006), "Home Depot in Chile: Case study," *Journal of Business Research*, 59 (3), 391–393.

——— (2009), "Retail internationalisation from emerging markets: case study evidence from Chile," *International Marketing Review*, 26 (2), 221–243.

Bianchi, Constanza C. and Enrique Ostale (2006), "Lessons learned from unsuccessful internationalization attempts: Examples of multinational retailers in Chile," *Journal of Business Research*, 59 (1), 140–147.

Bianchi, Constanza C. and Stephen J. Arnold (2004), "An Institutional Perspective on Retail Internationalization Success: Home Depot in Chile," *International Review of Retail, Distribution and Consumer Research*, 14 (2), 149–169.

Birkinshaw, Julian M. and Allen J. Morrison (1995), "Configurations of strategy and structure in subsidiaries of multinational corporations," *Journal of International Business Studies*, 26 (4), 729–753.

Birkinshaw, Julian M, Allen J. Morrison and John Hulland (1995), "Structural and Competitive Determinants of a Global Integration Strategy," *Strategic Management Journal*, 16 (8), 637–655.

Blomstermo, Anders, Deo D. Sharma and James Sallis (2006), "Choice of foreign market entry mode in service firms," *International Marketing Review*, 23 (2), 211–229.

Boddewyn, Jean J, Robin Soehl and Jacques Picard (1986), "Standardization in International Marketing: Is Ted Levitt in Fact Right?," *Business Horizons*, 29 (6), 69–75.

Bouquet, Cyril, Louis Hébert and Andrew Delios (2004), "Foreign expansion in service industries Sepapability and human capital intensity," *Journal of Business Research*, 57 (1), 35–46.

Bourlakis, Michael A. and Constantine A. Bourlakis (2001), "Deliberate and emergent logistics strategies in food retailing: a case study of the Greek multiple food retail sector," *Supply Chain Management: An International Journal*, 6 (4), 189–200.

Boyacigiller, Nakiye (1990), "The Role of Expatriates in the Management of Interdependence, Complexity and Risk in Multinational Corporations," *Journal of International Business Studies*, 21 (3), 357–381.

Brouthers, Keith D. (2002), "Institutional, Cultural and Transaction Cost Influence on Entry Mode Choice and Performance," *Journal of International Business Studies*, 33 (2), 203–221.

Brouthers, Keith D. and Jean-Francois Hennart (2007), "Boundaries of the firm: Insights from international entry mode research," *Journal of Management*, 33 (3), 395–425.

Brouthers, Keith D. and Lance E. Brouthers (2003), "Why Service and Manufacturing Entry Mode Choices Differ: The Influence of Transaction Cost Factors, Risk and Trust," *Journal of Management Studies*, 40 (5), 1179–1204.

Brouthers, Keith D, Lance E. Brouthers and Steve Werner (2003), "Transaction cost-enhanced entry mode choices and firm performance," *Strategic Management Journal*, 24 (12), 1239–1248.

——— (2008), "Resource-Based Advantages in an International Context," *Journal of Management*, 34 (2), 189–215.

Brown, Stephen W. and Steve L. Burt (1992), "Conclusion - Retail Internationalization, Past Imperfect, Future Imperative," *European Journal of Marketing*, 26 (8/9), 80–87.

Brun, Alessandro, Federico Caniato, Maria Caridi, Cecilia Castelli, Giovanni Miragliotta, Stefano Ronchi, Andrea Sianesi and Gianluca Spina (2008), "Logistics and supply chain management in luxury fashion retail: Empirical investigation of Italian firms," *International Journal of Production Economics*, 114 (2), 554–570.

Burt, Steve L. (1991), "Trends in the internationalization of grocery retailing: the European experience," *International Review of Retail, Distribution and Consumer Research*, 1 (4), 487–515.

——— (1993), "Temporal trends in the internationalization of British retailing," *International Review of Retail, Distribution and Consumer Research*, 3 (4), 391–410.

Burt, Steve L. and Alexis Mavrommatis (2006), "The International Transfer of Store Brand Image," *International Review of Retail, Distribution and Consumer Research*, 16 (4), 395–413.

Burt, Steve L. and Jose Carralero-Encinas (2000), "The role of store image in retail internationalisation," *International Marketing Review*, 17 (4/5), 433–453.

Burt, Steve L. and Leigh Sparks (2002), "Corporate Branding, Retailing, and Retail Internationalization," *Corporate Reputation Review*, 5 (2/3), 194–212.

Burt, Steve L. and Robin Limmack (2001), "Takeovers and shareholder returns in the retail industry," *International Review of Retail, Distribution and Consumer Research*, 11 (1), 1–21.

Burt, Steve L, Keri Davies, Andrew McAuley and Leigh Sparks (2005), "Retail Internationalisation: From Formats to Implants," *European Management Journal*, 23 (2), 195–202.

Burt, Steve L, Ulf Johansson and Åsa Thelander (2011), "Standardized marketing strategies in retailing? IKEA's marketing strategies in Sweden, the UK and China," *Journal of Retailing and Consumer Services*, 18 (3), 183–193.

Buzzell, Robert D. (1968), "Can you standardize multinational marketing?," *Harvard Business Review*, 46 (November-December), 102–113.

Canabal, Anne and George O. White (2008), "Entry mode research: Past and future," *International Business Review*, 17 (3), 267–284.

Cao, Lan L. and Marc Dupuis (2009), "Core competences, strategy and performance: the case of international retailers in China," *International Review of Retail, Distribution and Consumer Research*, 19 (4), 349–369.

Carlsson, Johan, Axel Nordegren and Fredrik Sjöholm (2005), "International experience and the performance of Scandinavian firms in China," *International Business Review*, 14 (1), 21–40.

Carman, James M. and Eric Langeard (1980), "Growth strategies for service firms," *Strategic Management Journal*, 1 (1), 7–22.

Carruthers, Robert (2003), "Rapid response retail," *Marketing*, 3 (April), 20–21.

Caruana, Albert, Michael H. Morris and Anthony J. Vella (1998), "The Effect of Centralization and Formalization on Entrepreneurship in Export Firms," *Journal of Small Business Management*, 36 (1), 16–29.

Cavusgil, Tamer S. and Shaoming Zou (1994), "Marketing Strategy-Performance Relationship: An Investigation of the Empirical Link in Export Market Ventures," *Journal of Marketing*, 58 (1), 1–21.

Cavusgil, Tamer S, Shaoming Zou and G. M. Naidu (1993), "Product and promotion adaptation in export ventures: an empirical investigation," *Journal of International Business Studies*, 24 (3), 479-506.

Chan, Christine and Shige Makino (2007), "Legitimacy and Multi-Level Institutional Environments: Implications for Foreign Subsidiary Ownership Structure," *Journal of International Business Studies*, 38 (4), 621–638.

Chan, Polly, Carol Finnegan and Brenda Sternquist (2011), "Country and firm level factors in international retail expansion," *European Journal of Marketing*, 45 (6), 1005–1022.

Chandra, Aruna, David A. Griffith and John K. Ryans (2002), "The association between process and program advertising standardization: an illustration of

U.S. multinationals operating in India," *Advances in International Marketing*, 12 (1), 67–83.

Chaney, Isabella and Jos Gamble (2008), "Retail store ownership influences on Chinese consumers," *International Business Review*, 17 (2), 170–183.

Chang, Myong-Hun and Joseph E. Harrington (2000), "Centralization vs. Decentralization in a Multi-Unit Organization: A Computational Model of a Retail Chain as Multi-Agent Adaptive System," *Management Science*, 46 (11), 1427–1440.

Chang, Sea-Jin and Philip M. Rosenzweig (2001), "The choice of entry mode in sequential foreign direct investment," *Strategic Management Journal*, 22 (8), 747–776.

Chang, Sea-Jin, Arjen van Witteloostuijn and Lorraine Eden (2010), "From the Editors: Common method variance in international business research," *Journal of International Business Studies*, 41 (2), 178–184.

Chang, Yegmin and Howard Thomas (1989), "The impact of diversification strategy on risk-return performance," *Strategic Management Journal*, 10 (3), 271–284.

Chen, Yung-Ray, Chyan Yang, Sue-Ming Hsu and Yau-De Wang (2009), "Entry mode choice in China's regional distribution markets: Institution vs. transaction costs perspectives," *Industrial Marketing Management*, 38 (7), 702–713.

Chin, Wynne W, Barbara L. Marcolin and Peter R. Newsted (2003), "A Partial Least Squares Latent Variable Modeling Approach for Measuring Interaction Effects: Results from a Monte Carlo Simulation Study and an Electronic-Mail Emotion/Adoption Study," *Information Systems Research*, 14 (2), 189–217.

Christopher, Martin, Robert Lowson and Helen Peck (2004), "Creating agile supply chains in the fashion industry," *International Journal of Retail & Distribution Management*, 32 (8), 367–376.

Chung, Henry F. L. (2003), "International Standardization Strategies: The Experiences of Australian and New Zealand Firms Operating in the Greater China Markets," *Journal of International Marketing*, 11 (3), 48–82.

——— (2008), "The Impact of a Centralised Organisational Structure on Marketing Standardisation Strategy and Performance: The Experience of Price, Place and Management Processes," *Journal of Global Marketing*, 21 (2), 83–107.

——— (2009), "Structure of marketing decision making and international marketing standardisation strategies," *European Journal of Marketing*, 43 (5/6), 794–825.

Churchill, Gilbert A. (1979), "A Paradigm for Developing Better Measures of Marketing Constructs," *Journal of Marketing Research*, 16 (1), 64–73.

Clarke, Ian and Peter Rimmer (1997), "The Anatomy of Retail Internationalisation: Daimaru's Decision to Invest in Melbourne, Australia," *Service Industries Journal*, 17 (3), 361–382.

Coe, Neil M. (2004), "The internationalisation/globalisation of retailing: towards an economic - geographical research agenda," *Environment and Planning A*, 36 (9), 1571–1594.

Coe, Neil M. and Martin Hess (2005), "The internationalization of retailing: implications for supply network restructuring in East Asia and Eastern Europe," *Journal of Economic Geography*, 5 (4), 449–473.

Coe, Neil M. and Young-Sook Lee (2006), "The Strategic Localization of Transnational Retailers: The Case of Samsung-Tesco in South Korea," *Economic Geography*, 82 (1), 61–88.

Cohen, Jacob (1988), *Statistical power analysis for the behavioral sciences.* Hillsdale: Lauwrence Erlbaum Associates.

Cohen, Jacob, Patricia Cohen, Stephen G. West and Leona S. Aiken (2003), *Applied Multiple Regression/Correlation Analysis for the Behavioral Sciences.* Mahwah: Lauwrence Erlbaum Associates.

Colla, Enrico and Marc Dupuis (2002), "Research and managerial issues on global retail competition: Carrefour/Wal-Mart," *International Journal of Retail and Distribution Management*, 30 (2), 103–111.

Colombo, Massimo G. (1995), "Firm Size and Cooperation: The Determinants of Cooperative Agreements in Information Technology Industries," *International Jounal of the Economics of Business*, 2 (1), 3–28.

Contractor, Farok J. and Sumit K. Kundu (1998), "Modal Choice in a World of Alliances: Analyzing Organizational Forms in the International Hotel Sector," *Journal of International Business Studies*, 29 (2), 325–357.

Corstjens, Judy, Marcel Corstjens and Rajiv Lal (1995), "Retail competition in the fast-moving consumer goods industry: the case of France and the UK," *European Management Journal*, 13 (4), 363–373.

Cray, David (1984), "Control and coordination in multinational corporations," *Journal of International Business Studies*, 15 (2), 85–98.

Currah, Andrew and Neil Wrigley (2004), "Networks of organizational learning and adaptation in retail TNCs," *Global Networks*, 4 (1), 1–23.

Dalton, Dan R, William D. Todor, Michael J. Spendolini, Gordon J. Fielding and Lyman W. Porter (1980), "Organization structure and performance: A critical review," *Academy of Management Review*, 5 (1), 49-64.

Danneels, Erwin (1996), "Market segmentation: normative model versus business reality," *European Journal of Marketing*, 30 (6), 36–51.

Davis, Peter S, Ashay B. Desai and John D. Francis (2000), "Mode of International Entry: An Isomorphism Perspective," *Journal of International Business Studies*, 31 (2), 239–258.

Dawson, John A. (1994), "Internationalization of Retailing Operations," *Journal of Marketing Management*, 10 (4), 267–282.

——— (2001), "Strategy and Opportunism in European Retail Internationalization," *British Journal of Management*, 12 (4), 253–266.

——— (2007), "Scoping and conceptualizing retailer internationalization," *Journal of Economic Geography*, 7 (4), 373–397.

Delios, Andrew and Paul W. Beamish (1999), "Ownership Strategy of Japanese Firms: Transactional, Institutional, and Experience Influences," *Strategic Management Journal*, 20 (10), 915–933.

Deloitte (2011), *Leaving home - Global Powers of Retailing 2011. Global retail perspectives from Deloitte*.

Demirbag, Mehmet, Keith W. Glaister and Ekrem Tatoglu (2007), "Institutional and transaction cost influences on MNEs' ownership strategies of their affiliates: Evidence from an emerging market," *Journal of World Business*, 42 (4), 418–434.

Deshpandé, Rohit (1982), "The Organizational Context of Market Research Use," *Journal of Marketing*, 46 (4), 91–101.

Diamantopoulos, Adamantios and Heidi M. Winklhofer (2001), "Index construction with formative indicators: an alternative to scale development," *Journal of Marketing Research*, 38 (2), 269–277.

DiMaggio, Paul J. and Walter W. Powell (1983), "The Iron Cage Revisited: Institutional Isomorphism and Collective Rationality in Organizational Fields," *American Sociological Review*, 48 (2), 147–160.

Doherty, Anne M. (1999), "Explaining international retailers' market entry mode strategy: internalization theory, agency theory and the importance of information asymmetry," *International Review of Retail, Distribution and Consumer Research*, 9 (4), 379–402.

——— (2000), "Factors Influencing International Retailers' Market Entry Mode Strategy: Qualitative Evidence from the UK Fashion Sector," *Journal of Marketing Management*, 16 (1), 223–245.

——— (2007), "The internationalization of retailing - Factors influencing the choice of franchising as a market entry strategy," *International Journal of Service Industry Management*, 18 (2), 184-205.

Douglas, Susan P. and Yoram Wind (1987), "The myth of globalization," *Columbia Journal of World Business*, 22 (4), 19–29.

Dunning, John H. (1988), "The Eclectic Paradigm of International Production: A Restatement and Some Possible Extensions," *Journal of International Business Studies*, 19 (1), 1–31.

Dupuis, Marc and Nathalie Prime (1996), "Business distance and global retailing: a model for analysis of key success/failure factors," *International Journal of Retail and Distribution Management*, 24 (11), 30–38.

Edvinsson, Leif and Michael S. Malone (1997), *Intellectual Capital: Realizing Your Company's True Value by Finding its Hidden Brainpower.* New York: Harper Business.

Einarsson, Ágúst (2008), "The retail sector in the Nordic countries: A description of the differences, similarities, and uniqueness in the global market," *Journal of Retailing and Consumer Services*, 15 (6), 443–451.

Ekeledo, Ikechi and K. Sivakumar (2004), "International market entry mode strategies of manufacturing firms and service firms: A resource-based perspective," *International Marketing Review*, 21 (1), 68–101.

El-Amir, Ayman and Steve L. Burt (2008), "Sainsbury's in Egypt: the strange case of Dr Jekyll and Mr Hyde?," *International Journal of Retail and Distribution Management*, 36 (4), 300–322.

Erramilli, Krishna M. (1990), "Entry Mode Choice in Service Industries," *International Marketing Review*, 7 (5), 50–62.

——— (1991), "The experience factor in foreign market entry behavior of service firms," *Journal of International Business Studies*, 22 (3), 479–501.

Erramilli, Krishna M. and Cha P. Rao (1993), "Service Firms‘ International Entry Mode Choice: A Modified Transaction-Cost Analysis Approach," *Journal of Marketing*, 57 (3), 19–38.

Estrin, Saul, Delia Baghdasaryan and Klaus E. Meyer (2009), "The impact of institutional and human resource distance on international entry strategies," *Journal of Management Studies*, 46 (7), 1171–1196.

Etgar, Michael and Dalia Rachman-Moore (2008), "International expansion and retail sales: an empirical study," *International Journal of Retail and Distribution Management*, 36 (4), 241–259.

Evans, Jody and Felix T. Mavondo (2002), "Psychic Distance and Organizational Performance: An Empirical Examination of International Retailing Operations," *Journal of International Business Studies*, 33 (3), 515–532.

Evans, Jody and Kerrie Bridson (2005), "Explaining retail offer adaptation through psychic distance," *International Journal of Retail and Distribution Management*, 33 (1), 69–78.

Evans, Jody, Alan Treadgold and Felix T. Mavondo (2000), "Psychic distance and the performance of international retailers: a suggested theoretical framework," *International Marketing Review*, 17 (4/5), 373–391.

Evans, Jody, Felix T. Mavondo and Kerrie Bridson (2008), "Psychic Distance: Antecedents, Retail Strategy Implications, and Performance Outcomes," *Journal of International Marketing*, 16 (2), 32–63.

Fam, Kim-Shyan and Zhilin Yang (2006), "Primary influences of environmental uncertainty on promotions budget allocation and performance: A cross-country study of retail advertisers," *Journal of Business Research*, 59 (2), 259–267.

Federal Statistical Office (2003), "German Classification of Economic Activities," (accessed January 21, 2012), [available at http://www.destatis.de/jetspeed/portal/cms/Sites/destatis/Internet/DE/Content/Klassifikationen/GueterWirtschaftklassifikationen/klassifikationwz2003englisch,property=file.pdf].

Fernie, John (1992), "Distribution Strategies of European Retailers," *European Journal of Marketing*, 26 (8/9), 35–47.

Fernie, John and Stephen J. Arnold (2002), "Wal-Mart in Europe: prospects for Germany, the UK and France," *International Journal of Retail and Distribution Management*, 30 (2), 92–102.

Fornell, Claes and David F. Larcker (1981), "Evaluating Structural Equation Models with Unobservable Variables and Measurement Error," *Journal of Marketing Research*, 18 (1), 39–50.

Fornell, Claes and Fred L. Bookstein (1982), "Two Structural Equation Models: LISREL and PLS Applied to Consumer Exit-Voice Theory," *Journal of Marketing Research*, 19 (4), 440–452.

Gamble, Jos (2009), "Demanding customers in the Chinese context," *Asia Pacific Business Review*, 15 (1), 93–105.

——— (2010), "Transferring Organizational Practices and the Dynamics of Hybridization: Japanese Retail Multinationals in China," *Journal of Management Studies*, 47 (4), 705–732.

Ganesan, Shankar, Morris George, Sandy D. Jap, Robert W. Palmatier and Barton A. Weitz (2009), "Supply Chain Management and Retailer Performance: Emerging Trends, Issues, and Implications for Research and Practice," *Journal of Retailing*, 85 (1), 84–94.

García-Canal, Esteban and Mauro F. Guillén (2008), "Risk and The Strategy of Foreign Location Choice in Regulated Industries," *Strategic Management Journal*, 29 (10), 1097–1115.

Garnier, Gérard H. (1982), "Context and Decision Making Autonomy in the Foreign Affiliates of U.S. Multinational Corporations," *Academy of Management Journal*, 25 (4), 893–908.

Gerbing, David W. and James C. Anderson (1988), "An Updated Paradigm for Scale Development Incorporating Unidimensionality and Its Assessment," *Journal of Marketing Research*, 25 (2), 186–192.

Ghoshal, Sumantra and Nitin Nohria (1993), "Horses for courses: organisational forms for multinationaloperationsReview," *Sloan management review*, 34 (2), 23–35.

Gielens, Katrijn and Marnik G. Dekimpe (2001), "Do international entry decisions of retail chains matter in the long run?," *International Journal of Research in Marketing*, 18 (3), 235–259.

——— (2007), "The Entry Strategy of Retail Firms into Transition Economies," *Journal of Marketing*, 71 (2), 196–212.

Gielens, Katrijn, Linda van de Gucht, Jan-Benedict E. M. Steenkamp and Marnik G. Dekimpe (2008), "Dancing with a Giant: The Effect of Wal-Mart's Entry into the United Kingdom on the Performance of European Retailers," *Journal of Marketing Research*, 45 (5), 519–534.

Godley, Andrew and Scott R. Fletcher (2000), "Foreign entry into British retailing, 1850-1994," *International Marketing Review*, 17 (4/5), 392–400.

Goldman, Arieh (1981), "Transfer of a Retailing Technology into the Less Developed Countries: The Supermarket Case," *Journal of Retailing*, 57 (2), 5–29.

——— (2000), "Supermarkets in China: the case of Shanghai," *International Review of Retail, Distribution and Consumer Research*, 10 (1), 1–21.

——— (2001), "The transfer of retail formats into developing economies: The example of China," *Journal of Retailing*, 77 (2), 221–242.

Govindarajan, Vijay (1986), "Decentralization, Strategy, and Effectiveness of Strategic Business Units in Multibusiness Organizations," *Academy of Management Review*, 11 (4), 844–856.

Green, Kenneth W, Dwayne Whitten and Anthony R. Inman (2008), "The impact of logistics performance on organizational performance in a supply chain context," *Supply Chain Management: An International Journal*, 13 (4), 317–327.

Gregory, Robert (2010), "Executive opinion - Does e-commerce represent the future for internationalisation?," *Planet Retail*, 1–9.

Grewal, Rajdeep and Ravi Dharwadkar (2002), "The Role of Institutional Environment in Marketing Channels," *Journal of Marketing*, 66 (3), 82–97.

Griffith, David A, Aruna Chandra and John K. Ryans (2003), "Examining the Intricacies of Promotion Standardization: Factors Influencing Advertising Message and Packaging," *Journal of International Marketing*, 11 (3), 30–47.

Griffith, David A, Michael Y. Hu and John K. Ryans (2000), "Process standardization across intra-and inter-cultural relationships," *Journal of International Business Studies*, 31 (2), 303–324.

Grönroos, Christian (1997), "From Marketing Mix to Relationship Marketing – towards a Paradigm Shift in Marketing," *Management Decision*, 35 (4), 322–339.

Hadjimarcou, John and John Barnes (1998), "Retailing to Foreign National Consumers in the Border Zone," *Journal of Global Marketing*, 11 (3), 85–106.

Hair, Joseph F, William C. Black, Barry J. Babin and Rolph E. Anderson (2010), *Multivariate Data Analysis: A Global Perspective.* Upper Saddle River, NJ: Pearson.

Håkanson, Lars and Björn Ambos (2010), "The antecedents of psychic distance," *Journal of International Management*, 16 (3), 195–210.

Hannan, Michael T. and John Freeman (1984), "Structural inertia and organizational change," *American Sociological Review*, 49 (2), 149–164.

Harris, Lloyd C. (2000), "The organizational barriers to developing market orientation," *European Journal of Marketing*, 34 (5/6), 598–624.

Harzing, Anne-Wil (2000), "An Empirical Analysis and Extension of the Bartlett and Ghoshal Typology of Multinational Companies," *Journal of International Business Studies*, 31 (1), 101–119.

Haugland, Sven A. (2010), "The integration-responsiveness framework and subsidiary management: A commentary," *Journal of Business Research*, 63 (1), 94–96.

Haunschild, Pamela R. and Anne S. Miner (1997), "Modes of Interorganizational Imitation: The Effects of Outcome Salience and Uncertainty," *Administrative Science Quarterly*, 42 (3), 472–500.

Helfferich, Evert, Marjolein Hinfelaar and Hans Kasper (1997), "Towards a clear terminology on international retailing," *International Review of Retail, Distribution and Consumer Research*, 7 (3), 287–307.

Hempel, Paul S, Zhi-Xue Zhang and Yulan Han (2012), "Team Empowerment and the Organizational Context Decentralization and the Contrasting Effects of Formalization," *Journal of Management*, 38 (2), 475–501.

Henderson, Jeffrey, Peter R. Dickson, Martin Hess, Neil M. Coe and Henry W.-C. Yeung (2002), "Global production networks and the analysis of economic development," *Review of International Political Economy*, 9 (3), 436–464.

Henisz, Witold J. (2000), "The Institutional Environment for Economic Growth," *Economics and Politics*, 12 (1), 1–31.

Henisz, Witold J. and Andrew Delios (2001), "Uncertainty, Imitation and Plant Location: Japanese Multinational Corporations, 1990-1996," *Administrative Science Quarterly*, 46 (3), 443–475.

Henseler, Jörg, Christian M. Ringle and Rudolf R. Sinkovics (2009), "The Use of Partial Least Squares Path Modeling In International Marketing," *Advances in International Marketing*, 20 (1), 277–319.

Hernandez, Tony and David Bennison (2000), "The art and science of retail location decisions," *International Journal of Retail and Distribution Management*, 28 (8), 357–367.

Herrmann, Pol and Deepak K. Datta (2002), "CEO Successor Characteristics and the Choice of Foreign Market Entry Mode: An Empirical Study," *Journal of International Business Studies*, 33 (3), 551–569.

Hollander, Stanley C. (1970), *Multinational Retailing.* East Lansing: Michigan State University.

House, Robert J, Paul J. Hanges, Mansour Javidan, Peter W. Dorfman and Vipin Gupta (2007), *Culture, Leadership, and Organizations: The Globe Study of 62 Societies.* Thousand Oaks, CA: Sage.

Huang, Ying and Brenda Sternquist (2007), "Retailers' foreign market entry decisions: An institutional perspective," *International Business Review*, 16 (5), 613–629.

Hulland, John (1999), "Use of Partial Least Squares (PLS) in strategic management research: A review of four recent studies," *Strategic Management Journal*, 20 (2), 195–204.

Hult, G. T. M, David J. Ketchen, David A. Griffith, Brian R. Chabowski, Mary K. Hamman, Bernadine J. Dykes, Wesley A. Pollitte and Tamer S. Cavusgil (2008), "An assessment of the measurement of performance in international business research," *Journal of International Business Studies*, 39 (6), 1064–1080.

Hutchinson, Karise, Barry Quinn and Nicholas Alexander (2006), "SME retailer internationalisation: case study evidence from British retailers," *International Marketing Review*, 23 (1), 25–53.

Jaccard, James (2001), *Interaction effects in logistic regression.* Thousand Oaks, CA: Sage.

Jain, Subhash C. (1989), "Standardization of International Marketing Strategy: Some Research Hypotheses," *Journal of Marketing*, 53 (1), 70–79.

Jarillo, Carlos J. (1988), "On strategic networks," *Strategic Management Journal*, 9 (1), 31–41.

Jaworski, Bernard J. and Ajay K. Kohli (1993), "Market Orientation: Antecedents and Consequences," *Journal of Marketing*, 57 (3), 53–70.

Jensen, Robert J. and Gabriel Szulanski (2007), "Template use and the effectiveness of knowledge transfer," *Management Science*, 53 (11), 1716–1730.

Jiménez, Alfredo (2010), "Does political risk affect the scope of the expansion abroad? Evidence from Spanish MNEs," *International Business Review*, 19 (6), 619–633.

Johanson, Jan and Finn Wiedersheim-Paul (1975), "The internationalization of the firm - Four Swedish cases," *Journal of Management Studies*, 12 (3), 305–322.

Johanson, Jan and Jan-Erik Vahlne (1977), "The Internationalization Process of the Firm-A Model of Knowledge Development and Increasing Foreign Market Commitments," *Journal of International Business Studies*, 8 (1), 23–32.

——— (2003), "Business Relationship Learning and Commitment in the Internationalization Process," *Journal of International Entrepreneurship*, 1 (1), 83–101.

Johansson, Ulf (2002), "Food retail buying processes – a study of the UK, Italy and Sweden," *International Journal of Retail and Distribution Management*, 30 (12), 575–585.

Johnson, Joseph and Gerard J. Tellis (2008), "Drivers of Success for Market Entry into China and India," *Journal of Marketing*, 72 (3), 1–13.

Jones, Marian V. and Nicole E. Coviello (2005), "Internationalisation: conceptualising an entrepreneurial process of behaviour in time," *Journal of International Business Studies*, 36 (3), 284–303.

Jonsson, Anna and Nicolai J. Foss (2011), "International expansion through flexible replication: Learning from the internationalization experience of IKEA," *Journal of International Business Studies*, 42 (9), 1079–1102.

Kacker, Madhav (1988), "International Flow of Retailing Know-How: Bridging the Technology Gap in Distribution," *Journal of Retailing*, 64 (1), 41–67.

Katsikeas, Constantine S, Saeed Samiee and Marios Theodosiou (2006), "Strategy Fit and Performance Consequences of International Marketing Standardization," *Strategic Management Journal*, 27 (9), 867–890.

Kaufmann, Patrick J. and Sevgin Eroglu (1999), "Standardization and Adaptation in Business Format Franchising," *Journal of Business Venturing*, 14 (1), 69–85.

Kline, Theresa J. B, Lorne M. Sulsky and Sandra D. Rever-Moriyama (2000), "Common method variance and specification errors: A practical approach to detection," *Journal of Psychology*, 134 (4), 401–421.

Kogut, Bruce and Harbir Singh (1988), "The effect of national culture on the choice of entry mode," *Journal of International Business Studies*, 19 (3), 411–432.

Kostova, Tatiana (1999), "Transnational transfer of strategic organizational practices: A contextual perspective," *Academy of Management Review*, 24 (2), 308–324.

Kostova, Tatiana and Kendall Roth (2002), "Adoption of an organizational practice by subsidiaries of multinational corporations: Institutional and relational effects," *Academy of Management Journal*, 45 (1), 215–233.

Kostova, Tatiana and Srilata Zaheer (1999), "Organizational Legitimacy under Conditions of Complexity: The Case of the Multinational Enterprise," *Academy of Management Review*, 24 (1), 64–81.

Kumar, Nirmalya, Louis W. Stern and James C. Anderson (1993), "Conducting Interorganizational Research Using Key Informants," *Academy of Management Journal*, 36 (6), 1633–1651.

Lee, Martyn J. (1993), *Consumer Culture Born: the Cultural Politics of Consumption*. London: Routledge.

Leknes, Hanne M. and Chris Carr (2004), "Globalisation, International Configurations and Strategic Implications: The Case of Retailing," *Long Range Planning*, 37 (1), 29–49.

Lessassy, Leopold and Alain Jolibert (2007), "Internationalization of Retail Strategies," *Journal of Euromarketing*, 16 (3), 27–36.

Levitt, Theodoré (1983), "The Globalization of Markets," *Harvard Business Review*, 61 (3), 92–102.

Liang, Kung-Yee and Scott L. Zeger (1986), "Longitudinal data analysis using generalized linear models," *Biometrika*, 73 (1), 13–22.

Lin, Shao-Lung and An-Tien Hsieh (2010), "International strategy implementation: Roles of subsidiaries, operational capabilities, and procedural justice," *Journal of Business Research*, 63 (1), 52–59.

Lin, Xiaohua and Richard Germain (2003), "Organizational structure, context, customer orientation, and performance: lessons from Chinese state-owned enterprises," *Strategic Management Journal*, 24 (11), 1131–1151.

Liu, Hong and Peter J. McGoldrick (1996), "International retail sourcing: trend, nature, and process," *Journal of International Marketing*, 4 (4), 9-33.

Lowe, Michelle and Neil Wrigley (2009), "Innovation in retail internationalisation: Tesco in the USA," *International Review of Retail, Distribution and Consumer Research*, 19 (4), 331–347.

Lowson, Robert (2001), "Analysing the Effectiveness of European Retail Sourcing Strategies," *European Management Journal*, 19 (5), 543–551.

Lu, Jane W. (2002), "Intra- and Inter-organizational Imitative Behavior: Institutional Influences on Japanese Firms' Entry Mode Choice," *Journal of International Business Studies*, 33 (1), 19–37.

Lu, Yao, Elena E. Karpova and Ann M. Fiore (2011), "Factors influencing international fashion retailers' entry mode choice," *Journal of Fashion Marketing and Management*, 15 (1), 58–75.

Lynch, Daniel F, Scott B. Keller and John Ozment (2000), "The effects of logistics capabilities and strategy on firm performance," *Journal of Business Logistics*, 21 (2), 47–67.

MacKenzie, Scott B. and Richard A. Spreng (1992), "How does motivation moderate the impact of central and peripheral processing on brand attitudes and intentions?," *Journal of Consumer Research*, 18 (4), 519–529.

Madhok, Anoop (1997), "Cost, Value and Foreign Market Entry Mode: The Transaction and the Firm," *Strategic Management Journal*, 18 (1), 39–61.

——— (1998), "The nature of multinational firm boundaries: Transaction costs, firm capabilities and foreign market entry mode," *International Business Review*, 7 (3), 259–290.

Malone, Thomas W. (1999), "Is 'empowerment' just a fad? Control, decision-making, and information technology," *B T Technological Journal*, 17 (4), 141–144.

Manrodt, Karl B. and Kate Vitasek (2004), "Global process standardization: a case study," *Journal of Business Logistics*, 25 (1), 1–19.

Mårtenson, Rita (1987), "Is Standardisation of Marketing feasible in Culture-Bound Industries? A European Case Study," *International Marketing Review*, 4 (3), 7–17.

Martinez, Jon I. and J.Carlos Jarillo (1989), "The evolution of research on co-ordination mechanisms in multinational corporations," *Journal of International Business Studies*, 20 (3), 489–514.

Mathe, Hervé and Teo F. Dagi (1996), "Harnessing technology in global service businesses," *Long Range Planning*, 29 (4), 449–461.

McCarthy, Jerome E. (1964), *Basic Marketing.* Homewood, IL: Irwin.

McGauran, Anne-Marie (2001), "Retail is detail: cross-national variation in the character of retail selling in Paris and Dublin," *International Review of Retail, Distribution and Consumer Research*, 11 (4), 437–458.

McGoldrick, Peter J. (1998), "Spatial and Temporal Shifts in the Development of International Retail Images," *Journal of Business Research*, 42 (2), 189–196.

McKenzie, Brent and Bill Merrilees (2008), "Retail value chains: extension and development into transition economies: Stockmann in Estonia and Latvia," *Baltic Journal of Management*, 3 (3), 309–327.

McNeil, Ian R. (1978), "Contracts: adjustment of long-term economic relations under classical, neoclassical, and relational contract law," *North-Western University Law Review*, 72 (6), 854–902.

Menard, Scott W. (2002), *Applied logistic regression analysis.* Thousand Oaks: Sage.

Mentzer, John T, Soonhong Min and Zach G. Zacharia (2000), "The nature of interfirm partnering in supply chain management," *Journal of Retailing*, 76 (4), 549–568.

Metro Group AG (2011), "Shape 2012 is driving change. Annual report 2011," (accessed October 22, 2011), [available at www.metro-group.com].

Meyer, John W. and Brian Rowan (1977), "Institutionalized organizations: Formal structure as myth and ceremony," *American Journal of Sociology*, 83 (2), 340–363.

Meyer, Klaus E. (2001), "Institutions, Transaction Costs and Entry Mode Choice in Eastern Europe," *Journal of International Business Studies*, 32 (2), 357–367.

Meyer, Klaus E. and Hung V. Nguyen (2005), "Foreign Investment Strategies and Sub-national Institutions in Emerging Markets: Evidence from Vietnam," *Journal of Management Studies*, 42 (1), 63–93.

Meyer, Klaus E. and Mike W. Peng (2005), "Probing theoretically into Central and Eastern Europe: Transactions, Resources, and Institutions," *Journal of International Business Studies*, 36 (6), 600–621.

Meyer, Klaus E, Saul Estrin, Sumon K. Bhaumik and Mike W. Peng (2009), "Institutions, Resources, and Entry Strategies in Emerging Economies," *Strategic Management Journal*, 30 (1), 61–80.

Miller, Danny (1987), "Strategy Making and Structure: Analysis and Implications for Performance," *Academy of Management Journal*, 30 (1), 7–32.

Mintzberg, Henry (1979), *The structuring of organizations.* Englewood Cliffs: Prentice Hall.

Mitronen, Lasse and Kristian Möller (2003), "Management of hybrid organisations: a case study in retailing," *Industrial Marketing Management*, 32 (5), 419–429.

Mooij, Marieke de and Geert Hofstede (2002), "Convergence and divergence in consumer behavior: implications for international retailing," *Journal of Retailing*, 78 (1), 61–69.

Moore, Christopher M, Anne M. Doherty and Stephen A. Doyle (2010), "Flagship stores as a market entry method: the perspective of luxury fashion retailing," *European Journal of Marketing*, 44 (1/2), 139–161.

Moore, Christopher M, Grete Birtwistle and Steve L. Burt (2004), "Channel power, conflict and conflict resolution in international fashion retailing," *European Journal of Marketing*, 38 (7), 749–769.

Morosini, Piero, Scott A. Shane and Harbir Singh (1998), "National cultural distance and cross-border acquisition performance," *Journal of International Business Studies*, 29 (1), 137–158.

Morrison, Allen J. and Kendall Roth (1993), "Relating Porter's Configuration/Coordination Framework to Competitive Strategy and Structural Mechanisms: Analysis and Implications," *Journal of Management*, 19 (4), 797–818.

Morschett, Dirk, Hanna Schramm-Klein and Bernhard Swoboda (2010), "Decades of research on market entry modes: What do we really know about external antecedents of entry mode choice?," *Journal of International Management*, 16 (1), 60–77.

Mulhern, Francis J. (1997), "Retail Marketing: From Distribution to integration," *International Journal of Research in Marketing*, 14 (2), 103–124.

Mutinelli, Marco and Lucia Piscitello (1998), "The entry mode choice of MNEs: an evolutionary approach," *Research Policy*, 27 (5), 491–506.

Nelson, Richard R. and Sidney G. Winter (2008), *An Evolutionary Theory of Economic Change.* Cambrige: Harvard University Press.

Newbert, Scott L. (2007), "Empirical research on the resource based view of the firm: an assessment and suggestions for future research," *Strategic Management Journal*, 28 (2), 121–146.

Nohria, Nitin and Sumantra Ghoshal (1994), "Differentiated Fit and Shared Values: Alternatives for Managing Headquarters-Subsidiary Relations," *Strategic Management Journal*, 15 (6), 491–502.

North, Douglass C. (1990), *Insitutions, Institutional Change and Economic Performance.* Cambrige: Cambrige University Press.

Nunally, Jum C. and Ira H. Bernstein (1967), *Psychometric Theory.* New York u.a.: McGrawHill.

——— (1978), *Psychometric Theory.* New York u.a.: McGrawHill.

O'Grady, Shawna and Henry W. Lane (1996), "The Psychic Distance Paradox," *Journal of International Business Studies*, 27 (2), 309–333.

Oliver, Christine (1996), "The institutional embeddedness of economic activity," *Advances in Strategic Management*, 13 (1), 163–186.

——— (1997), "Sustainable Competitive Advantage. Combining Institutional and Resource-Based-Views," *Strategic Management Journal*, 18 (9), 697–713.

Oviatt, Benjamin M. and Patricia P. McDougall (2005), "Defining International Entrepreneurship and Modeling the Speed of Internationalization," *Entrepreneurship Theory and Practice*, 29 (5), 537–554.

Özsomer, Ayşegül and Bernard L. Simonin (2004), "Marketing program standardization: A cross-country exploration," *International Journal of Research in Marketing*, 21 (4), 397–419.

Özsomer, Ayşegül and Gregory E. Prussia (2000), "Competing Perspectives in International Marketing Strategy: Contingency and Process Models," *Journal of International Marketing*, 8 (1), 27–50.

Özsomer, Ayşegül, Muzzafer Bodur and Tamer S. Cavusgil (1991), "Marketing Standardization by Multinationals in an Emerging Market," *European Journal of Marketing*, 25 (12), 50–61.

Padmanabhan, Prasad and Kang R. Cho (1999), "Decision Specific Experience in Foreign Ownership and Establishment Strategies: Evidence from Japanese Firms," *Journal of International Business Studies*, 30 (1), 25–43.

Palmer, Mark (2005), "Crossing Threshold Periods in the Retail Life Cycle: Insights from Wal-Mart International," *European Management Journal*, 23 (6), 717–729.

Palmer, Mark, Martin Owens and Ronan de Kervenoael (2010), "Paths of the least resistance: understanding how motives form in international retail joint venturing," *Service Industries Journal*, 30 (6), 965–989.

Pan, Yue and George M. Zinkhan (2006), "Determinants of retail patronage: a meta-analytical perspective," *Journal of Retailing*, 82 (3), 229–243.

Park, Youngsun and Brenda Sternquist (2008), "The global retailer's strategic proposition and choice of entry mode," *International Journal of Retail and Distribution Management*, 36 (4), 281–299.

Paswan, Audhesh, María I. D. S. de Pineda and Francisco C. S. Ramirez (2010), "Small versus large retail stores in an emerging market—Mexico," *Journal of Business Research*, 63 (7), 667–672.

Pedersen, Torben, Bent Petersen and Gabriel R. G. Benito (2002), "Change of foreign operation method: impetus and switching costs," *International Business Review*, 11 (3), 325–345.

Pederzoli, Daniele (2008), "The internationalisation of voluntary groups: An exploratory analysis of selected value chain aspects," *Journal of Retailing and Consumer Services*, 15 (2), 118–126.

Peña-Vinces, Jesus, Gabriel Cepeda-Carrión and Wynne W. Chin (2012), "Effect of ITC on the international competitiveness of firms," *Management Decision*, 50 (6), 4-4.

Penrose, Edith (1995), *The theory of the Growth of the Firm.* Oxford: Oxford University Press.

Peter, Paul J. (1981), "Construct Validity: A Review of Basic Issues and Marketing Practices," *Journal of Marketing Research*, 18 (2), 133–145.

Peterson, Robert A. (1994), "A meta-analysis of Cronbach's coefficient alpha," *Journal of Consumer Research*, 21 (2), 381–391.

Pfeffer, Jeffrey and Gerald R. Salancik (1978), *The External Control of Organizations: A Resource Dependence Perspective.* New York: Harper & Row.

Picot-Coupey, Karine (2006), "Determinants of international retail operation mode choice: Towards a conceptual framework based on evidence from French specialised retail chains," *International Review of Retail, Distribution and Consumer Research*, 16 (2), 215–237.

Planet Retail (2008), "Top 20 Rankings, 2008: Surviving the uncertainty,"

——— (2011a), "Global Retail Intelligence," (accessed October 14, 2011), [available at www.planetretail.net].

——— (2011b), "World retail sales: 2006-2015," Planet Retail.

Podsakoff, Philip M. and Dennis W. Organ (1986), "Self-Reports in Organizational Research: Problems and Prospects," *Journal of Management*, 12 (4), 531–544.

Podsakoff, Philip M, Scott B. MacKenzie, Lee Jeong-Yeon and Nathan P. Podsakoff (2003), "Common method biases in behavioral research: A critical review of the literature and recommended remedies," *Journal of Applied Psychology*, 88 (5), 879-893.

Powell, Walter W. (1987), "Hybrid organizational arrangements: new form or transitional development?," *California Management Review*, 30 (1), 67–87.

Priem, Richard L. and John E. Butler (2001), "Is the resource-based" view" a useful perspective for strategic management research?," *Academy of Management Review*, 26 (1), 22–40.

Puck, Jonas F, Dirk Holtbruegge and Alexander T. Mohr (2009), "Beyond entry mode choice: Explaining the conversion of joint ventures into wholly owned subsidiaries in the Peoples Republic of China," *Journal of International Business Studies*, 40 (3), 388-404.

Pugh, Derek S, David J. Hickson, Christopher R. Hinings and Christopher Turner (1968), "Dimensions of Organization Structure," *Administrative Science Quarterly*, 13 (1), 65–105.

Quester, Pascale G. and Jodie Conduit (1996), "Standardization, Centralization and Marketing in Multinational Companies," *International Business Review*, 5 (4), 395–421.

Quinn, Robert E. and Kim Cameron (1983), "Organizational life cycles and shifting criteria of effectiveness: Some preliminary evidence," *Management Science*, 29 (1), 33–51.

Quintens, Lieven, Pieter Pauwels and Paul Matthyssens (2006), "Global purchasing strategy: Conceptualization and measurement," *Industrial Marketing Management*, 35 (7), 881–891.

Reinartz, Werner, Michael Haenlein and Jörg Henseler (2009), "An empirical comparison of the efficacy of covariance-based and variance-based SEM," *International Journal of Research in Marketing*, 26 (4), 332–344.

Roberts, Graham H. (2005), "Auchan's entry into Russia: prospects and research implications," *International Journal of Retail and Distribution Management*, 33 (1), 49–68.

Rogers, Helen, Pervez N. Ghauri and Katharine L. George (2005), "The Impact of Market Orientation on the Internationalization of Retailing Firms: Tesco in Eastern Europe," *International Review of Retail, Distribution and Consumer Research*, 15 (1), 53–74.

Root, Franklin R. (1987), *Entry Strategies for International Market.* Washington DC: Heath and Company.

——— (1995), *Entry Strategies for International Markets.* Lexington: Lexington Books.

Rosenbloom, Bert (1991), *Marketing Channels.* Orlando: Dryden Press.

Rosenzweig, Philip M. and Jitendra V. Singh (1991), "Organizational Environments and the Multinational Enterprise," *Academy of Management Review*, 16 (2), 340–361.

Ruberty, Jill (1994), "The British production regime: a societal-specific system?," *Economy and Society*, 23 (3), 335–354.

Ruekert, Robert W, O. C. Walker and Kenneth J. Roering (1985), "The Organization of Marketing Activities: A Contingency Theory of Structure and Performance," *Journal of Marketing*, 49 (1), 13–25.

Sambharya, Rakesh B. (1996), "Foreign Experience of Top Management Teams and International Diversification Strategies of U.S. Multinational Corporations," *Strategic Management Journal*, 17 (9), 739–746.

Samiee, Saeed and Kendall Roth (1992), "The Influence of Global Marketing Standardization on Performance," *Journal of Marketing*, 56 (2), 1–17.

Samiee, Saeed, Leslie S. C. Yip and Sherriff T. K. Luk (2004), "VIEWPOINT, International marketing in Southeast Asia, Retailing trends and opportunities in China," *International Marketing Review*, 21 (3), 247–254.

Sanchez-Peinado, Esther, José Pla-Barber and Louis Hébert (2007), "Strategic Variables That Influence Entry Mode Choice in Service Firms," *Journal of International Marketing*, 15 (1), 67–91.

Sarkar, Mitrabarun and Tamer S. Cavusgil (1996), "Trends in international business thought and literature: A review of international market entry mode research: Integration and synthesis," *The International Executive*, 38 (6), 825–847.

Schilke, Oliver and Anthony Goerzen (2010), "Alliance Management Capability: An Investigation of the Construct and Its Measurement," *Journal of Management*, 36 (5), 1192–1219.

Schilke, Oliver, Martin Reimann and Jacquelyn S. Thomas (2009), "When Does International Marketing Standardization Matter To Firm Performance?," *Journal of International Marketing*, 17 (4), 24-46.

Schmid, Stefan and Thomas Kotulla (2011), "50 years of research on international standardization and adaptation - From a systematic literature analysis to a theoretical framework," *International Business Review*, 20 (5), 491–507.

Schramm-Klein, Hanna and Dirk Morschett (2006), "The relationship between marketing performance, logistics performance and company performance for retail companies," *International Review of Retail, Distribution and Consumer Research*, 16 (02), 277–296.

Schuiling, Isabelle and Jean-Nöel Kapferer (2004), "Real differences between local and international brands: strategic implications for international marketers," *Journal of International Marketing*, 12 (4), 97–112.

Schwens, Christian and Ruediger Kabst (2009), "How early opposed to late internationalizers learn: Experience of others and paradigms of interpretation," *International Business Review*, 18 (5), 509–522.

Schwens, Christian, Julia Eiche and Ruediger Kabst (2011), "The Moderating Impact of Informal Institutional Distance and Formal Institutional Risk on SME Entry Mode Choice," *Journal of Management Studies*, 48 (2), 331–351.

Scott, W. R. (1995), *Institutions and organizations.* Thousand Oaks, CA: Sage.

Seevers, Matthew T, Steven J. Skinner and Robert Dahlstrom (2010), "Performance Implications of a Retail Purchasing Network: The Role of Social Capital," *Journal of Retailing*, 86 (4), 310–321.

Segal-Horn, Susan and Heather Davison (1992), "Global Markets, the Global Consumer and International Retailing," *Journal of Global Marketing*, 5 (3), 31–61.

Sharma, Deo D. and Anders Blomstermo (2003), "The internationalization process of born globals: a network view," *International Business Review*, 12 (6), 739–753.

Shenkar, Oded (2001), "Cultural Distance Revisited: Towards a More Rigorous Conceptualization and Measurement of Cultural Differences," *Journal of International Business Studies*, 32 (3), 519–535.

Shoham, Aviv (1996), "Marketing-Mix Standardization: Determinants of Export Performance," *Journal of Global Marketing*, 10 (2), 53–73.

——— (1999), "Bounded Rationality, Planning, Standardization of International Strategy, and Export Performance: A Structural Model Examination," *Journal of International Marketing*, 7 (2), 24–50.

Simon, Herbert A. (1959), "Theories of decision-making in economics and behavioral science," *American Economic Review*, 49 (3), 253–283.

Sine, Wesley D, Hitoshi Mitsuhashi and David A. Kirsch (2006), "Revisiting Burns and Stalker: Formal Structure and New Venture Performance in Emerging Economic Sectors," *Academy of Management Journal*, 49 (1), 121–132.

Singh, Jitendra V. (1986), "Performance, Slack, and Risk Taking in Organizational Decision Making," *Academy of Management Journal*, 29 (3), 562–585.

Snijders, Tom A. and Roel J. Bosker (1999), *Multilevel analysis: An introduction to basic and advanced multilevel modeling.* Thousand Oaks: Sage.

Sobel, Michael E. (1987), "Direct and Indirect Effects in Linear Structural Equation Models," *Sociological Methods and Research*, 16 (1), 155–176.

Sorenson, Ralph Z. and Ulrich E. Wiechmann (1975), "How multinationals view marketing standardization," *Harvard Business Review*, 53 (May-June), 38–167.

Sousa, Carlos M. P. and Frank Bradley (2005), "Global markets: does psychic distance matter?," *Journal of Strategic Marketing*, 13 (1), 43-59.

Sousa, Carlos M. P. and Jorge Lengler (2009), "Psychic distance, marketing strategy and performance in export ventures of Brazilian firms," *Journal of Marketing Management*, 25 (5/6), 591–610.

Srivastava, Rajendra K, Tasadduq A. Shervani and Liam Fahey (1999), "Marketing, Business Processes, and Shareholder Value: An Organizationally Embedded View of Marketing Activities and the Discipline of Marketing," *Journal of Marketing*, 63 (Special Issue), 168–179.

Stinchcombe, Arthur L. (1965), "Social structure and organizations," in *Handbook of organizations*, James G. March, ed. Chicago, IL: Rand McNelly & Co, 142–192.

Stöttinger, Barbara and Bodo B. Schlegelmilch (2009), "Psychic distance: a concept past its due date?," *International Marketing Review*, 17 (2), 169–173.

Suh, Yong-Gu and Elizabeth Howard (2009), "Restructuring retailing in Korea: the case of Samsung-Tesco," *Asia Pacific Business Review*, 15 (1), 29–40.

Swoboda, Bernhard and Michael Anderer (2008), "Coordinating the international retailing firm: Exploratory models and evaluations of structural, systemic, and cultural options," *Journal of Retailing and Consumer Services*, 15 (2), 104–117.

Swoboda, Bernhard and Sandra Schwarz (2006), "Dynamics of the internationalisation of European retailing – From a national to a European perspective," in *Strategic Management – New Rules for Old Europe*, Christian Scholz and Joachim Zentes, eds. Wiesbaden: Gabler, 159–200.

Swoboda, Bernhard, Edith Olejnik and Dirk Morschett (2011), "Changes in foreign operation modes: Stimuli for increases versus reductions," *International Business Review*, 20 (5), 578–590.

Swoboda, Bernhard, Joachim Zentes and Stefan Elsner (2009), "Internationalisation of Retail Firms: State of the Art after 20 Years of Research," *Marketing - Journal of Research and Management*, 5 (2), 105–126.

Swoboda, Bernhard, Sandra Schwarz and Frank Hälsig (2009), "Towards a conceptual model of country market selection: Selection processes of retailers and C&C wholesalers," *International Review of Retail, Distribution and Consumer Research*, 17 (3), 253–282.

Swoboda, Bernhard, Stefan Elsner and Dirk Morschett (2012), "Preferences and performance of international strategies in retail sectors: an empirical study," *Long Range Planning*, DOI: 10.1016/j.lrp.2012.05.002..

Swoboda, Bernhard, Thomas Foscht and Gérard Cliquet (2008), "International value chain processes by retailers and wholesalers - A general approach," *Journal of Retailing and Consumer Services*, 15 (2), 63-77.

Swoboda, Bernhard, Thomas Foscht and Karin Pennemann (2009), *HandelsMonitor 2009: Internationalisierung des Handels – Erfolgreiches „Going" und „Being International".* Frankfurt am Main: Deutscher Fachverlag.

Szulanski, Gabriel and Robert J. Jensen (2008), "Growing through copying: The negative consequences of innovation on franchise network growth," *Research Policy*, 37 (10), 1732–1741.

Tacconelli, Wance and Neil Wrigley (2009), "Organizational Challenges and Strategic Responses of Retail TNCs in Post-WTO-Entry China," *Economic Geography*, 85 (1), 49–73.

Tan, Benjamin, Krishna M. Erramilli and Tan W. Liang (2001), "The Influence of dissemination risks, strategic control and global management skills on firms' modal decision in host countries," *International Business Review*, 10 (3), 323–340.

Theodosiou, Marios and Leonidas C. Leonidou (2003), "Standardization versus adaptation of international marketing strategy: an integrative assessment of the empirical research," *International Business Review*, 12 (2), 141-171.

Tihanyi, Laszlo, David A. Griffith and Craig J. Russell (2005), "The Effect of Cultural Distance on Entry Mode Choice, International Diversification, and MNE Performance: A Meta-Analysis," *Journal of International Business Studies*, 36 (3), 270–283.

Tokatli, Nebahat (2007), "Global sourcing: insights from the global clothing industry the case of Zara, a fast fashion retailer," *Journal of Economic Geography*, 8 (1), 21–38.

Townsend, Janell D, Sengun Yeniyurt, Seyda Z. Deligonul and Tamer S. Cavusgil (2004), "Exploring the Marketing Program Antecedents of Performance in a Global Company," *Journal of International Marketing*, 12 (4), 1–24.

Tse, David K, Yigang Pan and Kevin Y. Au (1997), "How MNCs Choose Entry Modes and Form Alliances: The China Experience," *Journal of International Business Studies*, 28 (4), 779–805.

Uhlenbruck, Klaus, Peter Rodriguez, Jonathan Doh and Lorraine Eden (2006), "The impact of corruption on entry strategy: Evidence from telecommunication projects in emerging economies," *Organization Science*, 17 (3), 402–414.

Venkatraman, N. and John H. Grant (1986), "Construct Measurement in Organizational Strategy Research: A critique and Proposal," *Academy of Management Review*, 11 (1), 71–87.

Verity, Julie (2005), "Interpreting the successful transformation of Shell's advertising activity 1997-2002," *Management Decision*, 43 (1), 72–85.

Vermeulen, Freek and Harry G. Barkema (2001), "Learning through acquisitions," *Academy of Management Journal*, 44 (3), 457–476.

——— (2002), "Pace, Rhythm, and Scope: Process Dependence in Building a Profitable Multinational Corporation," *Strategic Management Journal*, 23 (7), 637–653.

Vida, Irena (2000), "An empirical inquiry into international expansion of US retailers," *International Marketing Review*, 17 (4/5), 454–475.

Vida, Irena, James Reardon and Ann Fairhurst (2000), "Determinants of International Retail Involvement: The Case of Large U.S. Retail Chains," *Journal of International Marketing*, 8 (4), 37–60.

Vorhies, Douglas W. and Neil A. Morgan (2003), "A Configuration Theory Assessment of Marketing Organization Fit with Business Strategy and Its Relationship with Marketing Performance," *Journal of Marketing*, 67 (1), 100–115.

Vrontis, Demetris, Alkis Thrassou and Iasonas Lamprianou (2009), "International marketing adaptation versus standardisation of multinational companies," *International Marketing Review*, 26 (4/5), 477–500.

Wagner, Hardy (2004), "Internationalization speed and cost efficiency: evidence from Germany," *International Business Review*, 13 (4), 447–463.

Walters, Peter G. P. (1986), "International marketing policy: discussion of the standardization construct and its relevance for corporate policy," *Journal of International Business Studies*, 17 (2), 55–69.

Wegner, Douglas and Antonio D. Padula (2010), "Governance and Management of Horizontal Business Networks: An Analysis of Retail Networks in Germany," *International Journal of Business and Management*, 5 (12), 74–88.

Welch, Denice E. and Lawrence S. Welch (1996), "The internationalization process and networks: a strategic management perspective," *Journal of International Marketing*, 4 (3), 11–28.

Welch, Lawrence S. (1990), "Internationalisation By Australian Franchisors," *Asia Pacific Journal of Management*, 7 (2), 101–121.

Wernerfelt, Birger (1984), "A resource-based view of the firm," *Strategic Management Journal*, 5 (2), 171–180.

White, Darin W. and Keith Absher (2007), "Positioning of retail stores in Central and Eastern European accession states: Standardization versus adaptation," *European Journal of Marketing*, 41 (3/4), 292–306.

Wigley, Stephen M. and Chu-Ling R. Chiang (2009), "Retail internationalisation in practice: per una in the UK and Taiwan," *International Journal of Retail and Distribution Management*, 37 (3), 250–270.

Williamson, Oliver E. (1985), *The economic institutions of capitalism. Firms, markets, relational contracting.* New York: The Free Press.

Winter, Sidney G. and Gabriel Szulanski (2001), "Replication as strategy," *Organization Science*, 12 (6), 730–743.

Wong, May M. I. and Chris Hendry (1997), "A study of the employment system of Japanese multinational retailers in Hong Kong," *International Journal of Human Resource Management*, 8 (5), 629–643.

Wrigley, Neil (1997a), "British food retail capital in the USA - Part 1: Sainsbury and the Shaw's experience," *International Journal of Retail and Distribution Management*, 25 (1), 7–21.

——— (1997b), "British food retail capital in the USA - Part 2: Giant prospects?," *British Food Journal*, 99 (11), 427–437.

Wrigley, Neil, Neil M. Coe and Andrew Currah (2005), "Globalizing retail: conceptualizing the distribution-based transnational corporation (TNC)," *Progress in Human Geography*, 29 (4), 437–457.

Xia, Jun, Justin Tan and David Tan (2008), "Mimetic entry and bandwagon effect: the rise and decline of international equity joint venture in China," *Strategic Management Journal*, 29 (2), 195–217.

Xu, Dean and Oded Shenkar (2002), "Institutional distance and the multinational enterprise," *Academy of Management Review*, 27 (4), 608–618.

Xu, Dean, Yigang Pan and Paul W. Beamish (2004), "The Effect of Regulative and Normative Distances on MNE Ownership and Expatriate Strategies," *Management International Review*, 44 (3), 285–307.

Xu, Shichun, Tamer S. Cavusgil and Chris J. White (2006), "The Impact of Strategic Fit Among Strategy, Structure, and Processes on Multinational Corporation Performance: A Multimethod Assessment," *Journal of International Marketing*, 14 (2), 1–31.

Yahagi, Toshiyuki and Malobi Kar (2009), "The process of international business model transfer in the Seven-Eleven group: US - Japan - China," *Asia Pacific Business Review*, 15 (1), 41–58.

Yiu, Daphne and Shige Makino (2002), "The Choice Between Joint Venture and Wholly Owned Subsidiary: An Institutional Perspective," *Organization Science*, 13 (6), 667–683.

Zentes, Joachim, Bernhard Swoboda and Thomas Foscht (2012), *Handelsmanagement.* München: Vahlen.

Zhao, Hongxin, Yadong Luo and Taewon Suh (2004), "Transaction Cost Determinants and Ownership-Based Entry Mode Choice: A Meta-Analytical Review," *Journal of International Business Studies*, 35 (6), 524–544.

Zou, Shaoming and Tamer S. Cavusgil (2002), "The GMS: A Broad Conceptualization of Global Marketing Strategy and Its Effect on Firm Performance," *Journal of Marketing*, 66 (4), 40–56.

Zucker, Lynne G. (1977), "The Role of Institutionalization in Cultural Persistence," *American Sociological Review*, 42 (5), 726–743.

——— (1983), "Organizations As Institutions," *Research in the Sociology of Organizstions*, 2, 1–47

Appendix

In addition to the correlation matrix illustrated in Table B-3, the following Table Appendix-1 includes the firm dummy variables to check for multicollinearity. Again, only a few correlations exist, but all values fall below the recommended threshold of 0.7 (Anderson, Sweeney and Williams 2010) and also the calculated VIF values are all lower than the recommended threshold of 10.0 (Diamantopoulos and Winklhofer 2001). Hence, it can be concluded that multicollinearity does not constitute a serious problem, even when incorporating the firm dummy variables.

Although the firm dummy approach is a commonly accepted method to check for unobserved firm heterogeneity, the disadvantages of this approach have to be acknowledged. Hence, a binary logistic regression based on Generalized Estimating Equations (GEE; according to Liang and Zeger 1986) has additionally been employed that is especially appropriate to investigate longitudinal data. Thus, the firm has been used as subject variable to control for unobserved firm heterogeneity as well as the ordered numbered of market entries as within-subject variable to control for the amount of market entries. By the use of robust standard errors, Table Appendix-3 provides the same solution as previously calculated in Table B-4 concerning the main effect and all moderators. The positive moderating impact of the internal environment is even more strongly significant than before. The stability of effects is ensured by incorporating stepwise the interaction terms in model 2 to model 5. Regarding the overall model fit, the quasi-likelihood information criterion (QIC) is a modification of the Akaike Information Criterion (AIC) to estimate the model fit by using binary logistic regression based on GEE. Similar to the AIC, the QIC is a reverse value for goodness of fit so that the smaller the value, the better the model fit. As the decreasing values of the QIC and the corrected QIC (QICC) indicate, model 6 shows the best fit or the fit is improved by incorporating the moderating effects, respectively.

Furthermore, although probit analyses lead in most cases to the same results as logit analyses (Menard 2002), the results have also been checked for robustness purposes with a binary probit regression also based on the GEE approach. Hence, the results provided in Table Appendix-2 are almost the same as calculated in Table Appendix-3 and Table B-4.

Variables	1	2	3	4	5	6	7	8	9	10	11	12	13	14	15
Variance inflation factor (VIF)	-	8.786	1.236	1.541	5.393	3.550	5.328	1.140	1.206	1.164	1.223	1.275	1.922	5.636	2.074
1 Entry mode	-														
2 Institutionalized entry mode	0.669**	-													
3 Political distance	-0.048	-0.039	-												
4 Cultural distance	0.117*	0.074	0.108†	-											
5 International experience	0.070	0.172**	0.046	0.374**	-										
6 Internationalization speed	-0.111†	-0.123*	0.062	-0.139*	-0.409**	-									
7 Firm size	-0.149**	-0.287**	0.131*	-0.052	0.074	0.172**	-								
8 Market size	0.102†	0.025	-0.075	-0.211**	-0.115*	0.018	0.028	-							
9 Market growth	0.012	-0.026	0.216**	-0.079	0.020	-0.004	0.064	-0.064	-						
10Openness toward FDI	0.062	0.043	-0.069	-0.062	0.069	-0.109†	-0.015	-0.059	0.020	-					
11Industrial development	0.028	0.068	-0.231**	-0.092	-0.113*	-0.010	-0.123*	0.116*	-0.121*	0.116*	-				
12IEM x Political distance	-0.066	-0.049	-0.067	0.065	0.008	-0.109†	-0.165**	-0.005	-0.039	-0.015	0.074	-			
13IEM x Cultural distance	-0.144*	-0.262**	0.059	-0.060	-0.027	0.129*	0.160**	-0.036	0.111†	0.011	-0.016	0.062	-		
14IEM x International experience	-0.301**	-0.546**	0.003	-0.023	0.207**	-0.053	0.105†	-0.040	0.114*	0.001	-0.097†	0.058	0.518**	-	
15IEM x Internationalization speed	0.126*	0.120*	-0.077	0.101†	-0.043	-0.183**	-0.138*	-0.023	-0.089	-0.028	0.007	0.150**	-0.148*	-0.386**	-
16AEON	-0.111†	-0.249**	0.053	-0.059	-0.122*	0.092**	-0.070	-0.022	-0.179**	0.006	-0.075	-0.075	0.115*	0.272**	-0.190**
17Ahold	-0.293**	-0.240**	0.022	0.222**	0.032	0.050	-0.036	-0.066	-0.060	-0.018	0.013	0.005	-0.262**	-0.179**	0.010
18Aldi	0.158**	0.241**	-0.073	-0.050	0.117*	-0.246	-0.053	-0.013	0.006	0.134*	0.109†	-0.066	-0.077	0.086	-0.189**
19Auchan	0.062	0.205**	-0.014	-0.106†	-0.049	-0.145**	-0.058	0.029	0.038	0.100†	-0.028	-0.018	-0.126*	-0.104†	-0.094
20Carrefour	-0.162**	0.011	0.125*	-0.159**	0.108†	0.101†	0.004	0.000	0.009	-0.046	-0.019	0.036	-0.065	-0.176**	-0.058
21Casino	0.021	-0.105†	-0.027	-0.114*	-0.190**	0.155*	-0.077	0.082	0.018	-0.023	0.062	-0.027	0.062	0.077	0.004
22Costco	-0.213**	-0.336**	-0.056	-0.137*	-0.115*	0.008	-0.074	-0.002	0.082	-0.023	0.065	0.146*	0.331**	0.261**	0.003
23Delhaize	-0.047	-0.252**	-0.058	0.096†	0.027	-0.222**	-0.060	0.010	-0.132*	0.172**	-0.101†	0.096†	-0.151**	0.001	0.242**
24Edeka	0.008	-0.093	0.001	0.044	-0.131*	-0.062	-0.034	-0.007	-0.027	-0.022	0.072	0.051	-0.059	0.083	0.005
25Intermarché	0.110†	0.160**	-0.006	-0.108†	-0.135*	-0.031	-0.049	0.009	0.039	-0.019	0.007	0.003	-0.125*	-0.176**	-0.008
26Leclerc	-0.194**	-0.307**	-0.082	-0.100†	-0.127*	-0.038	-0.041	-0.003	-0.009	-0.020	-0.021	0.214**	0.242**	0.293**	0.092
27Schwarz Group	0.188**	0.285**	-0.090	0.028	-0.160**	0.163**	-0.105†	-0.035	-0.034	-0.017	0.085	-0.083	0.001	-0.225**	0.164**
28Metro	0.179**	0.226**	0.059	0.087	0.079	0.088	-0.062	-0.042	0.108†	-0.042	-0.094	0.059	0.054	0.008	0.071
29Rewe	0.087	0.102†	-0.048	0.056	-0.210**	0.337**	-0.017	-0.014	-0.150**	-0.022	0.052	-0.012	0.021	-0.145*	0.161**
30Tengelmann	0.017	-0.027	0.054	0.046	0.058	-0.216**	-0.024	-0.013	0.007	-0.017	0.005	0.042	0.039	0.023	0.004
31Tesco	0.100†	0.125*	-0.110†	-0.112†	-0.193**	0.212**	-0.046	0.182**	-0.010	-0.025	-0.022	-0.068	-0.088	-0.176**	0.119*
32Walmart	-0.194**	-0.379**	0.138*	-0.152**	-0.164**	0.211**	0.608**	0.061	0.032	-0.028	-0.057	-0.238**	0.254**	0.263**	-0.270**
33Spar	0.132*	0.138*	-0.018	0.264**	0.616**	-0.313**	-0.059	-0.076	-0.016	-0.038	-0.024	0.027	0.089	0.220**	-0.068

N = 301. Two-tailed Pearson correlations. † $p < 0.10$, * $p < 0.05$, ** $p < 0.01$, *** $p < 0.001$.

– cont'd. –

– cont'd. –

Variables	**16**	**17**	**18**	**19**	**20**	**21**	**22**	**23**	**24**	**25**	**26**	**27**	**28**	**29**	**30**	**31**	**32**	**33**
Variance inflation factor (VIF)	*1.750*	*2.300*	*2.249*	*1.789*	*3.591*	*1.839*	*2.288*	*2.227*	*1.558*	*1.438*	*2.181*	*2.527*	*2.418*	*2.344*	*1.64*	*1.910*	*7.216*	*2.879*
1 Entry mode																		
2 Institutionalized entry mode																		
3 Political distance																		
4 Cultural distance																		
5 International experience																		
6 Internationalization speed																		
7 Firm size																		
8 Market size																		
9 Market growth																		
10 Openness toward FDI																		
11 Industrial development																		
12 IEM x Political distance																		
13 IEM x Cultural distance																		
14 IEM x International experience																		
15 IEM x Internationalization speed																		
16 AEON	-																	
17 Ahold	*-0.036*	-																
18 Aldi	*-0.027*	*-0.074*	-															
19 Auchan	*-0.027*	*-0.074*	*-0.056*	-														
20 Carrefour	*-0.045*	*-0.123**	*-0.093*	*-0.093*	-													
21 Casino	*-0.027*	*-0.072*	*-0.054*	*-0.054*	*-0.090*	-												
22 Costco	*-0.017*	*-0.045*	*-0.034*	*-0.341*	*-0.056*	*-0.033*	-											
23 Delhaize	*-0.024*	*-0.064*	*-0.048*	*-0.048*	*-0.080*	*-0.047*	*-0.029*	-										
24 Edeka	*-0.018*	*-0.048*	*-0.037*	*-0.037*	*-0.060*	*-0.035*	*-0.022*	*-0.031*	-									
25 Intermarché	*-0.019*	*-0.052*	*-0.039*	*-0.039*	*-0.065*	*-0.038*	*-0.024*	*-0.034*	*-0.025*	-								
26 Leclerc	*-0.015*	*-0.041*	*-0.031*	*-0.031*	*-0.051*	*-0.030*	*-0.019*	*-0.025*	*-0.020*	*-0.021*	-							
27 Schwarz Group	*-0.033*	*-0.088*	*-0.067*	*-0.067*	*-0.110†*	*-0.064*	*-0.040*	*-0.057*	*-0.043*	*-0.046*	*-0.036*	-						
28 Metro	*-0.039*	*-0.106†*	*-0.080*	*-0.080*	*-0.133**	*-0.078*	*-0.048*	*-0.069*	*-0.052*	*-0.056*	*-0.044*	*-0.095†*	-					
29 Rewe	*-0.027*	*-0.072*	*-0.054*	*-0.054*	*-0.090*	*-0.052*	*-0.033*	*-0.047*	*-0.035*	*-0.038*	*-0.030*	*-0.064*	*-0.078*	-				
30 Tengelmann	*-0.029*	*-0.079*	*-0.060*	*-0.060*	*-0.099†*	*-0.058*	*-0.036*	*-0.051*	*-0.039*	*-0.042*	*-0.033*	*-0.071*	*-0.085*	*-0.058*	-			
31 Tesco	*-0.024*	*-0.064*	*-0.048*	*-0.048*	*-0.080*	*-0.047*	*-0.029*	*-0.042*	*-0.031*	*-0.034*	*-0.026*	*-0.057*	*-0.069*	*-0.047*	*-0.051*	-		
32 Walmart	*-0.027*	*-0.074*	*-0.056*	*-0.056*	*-0.093*	*-0.054*	*-0.034*	*-0.048*	*-0.037*	*-0.039*	*-0.031*	*-0.067*	*-0.080*	*-0.054*	*-0.060*	*-0.048*	-	
33 Spar	*-0.039*	*-0.106†*	*-0.080*	*-0.080*	*-0.133**	*-0.078*	*-0.048*	*-0.069*	*-0.052*	*-0.056*	*-0.044*	*-0.095†*	*-0.115**	*-0.078*	*-0.085*	*-0.069*	*-0.080*	-

N = 301. Two-tailed Pearson correlations. † $p < 0.10$, * $p < 0.05$, ** $p < 0.01$, *** $p < 0.001$.

Table Appendix-1: Correlations including Firm Dummy Variables

Source: Own source.

	Dependent variable: Full control mode = 1											
	Model 1		**Model 2**		**Model 3**		**Model 4**		**Model 5**		**Model 6**	
Measures	Beta	Wald-χ^2	Beta	Wald-χ^2	Beta	Wald-χ^2	Beta	Wald-χ^2	Beta	Wald-χ^2	Beta	Wald-χ^2
Independent variable												
Institutionalized entry mode	1.487***	(70.580)	1.683***	(107.724)	1.752***	(93.016)	1.763***	(84.889)	1.912***	(86.449)	2.064***	(200.054)
Moderator variables												
Political distance			-0.016ns	(0.018)	-0.088ns	(1.247)	-0.083ns	(1.118)	-0.097ns	(1.486)	-0.089ns	(0.993)
Cultural distance			0.554**	(8.708)	0.597***	(10.340)	0.576**	(8.980)	0.620***	(11.068)	0.597***	(13.212)
International experience			-0.448***	(20.051)	-0.458***	(19.169)	-0.455***	(18.787)	-0.570***	(45.862)	-0.514***	(28.067)
Internationalization speed			-0.263*	(5.318)	-0.268*	(5.031)	-0.269*	(5.199)	-0.265†	(3.501)	-0.166ns	(2.075)
Interaction terms												
Institutionalized entry mode x Political distance					-0.204*	(3.273)	-0.205*	(3.302)	-0.210*	(4.024)	-0.238*	(4.759)
Institutionalized entry mode x Cultural distance							-0.074ns	(0.148)	-0.204ns	(1.159)	-0.223ns	(0.951)
Institutionalized entry mode x International experience									0.469**	(7.075)	0.711***	(16.894)
Institutionalized entry mode x Internationalization speed											0.453***	(15.201)
Controls												
Firm size	0.138†	(2.777)	0.244***	(15.292)	0.245***	(14.003)	0.255**	(9.311)	0.268***	(11.695)	0.345***	(29.818)
Market size	0.424**	(7.365)	0.520***	(12.671)	0.541***	(17.571)	0.551***	(17.280)	0.553***	(17.241)	0.587***	(18.452)
Market growth	0.115*	(4.911)	0.144*	(4.476)	0.128†	(3.287)	0.129†	(3.804)	0.127*	(4.052)	0.109ns	(2.633)
Openness toward FDI	0.105***	(20.569)	0.257*	(11.157)	0.253***	(15.497)	0.258***	(14.113)	0.332**	(9.479)	0.342**	(6.932)
Industrial development	-0.136ns	(1.543)	-0.121ns	(1.434)	-0.104ns	(0.951)	-0.103ns	(0.962)	-0.114ns	(1.132)	-0.094ns	(0.666)
Constant term	0.867***	(25.263)	0.972***	(38.390)	0.971***	(40.180)	0.967***	(36.216)	0.919***	(44.132)	0.892***	(70.131)
Model indices												
N	301		301		301		301		301		301	
QIC	200.5		181.1		179.0		180.5		175.9		170.2	
QICC	200.3		186.7		186.1		188.2		186.6		185.1	

† $p < 0.10$, * $p < 0.05$, ** $p < 0.01$, *** $p < 0.001$, ns = not significant.

Table Appendix-2: Binary Probit Regression based on Generalized Estimating Equations (GEE)

Source: Own creation.

	Dependent variable: Full control mode = 1											
	Model 1		*Model 2*		*Model 3*		*Model 4*		*Model 5*		*Model 6*	
Measures	Beta	Wald-χ^2	Beta	Wald-χ^2	Beta	Wald-χ^2	Beta	Wald-χ^2	Beta	Wald-χ^2	Beta	Wald-χ^2
<u>*Independent variable*</u>												
Institutionalized entry mode	2.542***	(65.201)	2.922***	(95.849)	3.033***	(85.473)	3.043***	(80.725)	3.319***	(68.128)	3.678***	(142.174)
<u>*Moderator variables*</u>												
Political distance			-0.014ns	(0.004)	-0.152ns	(1.037)	-0.146ns	(0.997)	-0.164ns	(1.222)	-0.158ns	(0.966)
Cultural distance			1.004**	(10.758)	1.074**	(12.048)	1.038**	(8.643)	1.097**	(9.758)	1.067**	(11.522)
International experience			-0.811***	(19.953)	-0.819***	(19.374)	-0.818***	(18.942)	-1.007***	(36.065)	-0.929***	(23.060)
Internationalization speed			-0.485*	(5.509)	-0.493*	(5.211)	-0.494*	(5.370)	-0.487†	(3.436)	-0.275ns	(1.529)
<u>*Interaction terms*</u>												
Institutionalized entry mode x Political distance					-0.375*	(3.478)	-0.374*	(3.518)	-0.384*	(4.288)	-0.463*	(5.301)
Institutionalized entry mode x Cultural distance							-0.095ns	(0.070)	-0.352ns	(0.861)	-0.423ns	(0.830)
Institutionalized entry mode x International experience									0.773*	(4.928)	1.288***	(12.585)
Institutionalized entry mode x Internationalization speed											0.863***	(17.416)
<u>*Controls*</u>												
Firm size	0.262†	(3.308)	0.450***	(19.555)	0.438***	(16.571)	0.451**	(10.967)	0.481**	(11.926)	0.627***	(31.179)
Market size	0.726**	(7.013)	0.879***	(11.894)	0.907***	(15.678)	0.919***	(15.449)	0.928***	(15.814)	1.024***	(17.030)
Market growth	0.219*	(5.606)	0.278*	(5.841)	0.239†	(3.687)	0.249*	(4.103)	0.239*	(4.160)	0.207ns	(2.649)
Openness toward FDI	0.192***	(14.859)	0.468*	(4.667)	0.453**	(7.569)	0.460**	(6.792)	0.547*	(5.042)	0.611†	(3.475)
Industrial development	-0.218ns	(1.333)	-0.181ns	(1.283)	-0.149ns	(0.744)	-0.149ns	(0.768)	-0.160ns	(0.795)	-0.121ns	(0.376)
Constant term	1.433***	(19.575)	1.698***	(34.258)	1.707***	(35.736)	1.698***	(31.396)	1.622***	(36.473)	1.582***	(52.839)
<u>*Model indices*</u>												
N	301		301		301		301		301		301	
QIC	203.9		182.7		180.6		182.4		179.1		173.4	
QICC	203.1		188.7		188.0		190.1		188.7		187.0	

† $p < 0.10$, * $p < 0.05$, ** $p < 0.01$, *** $p < 0.001$, ns = not significant.

Table Appendix-3: Binary Logistic Regression based on Generalized Estimating Equations (GEE)

Source: Own creation.